THE JOSSEY-BASS
READER ON TEACHING

The Jossey-Bass Education Series

o

Foreword by
Ann Lieberman

JOSSEY-BASS
A Wiley Company
www.josseybass.com

Jossey-Bass books and products are available through most bookstores. To contact Jossey-Bass directly call our Customer Care Department within the U.S. at (800) 956-7739, outside the U.S. at 317-572-3986 or fax 317-572-4002.

Jossey-Bass also publishes its books in a variety of electronic formats. Some content that appears in print may not be available in electronic books.

Library of Congress Cataloging-in-Publication Data

The Jossey-Bass reader on teaching / foreword by Ann Lieberman.
       p.   cm. — (The Jossey-Bass education series)
    ISBN 0-7879-6240-6 (alk. paper)
    1. Teaching. I. Jossey-Bass Inc. II. Series.
  LB1025.3 .J684   2003
  371.823'41—dc21
                                              2002153382

PB Printing   10 9 8 7 6 5 4 3 2 1

CONTENTS

PART THREE
Developing Your Skills

SOURCES

PART ONE: WHAT DOES IT MEAN TO TEACH?
CHAPTER ONE
Parker J. Palmer. *The Courage to Teach: Exploring the Inner Landscape of a Teacher's Life.* San Francisco: Jossey-Bass Publishers, 1998.

CHAPTER TWO
William Ayers. *To Teach: The Journey of a Teacher.* New York: Teachers College Press, 2001.

CHAPTER THREE
Robert L. Fried. *The Passionate Teacher: A Practical Guide.* Boston: Beacon Press, 1995.

CHAPTER FOUR
Paulo Freire, tr. Donaldo Macedo, Dale Koike, Alexandre Oliveira. *Teachers as Cultural Workers: Letters to Those Who Dare Teach.* Colorado: Westview Press, 1998.

CHAPTER FIVE
Maxine Greene. "Teaching as Possibility: A Light in Dark Times." *The Journal of Pedagogy, Pluralism, and Practice,* 1997, 1(1).

PART TWO: BECOMING A TEACHER
CHAPTER SIX
Pearl Rock Kane (ed). *The First Year of Teaching: Real World Stories from America's Teachers.* New York: Walker and Company, 1991.

CHAPTER SEVEN
Pearl Rock Kane (ed). *The First Year of Teaching: Real World Stories from America's Teachers.* New York: Walker and Company, 1991.

CHAPTER EIGHT
Pearl Rock Kane (ed). *The First Year of Teaching: Real World Stories from America's Teachers.* New York: Walker and Company, 1991.

ABOUT THE AUTHORS

Sylvia Ashton-Warner (1908–1984) taught for many years in New Zealand, where she developed the model of "organic teaching" later described in *Teacher*. She wrote two educational books, five novels, and autobiographical works.

William Ayers is Distinguished Professor of Education and Senior University Scholar at the University of Illinois at Chicago. He is founder and director of the Center for Youth and Society, and codirector of the Small Schools Workshop. *To Teach: The Journey of a Teacher* was named Book of the Year by Kappa Delta Phi and won the Written Award for Distinguished Work in Biography and Autobiography.

Lisa Delpit is Benjamin E. Mays Chair of Urban Educational Leadership and director of the Alonzo A. Crim Center for Urban Educational Excellence at Georgia State University. She is a Spencer Fellow, 1990 recipient of a MacArthur "genius" grant, and 1993 recipient of the award for Outstanding Contribution to Education from the Harvard Graduate School of Education.

Paulo Freire (1921–1997) was an internationally respected adult educator and education scholar from Brazil. While exiled, Freire served as Visiting Professor at Harvard's Center for Studies in Education and Development, fellow at the Center for the Study of Development and Social Change, and Assistant Secretary of Education for the World Council of Churches in Switzerland. Upon his return to Brazil, Freire served on the faculty of the University of Sao Paulo and as minister of education for the City of Sao Paulo. His writings include *Pedagogy of the Oppressed* and *Pedagogy of Hope*.

Robert L. Fried is associate professor of education at Northeastern University. He works with teachers across the country and has served as a school principal, board member, English teacher, and field coordinator for the Coalition of Essential Schools.

Maxine Greene is professor of philosophy and education (emeritus) at Teachers College, Columbia University. She is founder of the Center for the Arts, Social Imagination, and Education at Teachers College, and serves as Philosopher-in-Residence at Lincoln Center Institute for the Arts in Education. She is the author of *Landscapes of Learning, The Dialectic of Freedom,* and *Releasing Imagination.*

Martin Haberman is Distinguished Professor in the School of Education (SOE) at the University of Wisconsin, Milwaukee. He is one of three founders of the SOE Urban Doctoral Program and is creator of the Metropolitan Milwaukee Teacher Education Program (MMTEP). Dr. Haberman has written seven books and over 200 articles and chapters.

Herbert Kohl is a veteran educator and writer who heads the Center for Teaching Excellence and Social Justice at the University of San Francisco. He has taught every grade from kindergarten to graduate school. His many writings on education include *The Discipline of Hope* and *36 Children.*

Patrick McWilliams experienced his first year of teaching at an independent school in New Hampshire. He currently teaches at a public boarding school in Illinois.

Andrew Dean Mullen spent his first year of teaching at a public school in Colorado. He currently teaches at an elementary school in Louisville, Kentucky.

James Nehring is a teacher who led the development of the Bethlehem Lab School in New York. His books include *The School Within Us* and *Upstart Startup.*

Vivian Gussin Paley is a former kindergarten teacher, winner of a MacArthur Award, and winner of the 1998 American Book Award for Lifetime Achievement given by the Before Columbus Foundation. She is the author of numerous books, including *You Can't Say You Can't Play* and *The Girl with the Brown Crayon.*

Parker J. Palmer is a writer and traveling teacher, senior associate of the American Association for Higher Education, and senior advisor to the

Fetzer Institute, for whom he designed the Teacher Formation Program for K–12 teachers. He is the author of *Let Your Life Speak, The Company of Strangers, The Active Life,* and *To Know as We Are Known.*

Vito Perrone is Theodore R. Sizer Senior Lecturer on Education, and director of teacher education at the Harvard Graduate School of Education. He is a senior fellow at the Carnegie Foundation for the Advancement of Teaching and has written extensively on progressivism in education, educational equity, curriculum, and testing and evaluation. His most recent book is *Lessons for New Teachers.*

Mike Rose is professor of social research methodology at the University of California, Los Angeles (UCLA) Graduate School of Education and Information Studies and an instructor for the UCLA Writing Program. His writings include *Lives on the Boundary: The Struggles and Achievements of America's Underprepared.*

Seymour B. Sarason is professor of psychology (emeritus) in the Department of Psychology and at the Institution for Social and Policy Studies at Yale University. His numerous books include *Teaching as a Performing Art* and *The Case for Change.*

Frank Smith is a writer and researcher who has served as a reporter, editor, novelist, and professor. He has written a number of books about education and language, including *Insult to Intelligence* and *Reading Without Nonsense.*

Brad Wilcox began his teaching career at an elementary school in Utah. He is now a member of the faculty at Brigham Young University, where he teaches undergraduate courses in elementary education and supervises student teachers.

ACKNOWLEDGMENTS

The Jossey-Bass Education Team would like to thank Ann Lieberman, Karen Kent, and Caryl Hurtig Casbon for their important contributions to this volume. Special thanks are due to Robert Fried, whose thoughtful commentary and astute suggestions were invaluable to this Reader.

We are also grateful to our project leader, Elisa Rassen, for pulling all the pieces and players together with intelligence, perseverance, and good humor.

FOREWORD

There is much wisdom to be found in the pages of this book, wisdom rooted in the knowledge of teachers and teaching, by authors who have been there and thought deeply about their experiences. They communicate by involving their readers in the world and work of teachers, a world that is at once simple and complex; intellectual and emotional; public and private.

This world of teaching is made up of the writings of many authors' chapters from books and essays that have influenced teachers and teaching over the years. They offer a variety of perspectives and insights into the realities of schools and teaching, students and teachers. Observe how a teacher learns to use the local setting to involve students in understanding their culture by building a curriculum based on the students' selection of topics. As students study their different topics, they write booklets that fill the classroom library, for their teacher is not only teaching reading and social studies but also building a learning community in her classroom. Another teacher advises prospective teachers of their "need to understand the kind of growth that they would like to nurture in their students." For him, connecting play and learning in a school setting is critical. Other teacher/writers encourage teachers to document their practice; ask questions of it; admit problems; and seek help.

Some of these teacher/writers deal with the fundamental nature of teaching, sharing with both prospective and veteran teachers the necessary risks that good teachers take in learning and practicing the craft and art of teaching. These fundamental learnings inspire us to feel that we can face the challenges of teaching "with our heads in the clouds and our feet on the ground."[1]

The Fundamentals of Teaching

Although many teachers come into teaching with high ideals, few are prepared for the challenges posed by the complexities of classroom life. Even fewer come to understand that their responses to these challenges will help determine what kind of a teacher they are to become. Some teachers settle for keeping students quiet and busy. Others burn out, often because they fail to see that teaching is not only about the teacher knowing the subject but about how a teacher engages students in learning. Teaching by providing opportunities for students to become involved in doing the work themselves requires teachers to relinquish their control. This is often a terrifying idea; it takes time for teachers to learn how to develop a variety of strategies that involve students: organizing small groups, having students do meaningful projects, building learning centers, and so on. None of this comes easy! We are reminded in so many different ways that the teacher, the subject, and the student form the critical "troika" that must be connected if education is to take place.

Our first serious encounter with teaching may cause us to struggle with fundamental questions: Who am I? What excites me about this work? What do I feel passionate about? It is in the process of answering these questions that we come to learn what can enthuse our students and engage them in the quest to know and discover. Discovering the fundamental truth that self-knowledge is critical to teaching helps us to understand what we need to know, where we can find support to help us, and how we can go about solving the teaching problems that we will inevitably face. For, as we find out from these teacher/writers, learning to teach is a lifetime affair involving constantly changing complexities of context, curriculum, and the communities of students.

The Complexities of Teaching

As teachers learn the fundamentals of teaching, they also become increasingly aware of its complexities and nuances. How do you build a "culture of acceptance" with students from a variety of cultures? In what ways can teachers honor the variety of experience that students bring to the classroom and still build a democratic learning community that works for all of the students? One teacher/writer involves us in her dramatic struggle to find ways to teach her students to read, to understand their fears, interests, anxieties, and the knowledge that they bring with them to class. She learns to listen as they struggle to give voice to their thoughts and feelings and eventually to read—to understand words, phrases, and ideas that have meaning to them. Learning to "read" our students then, helps our students learn to read. Furthermore it introduces us to the complexities of dealing with individuals and groups both personally and professionally.

Teaching offers us many choices. Resistance to change can be both an "opportunity and a trap." It can help us to see a problem as it really is and deal with it, or it can keep us from ever confronting the real problems that always exist in teaching groups of students. Because, although teaching is a calling that engages us as individuals in one of the noblest of professions, it is also a social activity subject to constraints posed by government and society that seek to standardize and bureaucratize the work.

Whether a teacher faces the inevitable challenges of teaching with "exhaustion, anger and despair" or with "optimism, joy and energy" may have much to do with a teacher becoming a member of an adult learning community. It is in such communities that teachers are able to gain knowledge, support, friendship, and confidence. For to stay alive as teachers, to continue to strive for excellence, to be scholars of good teaching, teachers must themselves be members of a learning community where they are able to practice and *feel* what it means to learn. The search for self-understanding, for new content and pedagogical knowledge, for new ways to make each classroom a learning community poses a lifetime of challenges for all those who teach. These teacher/writers involve us in their challenges, their hopes, and their successes, reminding us that as teachers, even as we provide for our students, we must continue to be learners ourselves. Keep this book by your side, whether you are a new or a veteran teacher. It inspires, it challenges, and it teaches us in ways that can move us to intelligent action.

Ann Lieberman
Senior Scholar at the Carnegie Foundation for the Advancement of
Teaching and Visiting Professor at Stanford

NOTE

1. This is a line taken from a song written by Ernie Sheldon entitled "Walking and Singing."

PART ONE

WHAT DOES IT
MEAN TO TEACH?

THE HEART OF A TEACHER

IDENTITY AND INTEGRITY IN TEACHING

Parker J. Palmer

Teaching Beyond Technique

AS SUMMER TOOK A SLOW turn toward fall, I walked into a college classroom and into my third decade of teaching.

I went to class that day grateful for another chance to teach; teaching engages my soul as much as any work I know. But I came home that evening convinced once again that I will never master this baffling vocation. Annoyed with some of my students and embarrassed by my own blunders, I pondered a recurring question: Might it be possible, at my age, to find a new line of work, maybe even something I know how to do?

The students in my first section were silent as monks. Despite my shameless pleading, I could not buy a response from them, and I soon found myself sinking into one of my oldest phobias: I must be very boring to anesthetize, so quickly, these young people who only moments earlier had been alive with hallway chatter.

In the second section they talked, but the talk flared into conflict as one student insisted that the concerns of another student were "petty" and did not deserve attention. I masked my irritation and urged open listening to diverse views, but the air was already polluted, and the dialogue died. That, of course, sank me into another ancient angst: how awkward I am at dealing with conflict when my students decide to start talking!

I have taught thousands of students, attended many seminars on teaching, watched others teach, read about teaching, and reflected on my own experience. My stockpile of methods is substantial. But when I walk into a new class, it is as if I am starting over. My problems are perennial, familiar to all teachers. Still, they take me by surprise, and my responses to them—though outwardly smoother with each year—feel almost as fumbling as they did when I was a novice.

After three decades of trying to learn my craft, every class comes down to this: my students and I, face to face, engaged in an ancient and exacting exchange called education. The techniques I have mastered do not disappear, but neither do they suffice. Face to face with my students, only one resource is at my immediate command: my identity, my selfhood, my sense of this "I" who teaches—without which I have no sense of the "Thou" who learns.

This [chapter] builds on a simple premise: *good teaching cannot be reduced to technique; good teaching comes from the identity and integrity of the teacher.*

The premise is simple, but its implications are not. It will take time to unfold what I do and do not mean by those words. But here is one way to put it: in every class I teach, my ability to connect with my students, and to connect them with the subject, depends less on the methods I use than on the degree to which I know and trust my selfhood—and am willing to make it available and vulnerable in the service of learning.

My evidence for this claim comes, in part, from years of asking students to tell me about their good teachers. Listening to those stories, it becomes impossible to claim that all good teachers use similar techniques: some lecture nonstop and others speak very little; some stay close to their material and others loose the imagination; some teach with the carrot and others with the stick.

But in every story I have heard, good teachers share one trait: a strong sense of personal identity infuses their work. "Dr. A is really *there* when she teaches," a student tells me, or "Mr. B has such enthusiasm for his subject," or "You can tell that this is really Prof. C's life."

One student I heard about said she could not describe her good teachers because they differed so greatly, one from another. But she could describe her bad teachers because they were all the same: "Their words float somewhere in front of their faces, like the balloon speech in cartoons."

With one remarkable image she said it all. Bad teachers distance themselves from the subject they are teaching—and in the process, from their students. Good teachers join self and subject and students in the fabric of life.

Good teachers possess a capacity for connectedness. They are able to weave a complex web of connections among themselves, their subjects, and their students so that students can learn to weave a world for themselves. The methods used by these weavers vary widely: lectures, Socratic dialogues, laboratory experiments, collaborative problem solving, creative chaos. The connections made by good teachers are held not in their methods but in their hearts—meaning *heart* in its ancient sense, as the place where intellect and emotion and spirit and will converge in the human self.

As good teachers weave the fabric that joins them with students and subjects, the heart is the loom on which the threads are tied, the tension is held, the shuttle flies, and the fabric is stretched tight. Small wonder, then, that teaching tugs at the heart, opens the heart, even breaks the heart—and the more one loves teaching, the more heartbreaking it can be. The courage to teach is the courage to keep one's heart open in those very moments when the heart is asked to hold more than it is able so that teacher and students and subject can be woven into the fabric of community that learning, and living, require.

If teaching cannot be reduced to technique, it is both good news and bad. The good news is that we no longer need suffer the boredom many of us feel when teaching is approached as a question of "how to do it." We rarely talk with each other about teaching at any depth—and why should we when we have nothing more than "tips, tricks, and techniques" to discuss? That kind of talk fails to touch the heart of a teacher's experience.

The good news gets even better. If teaching cannot be reduced to technique, I no longer need suffer the pain of having my peculiar gift as a teacher crammed into the Procrustean bed of someone else's method and the standards prescribed by it. That pain is felt throughout education today as we glorify the method *du jour,* leaving people who teach differently feeling devalued, forcing them to measure up to norms not their own.

I will never forget one professor who, moments before I was to start a workshop on teaching, unloaded years of pent-up workshop animus on me: "I am an organic chemist. Are you going to spend the next two days telling me that I am supposed to teach organic chemistry through role playing?" We must find an approach to teaching that respects the diversity of teachers and subjects, which methodological reductionism fails to do.

The good news is very good, but the bad news is daunting. If identity and integrity are more fundamental to good teaching than technique— and if we want to grow as teachers—we must do something alien to academic culture: we must talk to each other about our inner lives—risky stuff in a profession that fears the personal and seeks safety in the technical, the distant, the abstract.

I was reminded of that fear recently as I listened to a group of faculty argue about what to do when students share personal experiences in class—experiences that are related to the themes of the course but that some professors regard as "more suited to a therapy session than to a college classroom."

The house soon divided along predictable lines. On one side were the scholars, insisting that the subject is primary and must never be compromised for the sake of the students' lives. On the other side were the student-centered folks, insisting that the lives of students must always come first even if it means that the subject gets shortchanged. The more vigorously these camps promoted their polarized ideas, the more antagonistic they became—and the less they learned about pedagogy or about themselves.

The gap between these views seems unbridgeable—until we understand what creates it. At bottom, these professors were not debating teaching techniques. They were revealing the diversity of identity and integrity among themselves, saying, in various ways, "Here are my own limits and potentials when it comes to dealing with the relation between the subject and my students' lives."

If we stopped lobbing pedagogical points at each other and spoke about *who we are* as teachers, a remarkable thing might happen: identity and integrity might grow within us and among us, instead of hardening as they do when we defend our fixed positions from the foxholes of the pedagogy wars.

Teaching and True Self

The claim that good teaching comes from the identity and integrity of the teacher might sound like a truism, and a pious one at that: good teaching comes from good people.

But by identity and integrity I do not mean only our noble features, or the good deeds we do, or the brave faces we wear to conceal our confusions and complexities. Identity and integrity have as much to do with our shadows and limits, our wounds and fears, as with our strengths and potentials.

By *identity* I mean an evolving nexus where all the forces that constitute my life converge in the mystery of self: my genetic makeup, the nature of the man and woman who gave me life, the culture in which I was raised, people who have sustained me and people who have done me harm, the good and ill I have done to others and to myself, the experience of love and suffering—and much, much more. In the midst of that complex field, identity is a moving intersection of the inner and outer forces that make me who I am, converging in the irreducible mystery of being human.

By *integrity* I mean whatever wholeness I am able to find within that nexus as its vectors form and re-form the pattern of my life. Integrity requires that I discern what is integral to my selfhood, what fits and what does not—and that I choose life-giving ways of relating to the forces that converge within me: Do I welcome them or fear them, embrace them or reject them, move with them or against them? By choosing integrity, I become more whole, but wholeness does not mean perfection. It means becoming more real by acknowledging the whole of who I am.

Identity and integrity are not the granite from which fictional heroes are hewn. They are subtle dimensions of the complex, demanding, and lifelong process of self-discovery. *Identity* lies in the intersection of the diverse forces that make up my life, and *integrity* lies in relating to those forces in ways that bring me wholeness and life rather than fragmentation and death.

Those are my definitions—but try as I might to refine them, they always come out too pat. Identity and integrity can never be fully named or known by anyone, including the person who bears them. They constitute that familiar strangeness we take with us to the grave, elusive realities that can be caught only occasionally out of the corner of the eye.

Stories are the best way to portray realities of this sort, so here is a tale of two teachers, a tale based on people I have known, whose lives tell me more about the subtleties of identity and integrity than any theory could.

Alan and Eric were born into two different families of skilled craftspeople, rural folk with little formal schooling but gifted in the manual arts. Both boys evinced this gift from childhood onward, and as each grew in the skill of working with his hands, each developed a sense of self in which the pride of craft was key.

The two shared another gift as well: both excelled in school and became the first in their working-class families to go to college. Both did well as undergraduates, both were admitted to graduate school, both earned doctorates, and both chose academic careers.

But here their paths diverged. Though the gift of craft was central in both men's sense of self, Alan was able to weave that gift into his academic vocation, whereas the fabric of Eric's life unraveled early on.

Catapulted from his rural community into an elite private college at age eighteen, Eric suffered culture shock and never overcame it. He was insecure with fellow students and, later, with academic colleagues who came from backgrounds he saw as more "cultured" than his own. He learned to speak and act like an intellectual, but he always felt fraudulent among people who were, in his eyes, to the manor born.

But insecurity neither altered Eric's course nor drew him into self-reflection. Instead, he bullied his way into professional life on the theory that the best defense is a good offense. He made pronouncements rather than probes. He listened for weaknesses rather than strengths in what other people said. He argued with anyone about anything—and responded with veiled contempt to whatever was said in return.

In the classroom, Eric was critical and judgmental, quick to put down the "stupid question," adept at trapping students with trick questions of his own, then merciless in mocking wrong answers. He seemed driven by a need to inflict on his students the same wound that academic life had inflicted on him—the wound of being embarrassed by some essential part of one's self.

But when Eric went home to his workbench and lost himself in craft, he found himself as well. He became warm and welcoming, at home in the world and glad to extend hospitality to others. Reconnected with his roots, centered in his true self, he was able to reclaim a quiet and confident core—which he quickly lost as soon as he returned to campus.

Alan's is a different story. His leap from countryside to campus did not induce culture shock, in part because he attended a land-grant university where many students had backgrounds much like his own. He was not driven to hide his gift but was able to honor and transform it by turning it toward things academic: he brought to his study, and later to his teaching and research, the same sense of craft that his ancestors brought to their work with metal and wood.

Watching Alan teach, you felt that you were watching a craftsman at work—and if you knew his history, you understood that this feeling was more than metaphor. In his lectures, every move Alan made was informed by attention to detail and respect for the materials at hand; he connected ideas with the precision of dovetail joinery and finished the job with a polished summary.

But the power of Alan's teaching went well beyond crafted performance. His students knew that Alan would extend himself with great generosity to any of them who wanted to become an apprentice in his field, just as the elders in his own family had extended themselves to help young Alan grow in his original craft.

Alan taught from an undivided self—an integral state of being central to good teaching. In the undivided self, every major thread of one's life experience is honored, creating a weave of such coherence and strength that it can hold students and subject as well as self. Such a self, inwardly integrated, is able to make the outward connections on which good teaching depends.

But Eric failed to weave the central strand of his identity into his academic vocation. His was a self divided, engaged in a civil war. He projected that inner warfare onto the outer world, and his teaching devolved into combat instead of craft. The divided self will always distance itself from others, and may even try to destroy them, to defend its fragile identity.

If Eric had not been alienated as an undergraduate—or if his alienation had led to self-reflection instead of self-defense—it is possible that he, like Alan, could have found integrity in his academic vocation, could have woven the major strands of his identity into his work. But part of the mystery of selfhood is the fact that one size does not fit all: what is integral to one person lacks integrity for another. Throughout his life there were persistent clues that academia was not a life-giving choice for Eric, not a context in which his true self could emerge healthy and whole, not a vocation integral to his unique nature.

The self is not infinitely elastic—it has potentials and it has limits. If the work we do lacks integrity for us, then we, the work, and the people we do it with will suffer. Alan's self was enlarged by his academic vocation, and the work he did was a joy to behold. Eric's self was diminished by his encounter with academia, and choosing a different vocation might have been his only way to recover integrity lost.

Gandhi called his life "experiments with truth," and experimenting in the complex field of forces that bear on our lives is how we learn more about our integrity.[1] We learn experimentally that we thrive on some connections and wither with others, that we enhance our integrity by choosing relationships that give us life and violate it by assenting to those that do not.

Experimentation is risky. We rarely know in advance what will give us life and what will sap life away. But if we want to deepen our understanding of our own integrity, experiment we must—and then be willing to make choices as we view the experimental results.

"All real living is meeting," said Martin Buber, and teaching is endless meeting.[2] Staying open to new meetings, trying to distinguish those that have integrity from those that do not, is a tiring and sometimes frightening task. I am often tempted to protect my sense of self behind barricades of status or role, to withhold myself from colleagues or students or ideas and from the collisions we will surely have.

When I succumb to that temptation, my identity and integrity are diminished—and I lose the heart to teach.

When Teachers Lose Heart

Many of us became teachers for reasons of the heart, animated by a passion for some subject and for helping people learn. But many of us lose heart as the years of teaching go by. How can we take heart in teaching once more so that we can, as good teachers always do, give heart to our students?

We lose heart, in part, because teaching is a daily exercise in vulnerability. I need not reveal personal secrets to feel naked in front of a class. I need only parse a sentence or work a proof on the board while my students doze off or pass notes. No matter how technical my subject may be, the things I teach are things I care about—and what I care about helps define my selfhood.

Unlike many professions, teaching is always done at the dangerous intersection of personal and public life. A good therapist must work in a personal way, but never publicly: the therapist who reveals as much as a client's name is derelict. A good trial lawyer must work in a public forum but remain unswayed by personal opinion: the lawyer who allows private feelings about a client's guilt to weaken the client's defense is guilty of malpractice.

But a good teacher must stand where personal and public meet, dealing with the thundering flow of traffic at an intersection where "weaving a web of connectedness" feels more like crossing a freeway on foot. As we try to connect ourselves and our subjects with our students, we make ourselves, as well as our subjects, vulnerable to indifference, judgment, ridicule.

To reduce our vulnerability, we disconnect from students, from subjects, and even from ourselves. We build a wall between inner truth and outer performance, and we play-act the teacher's part. Our words, spoken at remove from our hearts, become "the balloon speech in cartoons," and we become caricatures of ourselves. We distance ourselves from students and subject to minimize the danger—forgetting that distance makes life more dangerous still by isolating the self.

This "self-protective" split of personhood from practice is encouraged by an academic culture that distrusts personal truth. Though the academy claims to value multiple modes of knowing, it honors only one—an "objective" way of knowing that takes us into the "real" world by taking us "out of ourselves."

In this culture, objective facts are regarded as pure, while subjective feelings are suspect and sullied. In this culture, the self is not a source to be tapped but a danger to be suppressed, not a potential to be fulfilled but an obstacle to be overcome. In this culture, the pathology of speech disconnected from self is regarded, and rewarded, as a virtue.

If my sketch of the academic bias against selfhood seems overdone, here is a story from a class that I taught at a large university some years ago.

I assigned my students a series of brief analytical essays involving themes in the texts we were going to be reading. Then I assigned a parallel series of autobiographical sketches, related to those themes, so that my students could see connections between the textbook concepts and their own lives.

After the first class, a student came up to me and inquired, "In those autobiographical essays you asked us to write, is it OK to use the word 'I'?"

I did not know whether to laugh or cry—but I knew that my response would have considerable impact on a young man who had just opened himself to ridicule. I told him that not only could he use the word "I," but I hoped he would use it freely and often. Then I asked what had led to his question.

"I'm a history major," he said, "and each time I use 'I' in a paper, they knock off half a grade."

The academic bias against subjectivity not only forces our students to write poorly ("It is believed . . . ," instead of "I believe . . . ") but also deforms their thinking about themselves and their world. In a single stroke, we delude our students into thinking that bad prose can turn opinions into facts, and we alienate them from their own inner lives.

Faculty often complain that students have no regard for the gifts of insight and understanding that are the true payoff of education—they care only about short-term outcomes in the "real" world: "Will this major get me a job?" "How will this assignment be useful in 'real' life?"

But those are not the questions deep in our students' hearts. They are merely the questions they have been taught to ask, not only by tuition-paying parents who want their children to be employable but also by an academic culture that distrusts and devalues inner reality. Of course our students are cynical about the inner outcomes of education: we teach them that the subjective self is unvalued and even unreal. Their cynicism simply proves that when academic culture dismisses inner truth and honors only the external world, students as well as teachers lose heart.

How can we who teach reclaim our hearts, for the sake of our students, ourselves, and educational reform? That simple question challenges the assumption that drives most reform—that meaningful change comes not from the human heart but from factors external to ourselves, from budgets, methodologies, curricula, and institutional restructuring. Deeper still, it challenges the assumptions about reality and power that drive Western culture.

The foundation of any culture lies in the way it answers the question "Where do reality and power reside?" For some cultures the answer is the gods; for some it is nature; for some it is tradition. In our culture, the answer is clear: reality and power reside in the external world of objects and events and in the sciences that study that world, while the inner realm of the heart is a romantic fantasy, an escape from harsh realities, perhaps, but surely not a source of leverage over the "real" world.

We are obsessed with manipulating externals because we believe that they will give us some power over reality and win us some freedom from its constraints. Mesmerized by a technology that seems to have done just that, we dismiss the inward world. We turn every question we face into an objective problem to be solved—and we believe that for every objective problem there is some sort of technical fix. That is why we train doctors to repair the body but not to honor the spirit; clergy to be CEOs but not spiritual guides; teachers to master techniques but not to engage their students' souls.

Yet at this point in history it should be clear that external "fixes" will not come soon enough to sustain the deepest passions of people who care about teaching. Institutions reform slowly, and as long as we wait, depending on "them" to do the job for us—forgetting that institutions are also "us"—we merely postpone reform and continue the slow slide into cynicism that characterizes too many teaching careers.

There is an alternative to waiting: we can reclaim our belief in the power of inwardness to transform our work and our lives. We became teachers because we once believed that ideas and insight are at least as real and powerful as the world that surrounds us. Now we must remind ourselves that inner reality can give us leverage in the realm of objects and events.

We will find such a reminder in the testimony of Václav Havel, poet and man of practical affairs, a leader in the Velvet Revolution that liberated Czechoslovakia from Soviet rule. It was a revolution that succeeded in the face of obstacles considerably more daunting than those stacked against educational reform.

Havel, now president of the Czech Republic, writes about spending years "under a rock" of institutional oppression that was dropped on the Czech people in the Communist coup of 1968. Then he speaks of the inward seed of human consciousness and how it grew into a flower of reform that cracked and crumbled the granite of totalitarianism a mere twenty years later: "The . . . experience I'm talking about has given me one certainty: . . . the salvation of this human world lies nowhere else than in the human heart, in the human power to reflect, in human meekness and in human responsibility. Without a global revolution in . . . human consciousness, nothing will change for the better, and the catastrophe toward which this world is headed . . . will be unavoidable."[3]

Havel helped the Czech people reclaim their hearts by reminding them who they, and all of us, are: not victims of external forces but persons possessed of an inner power that cannot be taken from us, though we can and do give it away.

Remembering ourselves and our power can lead to revolution, but it requires more than recalling a few facts. *Re-membering* involves putting ourselves back together, recovering identity and integrity, reclaiming the wholeness of our lives. When we forget who we are we do not merely drop some data. We *dis-member* ourselves, with unhappy consequences for our politics, our work, our hearts.

Academics often suffer the pain of dismemberment. On the surface, this is the pain of people who thought they were joining a community of scholars but find themselves in distant, competitive, and uncaring relationships with colleagues and students. Deeper down, this pain is more spiritual than sociological: it comes from being disconnected from our own truth, from the passions that took us into teaching, from the heart that is the source of all good work.

If we have lost the heart to teach, how can we take heart again? How can we re-member who we are, for our own sake and the sake of those we serve?

Mentors Who Evoked Us

If identity and integrity are found at the intersection of the forces that converge in our lives, revisiting some of the convergences that called us toward teaching may allow us to reclaim the selfhood from which good teaching comes. In this section and the next, I want to reflect on two such encounters—with the mentors who evoked us and with the subjects of study that chose us.

The power of our mentors is not necessarily in the models of good teaching they gave us, models that may turn out to have little to do with who we are as teachers. Their power is in their capacity to awaken a truth within us, a truth we can reclaim years later by recalling their impact on our lives.

If we discovered a teacher's heart in ourselves by meeting a great teacher, recalling that meeting may help us take heart in teaching once more.

In faculty workshops, I often ask people to introduce themselves by talking about a teacher who made a difference in their lives. As these stories are told, we are reminded of many facts about good teaching: that it comes in many forms, that the imprint of good teachers remains long after the facts they gave us have faded, and that it is important to thank our mentors, no matter how belatedly—partly because we owe them gratitude and partly as a cosmic counterpoint to the apparent ingratitude of our own students!

Then I ask the question that opens to the deeper purpose of this exercise: not "What made your mentor great?" but "What was it about *you* that allowed great mentoring to happen?" Mentoring is a mutuality that requires more than meeting the right teacher: the teacher must meet the right student. In this encounter, not only are the qualities of the mentor revealed, but the qualities of the student are drawn out in a way that is equally revealing.

One of my most memorable mentors was a man who seemed to break every "rule" of good teaching. He lectured at such length, and with such enthusiasm, that he left little room for questions and comments. Preoccupied with the world of thought, he listened poorly to students, not because he disdained them but because he was so eager to teach them by the only way he knew—sharing his knowledge and passions. His classes were mostly monologues, and his students rarely played any role other than audience.

He may sound like a pedagogical nightmare, but for reasons I could not articulate at the time, I was powerfully drawn to his teaching—indeed, he changed my life. Only years later did I understand my attraction and in that understanding are some clues to my identity.

I was the first in my family to attend college. My family valued education, but it offered no exemplars of the intellectual life that has turned out to be my birthright gift. I kept that gift sealed in the box it came in all the way through high school, graduating somewhere below the median of my class, with a major in extracurricular activities. Not until the second semester of college did I open the box, get excited about what was in it, and start doing well at schoolwork, going on to graduate school and into an academic career.

My loquacious professor in college gave me a first glimpse into this part of myself. My excitement in listening to him lay less in what he said—though his ideas were exhilarating—than in discovering a dormant dimension of my identity. It did not matter to me that he violated most rules of good group process and even some rules of considerate personal relations. What mattered was that he generously opened the life of his mind to me, giving full voice to the gift of thought. Something in me knew that this gift was mine as well, though it was years before I could fully trust that knowledge.

Long into my career I harbored a secret sense that thinking and reading and writing, as much as I loved them, did not quality as "real work." I taught and wrote, but I "justified" myself by working as an administrator for various institutions and projects—work that was practical and thus worthy, like that done by honored members of my family. Only in my mid-forties was I finally able to claim the life of the mind as the mainstay of my vocation, to trust the calling of my soul, a trust that deepened when I was able to decode this early experience of being mentored.

As we recall our mentors, not all of our self-insights are as happy as the one I have just drawn. We sometimes take the wrong lessons from the mentors who draw us when we are young and impressionable.

I witnessed such a case at a faculty workshop I led a few years ago. My on-campus host had taken pains to warn me about Professor X, a curmudgeonly and unpopular teacher, though brilliant in his scholarly field. Of the forty people in the workshop, my host said, Professor X had probably signed up not to learn about teaching but to debunk what we were doing.

In trepidation, I began the workshop with something "soft," inviting people to introduce themselves by talking about their mentors. By the time we got to Professor X, six or eight people had spoken, many with insight and feeling, and a spirit of openness filled the room. I tensed as he began to speak, fearing that this spirit was about to be killed. But it soon became clear that he, too, had been touched by the quality of the exchange.

He told the story of his mentor with the hesitancy that comes from speaking of sacred things and—as he talked about how hard he had tried to model his own career after his mentor's—he surprised us, and surely himself, by choking up.

Later, in private conversation with him, I learned the reason for his emotions. For twenty years, Professor X had tried to imitate his mentor's way of teaching and being, and it had been a disaster. He and his mentor were very different people, and X's attempt to clone his mentor's style had distorted his own identity and integrity. He had lost himself in an identity not his own—a painful insight that took courage to embrace, but one with the promise of growth.

Professor X's story gave me some insight into myself, an example of the mutual illumination that often occurs when we are willing to explore our inner dynamics with each other. Early in my career, I, too, had tried to emulate my mentor with nonstop lecturing, until I realized that my students were even less enthralled by my cheap imitation than some of my classmates had been by the genuine original.

I began to look for a way to teach that was more integral to my own nature, a way that would have as much integrity for me as my mentor's had for him—for the key to my mentor's power was the coherence between his method and himself. I began the long process of trying to understand my own nature as a teacher and to learn the techniques that might help it along.

Though I need sometimes to lecture and may even enjoy doing it, lecturing all the time simply bores me: I usually know what I am going to say, and I have heard it all before. But dialogical methods of teaching help keep me alive. Forced to listen, respond, and improvise, I am more likely to hear something unexpected and insightful from myself as well as others.

That does not mean that lecturing is the wrong way to teach. It simply means that my identity, unlike my mentor's, is more fulfilled in dialogue. When I was young and did not know who I was, I needed someone to model the intellectual gift that might be mine. But now, in midlife, knowing myself better, my identity demands that I use my gift in interaction and interdependence with others.

Here, I believe, is the proper and powerful role of technique: *as we learn more about who we are, we can learn techniques that reveal rather than conceal the personhood from which good teaching comes.* We no longer need to use technique to mask the subjective self, as the culture of professionalism encourages us to do. Now we can use technique to manifest more fully the gift of self from which our best teaching comes.

The self-knowledge that comes from these reflections is crucial to my teaching, for it reveals a complexity within me that is within my students as well. In my case, the "I" who teaches is both intimidated by and attracted to the life of the mind; for a long time it was bedeviled by a sense that the intellectual work it felt called to do was nonetheless a fraud. This "I," despite its intrigue with ideas, was once so unsure of itself that it welcomed a mentor whose performance barred participation. But today, this same "I" finds its own performance boring and needs to be nurtured in dialogue.

When I forget my own inner multiplicity and my own long and continuing journey toward selfhood, my expectations of students become excessive and unreal. If I can remember the inner pluralism of my own soul and the slow pace of my own self-emergence, I will be better able to serve the pluralism among my students at the pace of their young lives.

By remembering our mentors, we remember ourselves—and by remembering ourselves, we remember our students.

Looking back, I realize that I was blessed with mentors at every crucial stage of my young life, at every point where my identity needed to grow: in adolescence, in college, in graduate school, and early in my professional career. But a funny thing happened on the way to full adulthood: the mentors stopped coming. For several years I waited for the next one in vain, and for several years my own growth was on hold.

Then I realized what was happening. I was no longer an apprentice, so I no longer needed mentors. It was my turn to become a mentor to someone else. I needed to turn around and look for the new life emerging behind me, to offer to younger people the gift that had been given to me when I was young. As I did, my identity and integrity had new chances to evolve in each new encounter with my students' lives.

Mentors and apprentices are partners in an ancient human dance, and one of teaching's great rewards is the daily chance it gives us to get back on the dance floor. It is the dance of the spiraling generations, in which the old empower the young with their experience and the young empower the old with new life, reweaving the fabric of the human community as they touch and turn.

Subjects That Chose Us

Many of us were called to teach by encountering not only a mentor but also a particular field of study. We were drawn to a body of knowledge because it shed light on our identity as well as on the world. We did not merely find a subject to teach—the subject also found us. We may recover the heart to teach by remembering how that subject evoked a sense of self that was only dormant in us before we encountered the subject's way of naming and framing life.

Alice Kaplan is a teacher of French language and literature, and she has done this kind of remembering in a book called *French Lessons*. "Why do people want to adopt another culture?" she asks as she summarizes her journey into teaching and into life. "Because there's something in their own they don't like, that doesn't *name* them."[4] French culture gave Kaplan a way of claiming an identity and integrity she could not find in the culture to which she was born.

Recalling a course she taught in which a bigoted young man learned to appreciate the stranger through encountering another people in another language, Kaplan reflects: "Moments like this make me think that speaking a foreign language is . . . a chance for growth, for freedom, for liberation from the ugliness of our received ideas and mentalities."[5]

But Kaplan also understands the shadow side of a borrowed identity: "Learning French did me some harm by giving me a place to hide. If life got too messy, I could take off into my second world." But, she says, "writing about it has made me air my suspicions, my anger, my longings, to people for whom it's come as a total surprise."[6] The self-knowledge she gained by asking why she was attracted to her field helped her reconnect, wrestle with, and even redeem troubling events and relationships in her life, renewing her teacher's heart.

Reading Kaplan's reflections (richer by far in shadow and light than my brief review suggests), I was encouraged to make my own. My undergraduate majors were philosophy and sociology, and many of the details I once knew about those fields have long since leached away. But I still recall, thirty-five years later, the moment I discovered C. Wright Mills's idea of the "sociological imagination."[7] I was not merely taken with it—I was possessed by it.

The essence of his idea is simple, but it was radical to me: we cannot see what is "out there" merely by looking around. Everything depends on the lenses through which we view the world. By putting on new lenses, we can see things that would otherwise remain invisible.

Mills taught me how to view the world through the lenses of social theory, and when I took my first look, the world jumped out at me as if I had donned the 3-D movie glasses that Hollywood was hawking at the time. I saw the invisible structures and secret signals that shape our social lives, that have a power over us that I thought resided only in face-to-face relationships. I was astonished at this new vision of life in which people walked about, not freely, as I had imagined, but controlled by strings attached to their minds and hearts by invisible puppeteers.

Why was I so deeply drawn to the idea of the sociological imagination? Why did it become such a defining feature of my worldview? By reflecting on those questions, I have re-membered some key features of who I am.

Intellectually, the idea of the sociological imagination spoke to me because at age eighteen I had begun to understand that what you see is not necessarily what you get. I was a child of the 1950s, with its many social fictions, so it took time for me to see that the visible performance of individuals and groups was only the "on-stage" aspect of things, that reality has "backstage" dynamics far more influential than the performance we see up front.

But my attraction to Mills's concept was more than intellectual—it helped me come to terms with some of my deepest personal fears. As a young person, I found the on-stage world both seductive and intimidating. It was an arena of visibility where I wanted to perform and become known, but also an arena where my competence would be tested and surely found wanting. As I came to understand the backstage realities revealed by the sociological imagination, I was able to shake off some of my performance fears.

By looking backstage and seeing how human, how klutzy, how ordinary the mechanics of performance really are—how unlike the glitz and glamour of on-stage performance itself—I could ask myself, "If they can do it, why not me?" This backstage knowledge gave me the comfort of knowing that all heroes have feet of clay; it had the calming effect of the counsel given to nervous public speakers, "Imagine your audience naked."

But my attraction to the sociological imagination went deeper still—beyond intellectual interest, beyond performance fears, to a gap within my own soul. Mills's distinction between the on-stage show and backstage reality mirrored a great divide in my inner life. Outwardly, I had learned how to make my performance seem relatively smooth and accomplished, but inwardly, I felt anxious and fumbling and inept.

The constant contradiction between how I experienced myself and how other people viewed me created a painful, sometimes crippling sense of fraudulence. But the sociological imagination and its view of societal duplicity helped me understand how common that contradiction is, how basic to the human condition, and my sense of fraudulence became less onerous.

It has taken me a long time to turn Mills's insight from an analysis of our society toward an understanding of myself. The sociological imagination is easily used as one of those "debunking" tools, beloved of social science, that allows us to stand detached by the side of the road as the parade passes by, sniping at its silliness and pretending to be above it all.

For a long time, I stood off to the side as critic and judge, and now I understand why: I was projecting onto society all the fraudulence I felt but could not face in myself, and I was using that projection as a way of evading my own dividedness. I no longer want to live that way—which is why I take pains in my writing to counterbalance the truth of the sociological imagination.

Earlier in this chapter, I insisted that our inner world has a reality and a power that can keep us from being victims of circumstance and compel us to take responsibility for our own lives. In effect, I argued that the world of social structures and signals need not dictate our lives, that the sociological imagination that so entranced me as a young man (and has its grip on me yet) does not hold all the answers. In the very act of writing this chapter, I have been encountering my subject—and myself—anew, still respectful of the power of social facts but unwilling to use that knowledge as an escape from personal responsibility.

What I have learned about my identity as a teacher from this re-membering is, to some extent, encouraging: I would not be an advocate of the power of inner reality if I had not reached some degree of congru-ence between my on-stage and backstage lives.

But I have also learned that my conflict between on-stage and backstage reality is far from being resolved—it continues to come up in my teach-ing. That conflict was the theme of the teaching stories I told at the start of this chapter, stories whose drama, such as it is, lies in the tension between my external response to classroom events and my internal sense of incompetence.

One of my favorite essays on teaching is Jane Tompkins's "Pedagogy of the Distressed."[8] It seems to have been written directly to my divided condition. With wonderful candor, Tompkins says that her obsession as a teacher had not been with helping students learn what they wanted and needed to know but rather with "(a) showing the students how smart I was; (b) showing them how knowledgeable I was; and (c) showing them how well prepared I was for class. I had been putting on a performance whose true goal was not to help the students learn but to act in such a way that they would have a good opinion of me."

Then she asks, "How did it come to be that our main goal as acade-micians turned out to be performance?" Her answer rings true to me—fear: "Fear of being shown up for what you are: a fraud, stupid, ignorant, a clod, a dolt, a sap, a weakling, someone who can't cut the mustard."

That is how it sometimes is for me. Driven by fear that my backstage ineptitude will be exposed, I strive to make my on-stage performance slicker and smoother—and in the process, make it less and less likely that my students will learn anything other than how to cover up and show off. I conceal my own heart and am unable to weave the fabric of connected-ness that teaching and learning require.

Once again: when I seek my identity and integrity, what I find is not always a proud and shining thing. The discoveries I make about myself when I remember the encounters that have shaped and revealed my self-hood are sometimes embarrassing—but they are also real. Whatever the cost in embarrassment, I will know myself better, and thus be a better teacher, when I acknowledge the forces at play within me instead of allow-ing them to wreak witless havoc on my work.

Florida Scott-Maxwell, writing in her mid-eighties, made the point powerfully: "You need only claim the events in your life to make yourself yours. When you truly possess all you have been and done . . . you are fierce with reality."[9]

The Teacher Within

Encounters with mentors and subjects can awaken a sense of self and yield clues to who we are. But the call to teach does not come from external encounters alone—no outward teacher or teaching will have much effect until my soul assents. Any authentic call ultimately comes from the voice of the *teacher within,* the voice that invites me to honor the nature of my true self.

By the voice of the inward teacher, I do not mean *conscience* or *super-ego,* moral arbiter or internalized judge. In fact, conscience, as it is commonly understood, can get us into deep vocational trouble.

When we listen primarily for what we "ought" to be doing with our lives, we may find ourselves hounded by external expectations that can distort our identity and integrity. There is much that I ought to be doing by some abstract moral calculus. But is it my vocation? Am I gifted and called to do it? Is this particular ought a place of intersection between my inner self and the outer world, or is it someone else's image of how my life should look?

When I follow only the oughts, I may find myself doing work that is ethically laudable but not mine to do. A vocation that is not mine, no matter how externally valued, does violence to the self—in the precise sense that it *violates* my identity and integrity on behalf of some abstract norm. When I violate myself, I invariably end up violating the people I work with. How many teachers inflict their own pain on their students, the pain that comes from doing what never was, or no longer is, their true work?

In contrast to the strained and even violent concept of vocation as an ought, Frederick Buechner offers a more generous and humane image of vocation as "the place where your deep gladness and the world's deep hunger meet."[10]

In a culture that sometimes equates work with suffering, it is revolutionary to suggest that the best inward sign of vocation is deep gladness—revolutionary but true. If a work is mine to do, it will make me glad over the long haul, despite the difficult days. Even the difficult days will ultimately gladden me, because they pose the kinds of problems that can help me grow in a work if it is truly mine.

If a work does not gladden me in these ways, I need to consider laying it down. When I devote myself to something that does not flow from my identity, that is not integral to my nature, I am most likely deepening the world's hunger rather than helping to alleviate it.

There are times when we must work for money rather than meaning, and we may never have the luxury of quitting a job because it does not make us glad. But that does not release us from continually checking the violence we do to others and ourselves by working in ways that violate our souls. Nor does it relieve us from wondering whether preserving integrity is a luxury. What brings more security in the long run: holding this job or honoring my soul?

The teacher within is not the voice of conscience but of identity and integrity. It speaks not of what ought to be but of what is real for us, of what is true. It says things like, "This is what fits you and this is what doesn't"; "This is who you are and this is who you are not"; "This is what gives you life and this is what kills your spirit—or makes you wish you were dead." The teacher within stands guard at the gate of selfhood, warding off whatever insults our integrity and welcoming whatever affirms it. The voice of the inward teacher reminds me of my truth as I negotiate the force field of my life.

I realize that the idea of a teacher within strikes some academics as a romantic fantasy, but I cannot fathom why. If there is no such reality in our lives, centuries of Western discourse about the aims of education become so much lip-flapping. In classical understanding, education is the attempt to "lead out" from within the self a core of wisdom that has the power to resist falsehood and live in the light of truth, not by external norms but by reasoned and reflective self-determination. The inward teacher is the living core of our lives that is addressed and evoked by any education worthy of the name.

Perhaps the idea is unpopular because it compels us to look at two of the most difficult truths about teaching. The first is that what we teach will never "take" unless it connects with the inward, living core of our students' lives, with our students' inward teachers.

We can, and do, make education an exclusively outward enterprise, forcing students to memorize and repeat facts without ever appealing to their inner truth—and we get predictable results: many students never want to read a challenging book or think a creative thought once they get out of school. The kind of teaching that transforms people does not happen if the student's inward teacher is ignored.

The second truth is even more daunting: we can speak to the teacher within our students only when we are on speaking terms with the teacher within ourselves.

The student who said that her bad teachers spoke like cartoon characters was describing teachers who have grown deaf to their inner guide, who have so thoroughly separated inner truth from outer actions that they have lost touch with a sense of self. Deep speaks to deep, and when we have not sounded our own depths, we cannot sound the depths of our students' lives.

How does one attend to the voice of the teacher within? I have no particular methods to suggest, other than the familiar ones: solitude and silence, meditative reading and walking in the woods, keeping a journal, finding a friend who will listen. I simply propose that we need to learn as many ways as we can of "talking to ourselves."

That phrase, of course, is one we normally use to name a symptom of mental imbalance—a clear sign of how our culture regards the idea of an inner voice! But people who learn to talk to themselves may soon delight in the discovery that the teacher within is the sanest conversation partner they have ever had.

We need to find every possible way to listen to that voice and take its counsel seriously, not only for the sake of our work but for the sake of our own health as well. If someone in the outer world is trying to tell us something important and we ignore his or her presence, the person either gives up and stops speaking or becomes more and more violent in attempting to get our attention.

Similarly, if we do not respond to the voice of the inward teacher, it will either stop speaking or become violent: I am convinced that some forms of depression, of which I have personal experience, are induced by a long-ignored inner teacher trying desperately to get us to listen by threatening to destroy us. When we honor that voice with simple attention, it responds by speaking more gently and engaging us in a life-giving conversation of the soul.

That conversation does not have to reach conclusions to be of value: we do not need to emerge from talking to ourselves with clear goals, objectives, and plans. Measuring the value of inner dialogue by its practical outcomes is like measuring the value of a friendship by the number of problems that are solved when friends get together.

Conversation among friends has its own rewards: in the presence of our friends, we have the simple joy of feeling at ease, at home, trusted and able to trust. We attend to the inner teacher not to get fixed but to befriend the deeper self, to cultivate a sense of identity and integrity that allows us to feel at home wherever we are.

Listening to the inner teacher also offers an answer to one of the most basic questions teachers face: How can I develop the *authority* to teach, the capacity to stand my ground in the midst of the complex forces of both the classroom and my own life?

In a culture of technique, we often confuse authority with power, but the two are not the same. Power works from the outside in, but authority works from the inside out. We are mistaken when we seek authority outside ourselves, in sources ranging from the subtle skills of group process to that less than subtle method of social control called grading. This view of teaching turns the teacher into the cop on the corner, trying to keep things moving amicably and by consent but always having recourse to the coercive power of the law.

External tools of power have occasional utility in teaching, but they are no substitute for authority, the authority that comes from the teacher's inner life. The clue is in the word itself, which has *author* at its core. Authority is granted to people who are perceived as *authoring* their own words, their own actions, their own lives, rather than playing a scripted role at great remove from their own hearts. When teachers depend on the coercive powers of law or technique, they have no authority at all.

I am painfully aware of the times in my own teaching when I lose touch with my inner teacher and therefore with my own authority. In those times I try to gain power by barricading myself behind the podium and my status while wielding the threat of grades. But when my teaching is authorized by the teacher within me, I need neither weapons nor armor to teach.

Authority comes as I reclaim my identity and integrity, re-membering my selfhood and my sense of vocation. Then teaching can come from the depths of my own truth—and the truth that is within my students has a chance to respond in kind.

NOTES

1. Mohandas K. Gandhi, *An Autobiography, or the Story of My Experiments with Truth* (Ahmedabad, India: Navajivan Press, 1927).

2. Cited in Earl Schwartz, "Chronic Life," *Creative Nursing*, Feb. 1992, p. 58.

3. Václav Havel, speech delivered to joint meeting of the U.S. Congress, quoted in *Time*, Mar. 5, 1990, pp. 14–15.

4. Alice Kaplan, *French Lessons: A Memoir* (Chicago: University of Chicago Press, 1993), p. 209.

5. Kaplan, *French Lessons*, pp. 210–211.

6. Kaplan, *French Lessons*, p. 216.

7. C. Wright Mills, *The Sociological Imagination* (New York: Oxford University Press, 1959).

8. Jane Tompkins, "Pedagogy of the Distressed," *College English,* 1991, *52*(6).

9. Florida Scott-Maxwell, *The Measure of My Days* (New York: Penguin Books, 1983), p. 42.

10. Frederick Buechner, *Wishful Thinking: A Seeker's ABC* (San Francisco: HarperSanFrancisco, 1993), p. 119.

2

THE MYSTERY OF TEACHING

William Ayers

THE WORK OF A TEACHER—exhausting, complex, idiosyncratic, never twice the same—is, at its heart, an intellectual and ethical enterprise. Teaching is the vocation of vocations, a calling that shepherds a multitude of other callings. It is an activity that is intensely practical and yet transcendent, brutally matter-of-fact, and yet fundamentally a creative act. Teaching begins in challenge and is never far from mystery.

Teaching is highly personal—an intensely intimate encounter. The rhythm of teaching involves a complex journey, a journey of discovery and wonder, disappointment and fulfillment. A first step is becoming the student to your students; uncovering the fellow creatures who must be partners to the enterprise. Another is creating an environment for learning, a nurturing and challenging space in which to travel. And finally, the teacher must begin work on the intricate, many-tiered bridges that will fill up the space, connecting all the dreams, hopes, skills, experiences, and knowledge students bring to class with deeper and wider ways of knowing. Teaching requires a vast range of knowledge, ability, skill, judgment, and understanding—and it requires a thoughtful, caring person at its center.

Teaching is not something one learns to do, once and for all, and then practices, problem-free, for a lifetime, anymore than one knows how to have friends, and follows a static set of directions called "friendships" through each encounter. Teaching depends on growth and development, and it is practices in dynamic situations that are never twice the same. Wonderful teachers, young and old, will tell of fascinating insights, new understandings, unique encounters with youngsters, the intellectual puzzle and the ethical dilemmas that provide a daily challenge. Teachers, above all, must stay alive and engaged with all of this.

We are in a sense back at the beginning. It is perhaps even clearer that teaching involves a dazzling array of activities and experiences, a blizzard of actions and reactions, an attic-full of knowledge and skill. This is in part why I marvel at academics and policy-makers who so glibly prescribe for teachers, who provide tidy summaries on how to teach, who offer the "magic bullet" for instant classroom success, or who pursue projects that will finally capture and tame teaching into a set of neat propositions. I wish I knew only one thing about teaching as well as they seem to know everything. There is, in fact, a range of important skills and experiences needed to become an outstanding teacher—skills rarely acknowledged in colleges of education and never mentioned in schools. These are the subversive core of excellent teaching.

Stanislavsky (1936), the renowned Russian director and the father of method acting, argues that there are three widespread, common beliefs about acting that stand in the way of greatness. One is the belief that acting is a set of techniques and directions to be mastered. In other words, if you say your lines, move to the appointed spot on the stage, complete a specified gesture, then you are acting. Stanislavsky dismissed this as mechanical nonsense. Plenty of people can memorize lines and move around a stage, but great actors engage an audience, interact with them, and draw energy and inspiration from the relationship. Acting is dynamic.

A second obstacle is the notion that acting is mainly external. That is, you can act angry without ever having felt anger, or you can play a broken-hearted lover without ever knowing pain or loss. For Stanislavsky, actors must reach inside themselves and summon up particular aspects of their own knowledge and experience in order to act. Actors must be autobiographers, must in some sense play themselves, must find somewhere a seed of authenticity to build on. Only then can they move away from simple caricatures and learn to portray the complexities of living, human beings.

Finally, a barrier to great acting is the view that actors should, or even could learn their roles in some summative or final sense. In other words, once an actor's got Lady Macbeth, it is "hers." Stanislavsky argues that as soon as an actor believes she or he is master of the part, rigor mortis is already setting in. Being finished denies the uniqueness of each encounter with the character, destroys the dynamic and the creative core of acting. Any part must be learned anew, day by day, moment by moment, and year by year. It is never done. In essence, great acting is always in search of better acting, always beginning again.

Stanislavsky could well be advising teachers. Greatness in teaching, too, requires a serious encounter with autobiography: Who are you? How did you come to take on your views and outlooks? What forces helped to shape you? What was it like for you to be ten? What have you made of yourself? Where are you heading? An encounter with these kinds of questions is critical to outstanding teaching because teachers, whatever else they teach, teach themselves. Of all the knowledge teachers need to draw on, self-knowledge is most important (and least attended to). In this regard Rilke's (1934) advice to a young poet is appropriate:

> You are looking outward and that above all you should not do now. . . . There is only one single way. Go into yourself. Search for the reason that bids you write [or teach], find out whether it is spreading out its roots in the deepest places of your heart.

Greatness in teaching also requires getting over the notion that teaching is a set of techniques or disconnected methods. There are lots of people who write adequate lesson plans, keep order and quiet in their classrooms, deliver competent instruction in algebra or phonics, and are lousy teachers. Outstanding teachers engage youngsters, interact with them, draw energy and direction from them, and find ways to give them a reason to follow along. This is the difficult and serious work of teaching.

Greatness in teaching, as in acting or writing, is always in pursuit of the next utterance, the next performance, the next encounter. It is not—can never be—finished or summed up. Keeping track is in service of what is yet to come. Great teaching demands an openness to something new, something unique, something dynamic. In teaching it must always be, "Here I go again."

There are hundreds of other things one needs to know to become an outstanding teacher, many of which teachers will discover as they are needed. Here is a small sample:

○ *Creative insubordination.* I had been teaching at P.S. 269 for about four hours when the intercom squawked on for the seventh time: "If anyone drives a red station wagon, your lights are on." The seventh mindless interruption (the first had been a scratchy recording of the "Star Spangled Banner"); the seventh assault on our senses; the seventh reminder that our space was not our own and that learning was not respected. I got a screwdriver, pulled a table over to the wall, took apart the intercom, clipped the wires, and reassembled the whole thing. I then sent a student to the office with the bad news that our intercom was dysfunctional. It took three years to repair—three years of liberation from the box.

Every successful teacher I know (and every principal) can tell stories of creative insubordination—of regulations ignored, paper work "lost," procedures subverted. An enormous number of the existing regulations in schools serve bureaucracy but not youngsters. The guiding principle is simple: creative insubordination is justified if it serves student learning.

○ *Criticism/self-criticism.* In the lunchroom at P.S. 269 a colleague reprimanded a misbehaving seven-year-old girl by brandishing a pair of scissors and threatening to cut off her pony tail. I intervened, comforted the child, and pursued a complaint against him through an incredible wall of pressure to back down. It was unpleasant, but it opened an important conversation about appropriate and inappropriate discipline, about humiliation and abuse versus concern and community.

If teachers are never critical, they never have to test their deepest beliefs and values, and over time those values disappear. Soon they are acting like the teacher they once despised, they have become the people they once warned others about, and they have forgotten all the things that made them want to teach in the first place.

Similarly, if teachers are never self-critical they will lose their capacity for renewal and growth. They will become self-justifying and dogmatic. On the other side, if teachers are too self-critical they become powerless and timid. The tension is to end each day with a strong understanding of what could be improved, and to begin the next with forgiveness and hope.

Teachers are taught, in all kinds of ways, lessons in accommodation and conformity when they ought to be learning criticism and self-criticism. Teachers need to be critical because so much of schooling is inadequate or wrong; self-critical because there is always a new challenge, a new demand. Learning to be critical requires taking some risks, and these are neither simple nor easy to take. Again, the guiding principle is to be a resistance fighter on behalf of children, not to take risks simply to stay in shape.

○ *Finding allies.* Teaching is often isolated and isolating, and an assumption of teacher preparation is that it must always be this way. In fact, outstanding teaching is usually teaching against the grain, and teaching against the grain can best be accomplished with allies. This means supporters, friends, co-conspirators, and comrades. Learning how to find allies and build alliances can be life-saving.

○ *Learning from your own experience.* When we sent our first child off to school I experienced a jarring moment, an epiphany. I had been teaching young children for many years, advising parents on a wide range of issues, including the best and most painless ways to separate from their youngsters at school. When my own time came, I found that all my good advice to others was impossible to follow myself. Separation was tough. I felt like a midwife friend of mine who had assisted in the births of hundreds of babies before her own first child was born. In the middle of labor she cried out, "I've told hundreds of women, 'you can do it,' and it can't be done."

Teachers are encouraged to develop a professional stance that is outside their own experience. They are expected to assume a distanced superiority and to speak an arcane and inaccessible language. It is stronger and more fruitful to practice humility in the classroom, to have the courage to admit what you don't know, to invite others to teach you, and to stay close to your own experience. Good teaching requires audacity, but it also demands humility.

○ *Linking consciousness to conduct.* It is important to be both a dreamer and a doer, to hold onto ideals but also to struggle continually to enact those ideals in concrete situations. Many teachers begin with a romanticized idea of a "peaceable kingdom in the classroom," rather than a robust, interactive, dynamic space. They harbor the illusion that the classroom can be easily walled off from larger issues in the children's (and all of our) lives, and that their own good intentions will be enough to make their classrooms places of sweetness and light. When the classroom proves to be somewhat unpredictable, when issues from "out there" become enacted "in here," when teaching is more exhausting, demanding, and uncertain than ever imagined, teachers can become frustrated, disillusioned, and burned out.

The way out, I believe, is to expect that teaching in a humane, child-centered way is not easier but requires greater intelligence, reflection, justification, and commitment. It is teaching toward something better, and it requires, therefore, involvement in the wider world of children and families, of communities and neighborhoods, of society. Holding onto ideals is a way to resist acceding to the unacceptable things we find in the world; struggling alongside others to improve society is a way to become more focused and more effective as teachers, and also as citizens.

○ *Authentic friendship.* The ideal of friendship can be a guide for teaching, or it can be a trap. Teachers who start off desperately wanting to be "friends" with their students often end up being distant, authoritarian, and arbitrary, in part because they thought of friendship as a matter of being likable, popular, or nice. With this somewhat surface notion of friendship, it is easy to become inappropriate with students, to lose your bearings, or to become confused about how to act. Feeling betrayed, friends can turn easily into enemies.

One student teacher I worked with spoke openly about his living arrangements and sex life when talking with middle school students on the first day in their classroom. They had asked, and he was "being their friend." The incident, needless to say, was a disaster for him and for them. He had failed to really examine what it means to be a friend. Like a new kid on the block, he was prodded and provoked, and his desire to be popular led to his downfall.

A stronger sense of friendship is to think in terms of deep caring and compassion for others. Friendship, then, is a matter of solidarity between subjects, between human beings, and solidarity means criticism as well as acceptance. We share some intimate matters with certain friends, but not all. We don't want our friends doing something we take to be wrong, and so we are willing to raise questions and criticisms, even when that can be difficult. We don't want our friends to be weak or hopeless, and so we are willing to offer guidance and advice. Being popular or being liked every moment is not the point—a real friendship has bumpy and difficult times, too, and that can be the greater part of its strength.

○ *Balance and clarity.* There are literally thousands of good ideas floating around for making classrooms more decent and dynamic. The problem is that ideas come at teachers ninety miles an hour, and teachers need to choose what will work for them and their students. Trying to implement a new idea every day is not a particularly hopeful strategy. One problem is that big transformative ideas require sustained attention. "Whole language," for example, if taken seriously, could completely transform school practice, the shape of the day, the meaning of curriculum, everything. "Character education" could mean an entirely different school culture and ethos. If, on the other hand, they are the latest fads, something to fit into existing classroom practice, techniques and nothing more, then teachers can say things like, "We do whole language in ability groups from 9:00–9:30," or, "We do character education after lunch."

Teachers are typically trapped in the role of passive recipients rather than of active creators of their teaching. Teachers can resist this by operating out of the principle of "less is more," deciding what makes sense at the center of their own classroom life, and implementing that central core while resisting all the free-falling, well-meaning ideas. The best staff development, then, is not another workshop with an educational guru, but is visiting classrooms of other teachers you admire, or carving out time and space to reflect seriously on core principles and practices. Good schools are generally places where a lot of good teachers have been gathered together and allowed to teach. This means school leaders have attracted and recruited good teachers, and then run interference with bureaucratic regulations, state mandates, and the entire apparatus that undermines teaching.

Good schools are always unique: each the creation of particular teachers, administrators, parents, and youngsters working together to bring their vision of a better educational experience to life in classrooms. Good schools do not follow a generic, one-size-fits-all approach to education, but rely instead on a community of people working together, figuring out how to solve problems and improve their school on a daily basis, and then gathering the freedom to act on their conclusions. Reform must be crafted school by school, from the bottom up, and school improvement is generally a matter for the school community itself.

"Goodness" is complex and hard to measure on a simple scale, but there are several themes that, taken together, make a school more likely to be effective. Good schools tend to be organized around and powered by a set of *core values*. Values may be drawn from long tradition or from the specific needs and orientations of particular communities, but they must be embraced and owned by the community itself. Values cannot simply be tacked on, but must be explicit, obvious, and embodied in the daily life of the school.

Good schools have *high expectations for all learners*. The school community has straightforward goals that apply to all students and yet are flexible and personalized for each. They find ways to nurture and challenge the wide range of youngsters who actually arrive at school, and they don't consider the condition of the lives of their students a reasonable excuse for failure.

Good schools are places where *teachers are respected* and are expected to be responsible decision-makers. Teachers are not cogs in a machine, but feel themselves to be valuable, even indispensable. Each teacher feels a sense of authorship of her own teaching text, ownership of her own work.

Good schools are *geared to continuous improvement.* No school, no teaching, no curriculum is ever perfect; good schools are places where people are neither smug nor complacent. Good schools are always in the making.

I have tried to change, create, or improve schools and classrooms for much of my life. One thing I have learned along the way is that there are no guarantees—you dive into the work with faith and hope and fear. Another is that you must think big, question everything, and not merely tinker around the edges—rearranging the deck chairs on the Titanic might make for a more pleasant view, but it does not prevent the inevitable plunge to the ocean floor. At the same time, you must attend to details, to the needs and desires of specific people. You must think globally and act locally, head in the stars and feet on the ground. It's a stretch.

Recently, I have been working with an energetic group of parents and teachers to create a small public school within a large school building. Called the Imani School, this project is still more dream than reality, more faith than substance. *Imani* means "faith" in Swahili—the name was suggested by a teacher who keeps the faith for a brighter future as well as anyone I know.

The community drawn together to build this school is not made up of idle dreamers. Imani School is located in a poor, urban neighborhood. Many of the families live in depressed, dilapidated, and neglected housing projects. Most of the youngsters have witnessed violence firsthand, all are aware of the presence of exploitation and crime. One of the things that makes these teachers and parents so inspiring is precisely their willingness and ability to fight for a decent school and future for their children when there are so many reasons to give up.

An initial focus of the Imani School planning group was to "turn weaknesses into strengths." We organized small teams to tour and map the neighborhood, looking for community assets. The larger challenge was to name putative problems, and to see if they could be transformed into assets.

The park, fire house, and small commercial district are obvious community strengths. How can the school use them? Classes can take trips, perhaps, or organize a community campaign to keep the park clean. Some classes might "adopt" a restaurant or small business to study and support. These assets are worth naming, and it is valuable to figure out how to bring them more fully into the life of the school.

A deeper challenge is to try to look at problems from the other side. There are several vacant lots near the school—are these potential sites for gardens or play lots? The community has a high rate of unemployment—can some unemployed adults be organized to work in or around the school on specific projects? The planning group isn't certain, but attempting to turn weaknesses into strengths has expanded people's imaginative space.

One thing the group did early on was to try to discover our deep, collective values. We imagined that each of us had the power to magically bestow on all the people of the world three qualities, and we asked ourselves what they would be. These qualities could not be physical attributes like good health, material goods like wealth or a Rolls Royce, or specific religious affiliations. But beyond that, they could be anything at all.

We worked and worked on this activity, individually and in groups, and eventually achieved consensus on five qualities: compassion, curiosity, respect for others and self, creativity, and an ability to participate fully in society. This took a long time, and it represented a lot of conversation, struggle, compromise, and redefinition.

These qualities became for us our core values, a guide to future action. Since these were qualities we wanted for all people, qualities that would in some sense improve the world, we felt that they had to come alive and be readily apparent in school practice. We could not in good conscience teach the rules of grammar and ignore, for example, respect. How could curiosity become evident in the hallways? Would there be respect in the cafeteria? What would it look like? Was compassion going to be a part of every single interaction? How? None of this solved the problem of what to do in school, but it did provide a helpful lens through which to imagine and examine practice.

These core values led to an emphasis on democracy and active participation in social life. As one of the parents put it, "We should act as if we live in a democracy, and in that way make it become more so." Respect and fairness would be explicitly emphasized in the school, and teachers would strive to create classrooms where people can think and question freely, speak and write and read critically, work cooperatively, consider the common good and then act accordingly. Every class would need to have community service built into the day—the youngest children might tend a garden, for example, others would help in tutoring projects, the oldest would work in community organizations, and everyone would have to be involved in clean-up and maintenance.

The planning group emphasized the importance of experience as a teacher—hands-on learning, research projects involving first-person encounters and primary sources. There is a commitment from teachers to use the community and its residents as a school resource. Everyone teaches, everyone learns, and knowledge is keyed to action, experimentation, reflection, self-correction, discovery, and surprise. There is a desire to encourage youngsters to write their own stories and plays, to build on what they know and experience even when it is difficult or painful to do so. No student will be silenced.

Of course, developing an education based on experience is just the beginning. John Dewey (1938) noted that experience and education are not the same thing. We are all having experiences all the time, and yet some experiences may be disconnected events leading nowhere, or they may even be uneducative in the sense that they shut down or distort future growth. The challenge for teachers who are building an education based on experience is to create opportunities for students to have the kinds of experiences that will enable them to grow and develop into further experiences, and eventually to take control of their own learning. Allowing youngsters to tell their stories is one hopeful activity; providing them access to a wide range of materials is another. We know we are successful when students are willing to forge their own next steps, when they face the future with some love, some indignation, and a lot of courage.

Students at Imani School will be respected—valued for who they are, and honored for who they are becoming. Their projects, it is hoped, will shape much of the day, and their concrete efforts will keep the place running. Students will know that without them, the lunchroom would not be beautiful, the grounds would not be kept up, and nothing would work. This is in sharp contrast to schools where the very presence of students is seen mainly as a problem, an encumbrance, an obstacle to the smooth functioning of the place. Teachers at Imani School want to communicate a deeply held belief that they value children, that they find their own work meaningful precisely because of the presence and activity of youngsters. The planning group wants there to be neither a cult of youth, nor a cult of adulthood, but rather a sense of intergenerational dependence, care, responsibility, and commitment.

Imani School is being built. It is still in the planning stages, more possibility than reality, and it may not get where it hopes to go. But it seems to me to be on the right tack, a project that rejects the notion that school failure is inevitable, and, most importantly, acts in common purpose with parents and youngsters. No one at Imani is "saving children"—we are saving one another, and, perhaps with enough faith in people, saving the future.

Frederick Douglass tells a remarkable story of learning to read as a subversive activity. As a slave, Douglass had no rights and meager opportunities. Reading among slaves was strictly forbidden for it could open worlds and create unimaginable mischief. Besides, according to their overlords, slaves had no need of reading. They could be trained in the necessary menial and backbreaking work. Yet his master's wife, believing him to be an intelligent youngster, undertook to teach Douglass how to read the Bible in hopes that he would come closer to God. When the master discovered the crime, he exploded: "It will unfit him to be a slave!"

Education will unfit anyone to be a slave. That is because education is bold, adventurous, creative, vivid, illuminating—in other words, education is for self-activating explorers of life, for those who would challenge fate, for doers and activists, for citizens. Training is for slaves, for loyal subjects, for tractable employees, for willing consumers, for obedient soldiers. Education tears down walls; training is all barbed wire.

What we call education is usually no more than training. We are so busy operating schools that we have lost sight of learning. We mostly participate in certification mills, institutions founded on notions of control and discipline, lifeless and joyless places where people serve time and master a few basic skills on their way to a plain piece of paper that justifies and sanctions the whole affair. Sometimes, these places are merely mindless, and sometimes they are expressly malevolent.

A hundred years ago, this country developed a system of schools run out of the Interior Department called Indian Boarding Schools, a few of which survive to this day. The premise of these schools is that Native American children can be educated if they are stripped of everything Indian and taught to be like whites. Taken from their homes, these youngsters were punished severely for speaking their own languages, practicing their own religions, or attempting to contact their families. Everything Native had to be erased as a first step toward official learning. Some students, of course, went along, but many rebelled, refused to learn, and were labeled intractable.

The cost of education at an Indian Boarding School was great—dignity, individuality, humanity, maybe even sanity. The payoff was rather small: a menial job, a marginal place in the social order. Students had to submit to humiliation, degradation, and mutilation simply to learn how to function at the lowest levels of society. No wonder most refused: The price was high, the benefit meager.

It is not much different in many schools today. We claim to be giving students key skills and knowledge, and yet we deny them the one thing that is essential to their survival: something to live for. All the units in drug awareness, gang prevention, and mental health together are not worth that single hopeful thing.

When we as teachers recognize that we are partners with our students in life's long and complex journey, when we begin to treat them with the dignity and respect they deserve for simply being, then we are on the road to becoming worthy teachers. It is just that simple—and just that difficult.

Jane Addams, founder of Hull House, once asked, "How shall we respond to the dreams of youth?" It is a dazzling and elegant question, a question that demands an answer—a range of answers, really, spiraling outward in widening circles. It is a teacher's kind of question. It is a question to take with us as we plunge into teaching, full of dread and hope, alive to both, living a teacher's life, singular and mysterious, helping to create a generation unfit for slavery.

REFERENCES

Dewey, J. (1938). *Experience and education.* New York: Macmillan.

3

PASSIONATE TEACHING

Robert L. Fried

> *I believe I make a difference not only by helping kids connect
> math and science to their lives, but also in understanding how to
> reach their goals in life—how to be somebody.*

—Maria Ortiz, science teacher

The destiny of Maria Ortiz, now in her twenty-second year of teaching science at Lewis B. Fox Middle School in an inner-city neighborhood of Hartford, Connecticut, was probably decided on the very day she entered first grade, back in the village of Canóvanas, Puerto Rico, and encountered the woman she still refers to as "Mrs. Betancourt."

> She was not only a teacher, but a kind of mother to us—so loving to each kid that I can remember almost every single moment of first and second grade (I had her for two years) even though it was more than forty years ago. Every morning, she was waiting for us outside in the school yard. She hugged each kid like we were her long-lost children. Then she would gather us around her, like a mother hen with her chicks, and lead us inside.
>
> And waiting for us would be hot cocoa and soda crackers—she didn't believe we should have to wait for mid-morning snack time; we got our snack first thing. Then she would get us singing, all of us. And her songs were full of tricks to make us learn things even while we were singing and having fun: songs about the alphabet, about animals and numbers. We would get so involved in her projects—drawing,

building things, making a doll out of an old sock with buttons for its eyes—that we didn't realize how much we were learning. We *knew* we had to do schoolwork, but because of her warmth it didn't seem like work, it seemed like fun.

You see, I never planned to be a teacher. Since I liked science and was good at it, my parents wanted me to be a doctor. Instead, I studied pharmacology for four years in college and then started an apprenticeship in a drugstore. But as soon as I started practicing, I knew it wasn't for me. I didn't want to spend my life putting labels on bottles and selling them to customers for high prices.

So I went back to my dean and told him I was in the wrong profession and was quitting. He asked why, and I said, "A highly regarded doctor sent in a prescription for a woman, and although it was only for aspirin, he gave it a scientific name, and the druggist told me to cover over the 'Bayer Aspirin' label and charge her $20. I told him I wouldn't do it. If that's the kind of business it is, pharmacy is not for me. I have to have an opportunity to live!"

Then I thought I would change my major and become a science researcher. But my sister-in-law said, "Why don't you become a teacher?" Immediately Mrs. Betancourt flashed into my mind. And I said to myself: "Maybe that's what I *really* want to be—I want to be like *her!*"

So I began teaching right away. There was such a shortage of math and science teachers that they were willing to hire me even though I had never taken an education course and didn't know any methodology. I had to create everything myself, without relying on theories.

I started teaching science to students in grades 7 and 9, in a middle school in Hato Rey, near San Juan. As the newest teacher, naturally they gave me what they thought were the worst classes. (They didn't tell me that nine other teachers had already quit because they could not handle the kids.) I can still remember one of the students, Ismari Rivera. Our class was held in the art room, and when I came in, he was sitting atop the pottery wheel, slowly spinning around before an admiring audience of classmates. He gave me a look that said: "I dare you to get me off, or make me stop."

I decided to ignore him and busied myself at my desk. After a while, Ismari looked up and said: "Are you the new teacher?" I said, "Yes." He paused, and then asked, "Are you going to leave us, too?" I said, no, I wasn't going to leave. And he continued to spin on the wheel and I continued to ignore him and began talking to the kids.

For the first week or two, I said nothing at all about science. I was operating totally on instinct, and my instinct told me that I needed first of all to get to know who these kids really were. The principal had said that they were mentally retarded, but I soon found out that they were not that at all, just angry. We talked about the kind of sports and music they liked, and they told me all about who was in their families, and of course they asked about mine, and I told them.

At the end of the first week, I knew *so* much about their lives, and somehow, *that* changed their behavior. They probably saw me as the kind of older teenager that they might want to be, and they were grateful that I was so interested in them. They saw themselves as rebels in the school because there was so much anger around them, in their lives, in school, in their homes.

After a while, I could tell them that I was a science teacher and that my job was to teach the science curriculum. But I promised that we would take one day each week and pull our chairs into a circle and talk about whatever was on their minds. We set some rules: everybody had to promise to listen to each other and to take turns if they wanted to talk. When somebody mentioned a problem they were having, one by one the other kids could give suggestions or make helpful comments.

Ismari didn't like this. He had gotten down from the pottery wheel when the other kids stopped paying attention to him. But now he just sat in the corner and sulked. And I still decided it was best to ignore him. So eventually, he moved closer and closer, until he was in the circle.

I remember one girl, named Waleska, who told us she hated her father because he had killed her little sister. She said that he had backed up his car and it had run over her sister. She couldn't understand how he could have done that. And so we talked about it, and we all decided that it had been an accident, and that her father didn't mean it. Slowly, with our help, Waleska was able to understand this too. The circle gave them a chance to let their emotions out and deal with them. There was some crying, at times, by all of us. But there was also a lot of laughter.

And so I became a teacher, just like that. After a few years, I was offered a chance to come to America and teach for a year. I came to this school, in Hartford, in 1972. And I'm still here. I believe I make a difference not only by helping kids connect math and science to their lives, but also in understanding how to reach their goals in life—how to *be* somebody. It's strange: in Puerto Rico the kids seem so proud of themselves. But when they come here, they suffer a great blow to their esteem. We have to work very hard to help them convince themselves that their goals still matter, that nothing is impossible, that they can do it, that to be bilingual is to have power.

I don't feel fifty years old. I can still think like a teenager. There are three teachers in Hartford schools who were my students, here at Fox Middle, and another who's at the university, studying to be a teacher. And we owe it all to Mrs. Betancourt.

When I hear stories like this—and almost every school has its stories of inspired and devoted adults who reach out in ways that change people's lives—it occurs to me that we educators and social scientists have not yet found a way to capture what we hear and see. When we try to synthesize what has inspired us, to generalize from these individual stories and draw them into a theory or a technique, the images don't survive, like certain wildflowers that won't bloom if you try to transplant them.

We boil the stories down into their essences but their power slips away. We try to draw from them a methodology that seems so personal as to be nearly impossible to transmit to others, leaving us with fleeting impressions that can only be admired from a distance. We hear about the legendary Mrs. Betancourt in Puerto Rico, or about the work of Maria Ortiz amid the urban blight of Hartford, and we somehow end up putting a frame around their unique gifts and placing it up on a shelf, so it won't get trampled when the next bunch of kids comes storming or slouching into the classroom.

Our inability to translate great stories into a useful pedagogy is due to our encountering something that people find hard to identify, talk about, or hold onto intellectually. I believe that what we are dealing with is *passion*. And it all feels too special, too intense, too outside the boundaries of professional consideration.

But I am convinced that passion—our own as well as other people's—can be analyzed and put to work. The examples, strategies, and techniques I describe in these pages are instances of passion-in-action, ways of transforming those images into use in our daily work with children and young adults. I hope to celebrate passionate teaching and make it accessible to us in whatever roles we are called upon to play. My challenge is to enable readers to translate potentially exciting ideas and models into their own practical idioms, so that these will survive the inevitable clash with our workaday constraints.

Why passion, when we have so many other ways of thinking about teaching and learning? Passion seems a rather odd way to characterize what teachers ought to bring to their work. Bumping into one another on a Monday morning, not many of us are likely to ask: "So, are you feeling passionate enough for your classes today?" Isn't there enough irrationality and foolheadedness in education and most everywhere else these days without adding passion to the soup?

Yet as I look into hundreds of classrooms, watch teachers working with all kinds of students, when I ask myself what makes the greatest difference in the quality of student learning—it is a teacher's passion that leaps out. More than knowledge of subject matter. More than variety of teaching techniques. More than being well-organized, or friendly, or funny, or fair. *Passion.*

With teachers, as with anyone else who has a goal in life to do great things—to create works of art or defend the environment or right social wrongs or create new technologies—passionate people are the ones who make a difference in our lives. By the intensity of their beliefs and actions, they connect us with a sense of value that is within—and beyond—ourselves.

Sometimes that passion burns with a quiet, refined intensity; sometimes it bellows forth with thunder and eloquence. But in whatever form or style a teacher's passion emerges, students know they are in the presence of someone whose devotion to learning is exceptional. Even when that devotion has an intensity that may make students uncomfortable, they still know it is something important. It's what makes a teacher unforgettable.

Of some of our teachers, we remember their foibles and mannerisms; of others, their kindness and encouragement, or their fierce devotion to standards of work that we probably did not share at the time. And of those who inspired us most, we remember what they cared about, and that they cared about us and the person we might become. It is this quality of caring about ideas and values, this fascination with the potential for growth within people, this depth and fervor about doing things well and striving for excellence, that comes closest to what I mean in describing a "passionate teacher."

Here I can imagine an experienced teacher, someone with a pretty good reputation among colleagues and students, slamming this book shut and tossing it onto the teacher's-room table: "What's this guy want from us now—blood?! For eighteen years I've done my job, and done it pretty damn well. I not only teach them the stuff, I take the time to try to get to know the kids in my classes. Isn't it enough to be a caring teacher who's got the students' interests at heart, who helps them learn each in their own way, who gives everybody a chance to succeed? What business does anybody have asking me to be 'passionate' on top of everything else?"

Obviously no business at all. We should be more than grateful for each of the skilled, dedicated, caring teachers in our schools who do good enough work under conditions that are often demanding and stressful. I am tempted to say: "Oh, but this is not a book for *you*—it's for those other teachers, the ones who are just putting in their time and doing the minimum they need to get by."

But maybe it *is* part of my job in this book to make good teachers feel dissatisfied with being "good enough." Passion may just be the difference between being remembered as a "pretty good teacher" who made chemistry or algebra or tenth-grade English "sort of interesting"—or as the teacher who opened up a world of the mind to some students who had no one else to make them feel that they were capable of doing great things with test tubes, trumpets, trigonometry, or T. S. Eliot.

How, then, is a teacher "passionate"?

You can be passionate about your field of knowledge: in love with the poetry of Emily Dickinson or the prose of Marcus Garvey; dazzled by the spiral of DNA or the swirl of van Gogh's cypresses; intrigued by the origins of the Milky Way or the demise of the Soviet empire; delighted by the sound of Mozart or the sonority of French vowels; a maniac for health and fitness or wild about algebraic word problems . . .

You can be passionate about issues facing our world: active in the struggle for social justice or for the survival of the global environment; dedicated to the celebration of cultural diversity or to the search for a cure for AIDS . . .

You can be passionate about children: about the rate of violence experienced by young black males; about including children with disabilities in all regular school activities; about raising the low rate of high school completion by Latino children; about the insidious effects of sexism, racism, and social class prejudice on the spirits of all children; about the neglect of "average" kids in schools where those at the "top" and "bottom" seem to get all the attention; about the decline of literacy in an age of instant electronic gratification; about the wealth of hidden talent that goes unnoticed in so many children.

To be avowedly passionate about at least some of these things sets one apart from those who approach each day in a fog of fatigue, ritual, routine, or resignation, or who come to work wrapped in a self-protective cocoon. The passion that accompanies our attention to subjects, issues, and children is not just something we offer our students. It is also a gift we grant ourselves: a way of honoring our life's work, our profession. It says: "I know why I am devoting this life I've got to these children."

I want to distinguish passionate teaching from mere idiosyncrasies or foibles. Lots of teachers have "pet peeves" or fixations: points of grammar, disciplinary practices, eccentricities of dress or diction. These may, indeed, make them memorable to their students (for better or worse). But the passions I am speaking about convey much more. It is teachers' passions that help them and their students escape the slow death of "business as usual," the rituals of going through the motions, which in schools usually means checking that the homework was done, covering the curriculum, testing, grading, and quickly putting it all behind us. The example we set as passionate adults allows us to connect to young people's minds and spirits in a way that can have a lasting positive impact on their lives.

For me, passionate teachers include all those who ever entered the classroom because they loved kids, because they loved learning, because they wanted in some small way to change the world. Sadly, many who entered with high hopes have not been able to hold onto their passion for very long, because of the conditions under which they work. Others nurse their passions quietly, almost embarrassed to care so much or to hold to such high standards in a climate of school and society that looks for compromises and shortcuts. Still others have become embittered by the whole scene: students who won't do any work, administrators who manipulate, colleagues who complain all the time, officials who won't provide adequate funds, parents who can't seem to be bothered, and a society that would rather blame its schools than fund them.

Many disillusioned teachers began their careers as passionate people, only to have their spirits dampened, depleted, ground to dust. *The passion I talk about belongs as much to them as to the brightest-eyed newcomers or the cheeriest veterans.* It is their struggle, too. Our nation of children, faced with the ever-changing demands of being citizens, family members, and breadwinners in a twenty-first-century world, cannot afford for any of their teachers' passions to be eroded or squelched.

Who Are the Passionate Teachers?

What does passion look like when we see it at work in the classroom? Let's look briefly at some of the people whose stories appear in these pages.

We've just met Maria Ortiz. As I see it, her passion is to make sure that the students in her middle school, especially the girls, almost all of whom are African American or Latina, come to view science as a part of their lives and a part of their future. At a moment when so many forces around them are pushing these girls to abandon their education and their intellectual potential, Maria is determined to be that other voice—friendly and warm, but fiercely protective of the right of these young people to pursue a life of the mind.

For Tim Sullivan, the passion lies in a resolve that his fourth graders are going to be players on the field where classroom learning meets the real world: whether it's in lobbying for a seat-belt law, organizing and running a school store, or spray-painting "Stop, Look, Walk" on the sidewalk of every street corner near every elementary school in town.

David Ervin is a middle school music teacher in a middle-class college town who inspires the entire seventh grade to imagine, create, write, compose, organize, and stage an original musical play each year, with each of them playing a part.

Yvonne Griffin is passionately committed to her students' making choices in their relationships with other people. She is determined that they become young people who *make* things happen, rather than becoming people that things happen *to*.

Ed Clarke will not let any student he works with in his English classes write anything that is less than the best they can do. He flunks students in honors classes who try to slide by, while publishing the best poems and stories of even his least-skilled writers. Many of those who flunk come back the following year to work with him to get it right.

Alfredo Fuentes teaches math and wages a passionate struggle to convince everybody in the school that algebra is for *every* student, even those who have trouble with long division or don't yet know their multiplication tables.

When Dan Bisaccio was teaching science in a rural, working-class town in New Hampshire, his job was to show his students how to think and act like scientists, rather than simply to learn about science. The passion I witnessed in his teaching of evolution showed in his skill at coaching students to actively discover and debate Darwin's theories for themselves, not merely to read about and memorize them.

Susan Lukas teaches literature at an independent school with a diverse student body. She also writes poetry and fiction and edits manuscripts for other writers. Her passion as a teacher lies in assigning to her students works of literature that have very great meaning for her, and finding a way to encourage honest discussion about them with all her students, even those who are hostile to the authors and their message.

Christine Sullivan teaches writing to students in all four academic levels of a traditional rural/suburban high school. Her passion about student portfolio writing has led her students to discover their own learning styles, to minimize concern for letter grades while adopting a performance-based approach to learning, and to advocate for their own individual approaches to assignments given by other teachers.

Some of the most passionate teachers are quiet, intense, thoughtful people. They patiently insist on high standards of quality in a language lab or drafting class. They talk with students in conference about their work and where their talents and persistence might lead them. They stop to respond to a comment thrown out by a student that has more than a germ of truth in it. They bring in something from their current reading or their personal history that demonstrates the power of ideas.

On the other hand, a certain amount of abandon can also deliver the message. One teacher from Georgia announced at a workshop: "Ah intend this year to be jest a little bit *craaazy* about what ah'm teaching!" What he wanted his fellow teachers to hear was that he was eager to break out of the competent but comfortable mold he had built around himself, and to break up the unimaginable complacency of his students.

What impresses me about such teachers is that no particular set of teaching tricks or topics, much less a common personality type, epitomizes them. As individual as they are, what unites them are some ways they approach the mission of teaching; they organize their curricula and their daily work with students in practical ways that play to those different strengths. These practical observations—the tools of the passionate craft of teaching—will emerge, but let's look at two of them here:

1. Passionate teachers *organize and focus* their passionate interests *by getting to the heart of their subject* and sharing with their students some of what lies there—the beauty and power that drew them to this field in the first place and that has deepened over time as they have learned and experienced more. They are not after a narrow or elitist perspective, but rather a depth of engagement that serves as a base for branching out to other interests and disciplines.

2. Passionate teachers *convey their passion* to novice learners—their students—*by acting as partners in learning,* rather than as "experts in the field." As partners, they invite less experienced learners to search for knowledge and insightful experiences, and they build confidence and competence among students who might otherwise choose to sit back and watch their teacher do and say interesting things.

But how do we make passionate teaching happen? How do we shove aside all the stuff we're supposed to do and make room in our lesson plans for things we feel especially strongly about?

Giving Our Passions a Focus

Working within their disciplines, teachers best express their passions not only by what they celebrate but also by what they choose to ignore. "A man is rich," quoth Thoreau, "in terms of the number of things he can afford to leave alone." Passionate teachers put it thus: *A teacher is wise in terms of that part of the curriculum he or she conscientiously chooses not to cover.* Theodore Sizer, author of *Horace's Compromise* and *Horace's School,* calls this "the politics of subtraction" and says it is the toughest part of the reform agenda for schools.

Teachers can stop being the servants of a syllabus or curriculum produced somewhere else and take charge of a course or program of studies they have shaped out of their convictions of what is truly important and what they want students to remember and be able to use months and years later. We identify our passions within our subject area to separate what we care deeply about from what we are less excited about. We teach wholeheartedly those things that open up pathways to knowledge and engagement within our discipline for learners who have not yet come to appreciate them. We take courage from our deep interest in some things to pay less attention to other things, and we exercise a teacher's most solemn responsibility in choosing what to teach and what to ignore or pass over lightly.

We may want to ask our students to study, in depth, the Cuban Missile Crisis, rather than surveying the entire Cold War history. Or study the ecology of one small nearby pond instead of covering all the chapters in the biology text. Or learn a lot about Emily Dickinson and leave other nineteenth-century poets to be discovered later in the students' lives. Language arts teachers in an urban middle school decide that, for students in grades 6 through 8, learning how to write good, clear, convincing prose is so vital to students' future success that they want colleagues in science and social studies and math to teach writing across the curriculum, at the expense of some other things in the syllabus.

Unless, for example, we are teaching someone to operate a piece of dangerous machinery or to combine volatile chemicals in a laboratory, the act of teaching has more to do with preparing a learner to be an eager seeker of new skills than with nailing down pertinent data. Helping young people engage in the ideas and issues surrounding content is crucial to their ability to make meaning out of what they are learning. If it seems unconnected and boring, they will soon forget all or almost all of it and our teaching will have been for naught.

As teachers, we have only our passions to guard against students' inclination to find things adults care about boring and not worth remembering or putting to use. But it is not enough to focus on our passionate interests. We must show our students what it means to be passionate learners as well.

Conveying Our Passionate Interests

To students, teachers are critically important role models *because of what they are still learning,* not just because of what they already know. It is as experienced learners, with a high interest in and high standards for knowledge and skills, that we communicate the lasting value of these things to students. The obverse is also true: when we are no longer learning, we no longer teach, because we have lost the power to exemplify for young people what it means to be intellectually active. Even though we may still be able to present them with information, we have become purveyors of subject matter, "deliverers of educational services," in the jargon of the field.

Passionate teachers share their commitment to active learning by *showing,* not just telling. Teachers are, after all, role models of adults who care about issues of the mind. We are readers, writers, researchers, explorers of new knowledge, new ideas, new techniques and technologies, new ways of looking at old facts and theories. Our very excitement about these things helps young people reach beyond their social preoccupations and self-centeredness. Teachers are people who manage to earn a living by doing intellectual work for the betterment of society. We have found a career that, for all its shortcomings, allows us to open up the world for young people. Our greatest gift to students is to engage them through passionate teaching in areas of intense concern to us—intellectual, aesthetic, cultural, spiritual, political, environmental—and, by the example we set, to help them accept themselves as vibrant and thoughtful people.

A key to such engagement is the *learning partnership* that passionate teachers create with students. It is not enough for us to have these qualities; we must bring our students with us. A high school history teacher I know in a rural New Hampshire town brought her intense interest in archaeology into the classroom by bringing her students out into the woods in search of a long-forgotten graveyard. After watching her carefully, they pitched in to clean and prop up the headstones and then, a week later, followed her into the local historical society to search for the records of the people whose graves they had tended. Each student, again following her example, became a two-hundred-year-old former town resident and shared their life story in a presentation for townspeople.

There are any number of ways in which passionate teachers convey, through their personalities, the devotion they give to their work. Here are a few of the characteristics which will emerge again:

Passionate teachers love to work with young people, but they also care deeply about knowledge and ideas, so that they try never to let their compassion for a student serve as a reason for excusing that student's ignorance or lack of skill. They can be hard taskmasters precisely because they care for kids so deeply. Passionate teachers are alive to events both in the classroom and in the world outside school, and they bring those perspectives together in their work with students. They are always relating—and helping their students relate—learning with living, inviting students to forge their own meaning in the confrontation between life in school and life "out there in the real world."

Passionate teachers have the capacity for spontaneity and humor and for great seriousness, often at almost the same time. They join with kids in appreciating the abundant absurdity of human nature but are also sensitive to issues that deserve to be taken seriously, particularly fairness and decency in how people treat one another. They try to build a culture of mutual respect amid societal pressures to stigmatize and condemn unpopular persons and ideas and to dismiss young people and their concerns.

Passionate teachers are always taking risks, and they make at least as many mistakes as anybody else (probably more than most). What's different is how they react to their mistakes: they choose to acknowledge and learn from them, rather than to ignore or deny them. Thus, they help make the classroom a safer place for students to make their own mistakes and learn from them.

Finally, we know who passionate teachers are because they take their mission seriously and communicate their beliefs. They truly are passionate *teachers,* not just intense people who hide their passions behind a workaday mask and allow only the rare student to connect with them and benefit from their example.

Student Vulnerability and the Teacher's Role

The greatest value of our passionate concerns is that they invite students to feel emotionally alive in our presence. Children are, after all, sensitive to the same emotional currents as those I've just attributed to passionate adults: intensity, vulnerability, immediacy, risk. They may not always *want* to feel these things, but they can hardly help feeling them. School-age kids are emotionally "hanging out there" in all the physiological, social, and developmental stages they go through. They feel at times exposed, at risk, uncomfortable—anything but serene or self-satisfied.

It's so easy to forget this as we cope with children's often erratic personalities, especially in their teenage years. Even young teachers not many years removed from their own high school experience often forget what it was like to be a student. Even conscientious parents who recall their own rebelliousness expect their children to behave more consistently and more rationally. There is much pain in the loneliness, anxiety, and alienation that so many of us felt as teenagers: we want to put it out of our minds as soon as we can.

The reasons for a student's turmoil—family conflicts, worries about acceptance or sexuality, lack of meaning in life, lack of money to buy things, fears about violence—may be quite similar to, or different from, those of adults. But in most cases, what students seek from us is not that we identify with their problems (although they may seek our understanding and sympathy at times) but that we engage them around issues of importance and help them more easily accept themselves as vibrant and thoughtful people.

The pity is that we wear our success so hesitantly and that our achievements are arrayed in such drab colors. The pity is that today's teachers are heroes to so few of the young people who file into our classrooms. Schools would be wonderful places if the depth of caring about children and their future, the desire to be helpful, the reservoirs of good will that are so abundant within the teaching profession, could more often connect with the longing that young people have for acceptance, power, and respect. That schools are not so wonderful is due more to the climate created in them by social ills, lack of resources, ineffective practices, and misguided policies than by any want of caring on the part of most teachers.

Students *need* us, not because we have all the answers, but because we can help them discover the right questions. We don't always know what's good for them, but we can try to protect them from having to face life's dilemmas in ignorance or in despair—doing drugs, dropping out, drifting into a dead-end career or an unplanned parenthood. Those adults whom young people look to for guidance know how important they are to kids' futures. For all teachers, the recovery of passion can mean a recovery of our influence—dynamic and positive influence—in the lives of children.

By modeling, examining, and explaining our values and our passionate concerns in a way that does not harangue or intimidate them, we adults—teachers, parents, coaches, and mentors—encourage children and adolescents to feel okay about believing in and aspiring to thoughtfulness.

This, I argue, is what education *is*. There simply is no education without a commitment to developing the mind and the character of learners. And in our time and culture, perhaps as never before, that commitment must be a passionate one if we want young people to hear and heed that calling.

4

READING THE WORLD/
READING THE WORD

Paulo Freire

NO TOPIC COULD BE a better subject for this first letter to those who dare teach than the critical significance of teaching and the equally critical significance of learning. There is no *teaching* without *learning,* and by that I mean more than that the act of teaching demands the existence of those who teach and those who learn. What I mean is that teaching and learning take place in such a way that those who teach learn, on the one hand, because they recognize previously learned knowledge and, on the other, because by observing how the novice student's curiosity works to apprehend what is taught (without which one cannot learn), they help themselves to uncover uncertainties, rights, and wrongs.

The learning of those who teach does not necessarily take place through their apprentices' rectification of their mistakes. Their learning in their teaching is observed to the extent that, humble and open, teachers find themselves continually ready to rethink what has been thought and to revise their positions. Their learning lies in their seeking to become involved in their students' curiosity and in the paths and streams it takes them through. Some of the paths and streams that students' at times almost virgin curiosity runs through are pregnant with suggestions and questions never before noticed by teachers. But now, as they teach, not as *bureaucrats of the mind* but reconstituting the steps of their curiosity—the reason their conscious bodies, sensitive and touched, open up to the students' *guesses,* their innocence, and their discrimination—teachers who perform as such have a rich moment of learning in their teaching. Teachers first learn how to teach, but they learn how to teach as they teach something that is relearned as it is being taught.

The fact, however, that teachers learn how to teach a particular content must not in any way mean that they should venture into teaching without the necessary competence to do it. It does not give persons a license to teach what they do not know. Teachers' political, ethical, and professional responsibility puts them under an obligation to prepare and enable themselves before engaging in their teaching practice. Teaching requires constant preparation and development on the part of teachers, as is made clearer and clearer by their teaching experience, if well lived and apprehended. Such development is based on a critical analysis of their practice.

Let us begin from the learning, uncovering experience of those who are preparing for the teaching task, which necessarily involves *studying*. Obviously, my intention here is not to prescribe rules that must be strictly followed; that would be in shocking contradiction to everything I have talked about so far. On the contrary, what I am concerned with here is challenging its readers around certain points and aspects, demonstrating that there is always something different to be done in our educational day-to-day, whether we are involved in it as learners, and thus as teachers, or as teachers, and thus as learners as well.

I would not like to even give the impression that I am seeking to absolutely clarify the issues of *studying*, of *reading*, of *observing*, of *recognizing* the relationship between objects in order to get to know them. I will be trying to clarify some points that deserve our attention for a more critical understanding of these processes.

Let us begin with *studying*, which though involving *teaching* on the part of the teacher also involves a previous and concomitant learning on the part of the teacher and a learning either by students who are preparing to teach tomorrow or re-creating their knowledge to better teach today or by those who, children still, find themselves in the initial stages of their schooling.

An individual's preparation for learning, studying, is before anything else a critical, creative, re-creating activity. It does not matter whether one engages in it through reading a text that deals with and discusses a certain content proposed by a *school* or whether one starts from critical reflection on a certain social or natural occurrence that then leads to the reading of texts suggested by one's own curiosity or intellectual experience or suggested by others.

Thus, from a critical perspective, one that does not dichotomize between commonsense knowledge and the other more systematic, more precise knowledge but, rather, seeks a synthesis of opposites, the act of *studying* always implies that of reading, even if it is not reduced to it. Reading of the word enables us to read a previous reading of the world. But reading is not purely entertainment, nor is it a mechanical exercise in memorization of certain parts of a text.

If I am really studying, seriously reading, I cannot go past a page if I cannot grasp its significance relatively clearly. My solution does not lie in memorizing portions of paragraphs by mechanically reading—two, three, four times—portions of the text, closing my eyes and trying to repeat them as if the simple machinelike memorization could give me the knowledge I need.

Reading is an intellectual, difficult, demanding operation, but a gratifying one. Nobody studies authentically who does not take the critical position of being the subject of curiosity, of the reading, of the process of discovery. Reading is searching for, seeking to create an understanding of what is read; thus, among other fundamental points, the correct teaching of reading and writing is of great importance. It is not just that teaching reading is engaging; it is a creative experience around *comprehension,* comprehension and communication. And the experience of comprehension will be all the deeper if we can bring together, rather than dichotomizing, the concepts emerging from the school experience and those resulting from the day-to-day world. One critical exercise always required in reading, and necessarily also in writing, is that of easily moving from *sensory experience,* which characterizes the day-to-day, to *generalization,* which operates through school language, and then on to the tangible and concrete. One of the ways we can accomplish this exercise is through the practice that I have been referring to as "reading of a previous reading of the world," and here, "reading of the world" should be understood as the "reading" that precedes the reading of the word and that, equally concerned with the comprehension of objects, takes place in the domain of day-to-day life. The reading of the word, also a function of a search for text comprehension and thus of the objects contained therein, directs us now to a previous reading of the world. I must make it clear that this reading of the world, which is based on sensory experience, is not enough. But on the other hand, it must not be dismissed as inferior to the reading of the abstract world of concepts that proceeds from generalization to the tangible.

A literacy student from the northeast was discussing, in her culture circle, a codification[1] representing a man who created a clay vase with his own hands. The discussion involved the "reading" of a series of codifications, which in fact are representations of concrete reality, which is culture.

The concept of culture had already been apprehended by the group through the effort of *comprehension,* which characterizes the reading of the world or the *word.* The woman's memories of her previous experience and her sensory understanding of the process by which the man worked the clay to create the vase told her that the making of the vase was the sort of work with which he made a living. Just as the vase was only an object, it was the product of his work, which, once sold, made his and his family's lives viable.

Now, going beyond the sensory experience, the woman took a fundamental step: She reached the ability to *generalize,* which characterizes "school experience." Creating a vase through transformative work over clay was no longer only a means of survival but was also a means of creating *culture,* of creating *art.* For this reason, by revisiting her previous reading of the world, of the day-to-day activities in the world, that northeastern literacy student, proud and secure, said, "I create culture. I do this."

I have also had the opportunity to witness a similar experience from the point of view of the intelligence of people's behavior. I have referred to this fact before in my writing but there is no harm in bringing it up again.

I found myself on the island of São Tomé, in the Guinea Gulf off the western coast of Africa. I was with local educators, taking part in the first development program for literacy teachers.

The national commission had picked the small village of Porto Mont, a fishing community, as the center of all program activities. I suggested to the local educators that the development program not follow certain traditional methods that tend to separate theory from practice and that we not engage in any sort of work or activity that essentially dichotomized theory and practice either by underestimating *theory,* denying it any importance, by exclusively emphasizing *practice* as the only thing to really count, or by undermining practice by focusing only on theory. On the contrary, my intention was to have, from the very beginning, direct experimentation with the contradictions between theory and practice, which will be the object of analysis in one of my letters.

I refused, for this very reason, a schedule that reserved the initial moments for so-called theoretical presentations on fundamental content for the development of the future educators. In essence, that meant moments reserved for the speeches of the people deemed better able to speak before others.

My conviction lay elsewhere. I was thinking of a sequence of activities in which, in just one morning, we could discuss some key concepts—codification and decodification, for example—as if it were a time for *presentation* but without thinking even for a second that presentations were sufficient for the mastery of certain concepts. What was needed was a critical discussion of the practice in which the educators were about to engage.

Thus, with that basic idea accepted and put into practice, the future educators were asked to coordinate a discussion about codifications in a culture circle with twenty-five participants, who were aware that the activity addressed the professional development of educators. Prior to that, a discussion had been held about the political nature of their task, the task of helping us in a professional development effort, and they knew that they were going to be working with young people in a process of professional development. They knew that neither the teachers they were to work with nor they themselves had ever done anything like what they were going to do. The only difference that marked them was that the participants could only read from the world, while the young teachers in training read the word as well. They had never, however, discussed any codifications or taught literacy before.

Each afternoon in the program, four trainees took charge of the two-hour work sessions with the twenty-five participants. Those responsible for the program watched silently, taking notes. The theory behind the trainees' actions was revealed the following day during the four-hour evaluation and development seminars, when the mistakes, the errors, and the good points in their performance were discussed in the presence of the entire group.

The glitches and mistakes that had already been made and analyzed were hardly ever repeated. Theory emerged soaked in well-carried-out practice.

During one of these afternoon sessions—in a discussion about a codification depicting Porto Mont with its little houses lined up along the beach, facing the ocean, and a fisherman who walked away from his boat holding a fish—two of the participants stood up, as if they had planned it, walked to the window of the school where we were, looked at Porto Mont in the distance, and faced the codification that depicted the village once again and said, "Yeah, this is what Porto Mont is like, and we didn't even know it!"

Up until that point, their "reading" of that locale, of their private world, a reading made extremely close to the "text," which was the context of the village, had prevented them from *seeing* Porto Mont as it was. A certain dullness had veiled Porto Mont. The experiment they were conducting, of "taking some distance" from the object, the Porto Mont *codification*, allowed them to make a new reading, one more truthful to the text, to the context of Porto Mont. The taking of distance that the reading of the codification afforded them brought them closer to Porto Mont as a text being read. This new reading re-created their previous reading; that is why they said: "This is what Porto Mont is like, and we didn't even know it!" *Immersed* in the reality of their small world, they were unable to *see* it. By taking some distance, they *emerged* and were thus able to see it as they never had before.

To study is to uncover; it is to gain a more exact *comprehension* of an object; it is to realize its relationships to other objects. This implies a requirement for risk taking and venturing on the part of a student, the subject of learning, for without that they do not create or re-create.

For this reason also, as I have said so many times, *teaching* cannot be a process of transference of knowledge from the one teaching to the learner. This is the mechanical transference from which results machine-like memorization, which I have already criticized. Critical study correlates with teaching that is equally critical, which necessarily demands a critical way of comprehending and of realizing the reading of the word and that of the world, the reading of text and of context.

This critical way of comprehending and realizing the reading of the word and of the world lies, on the one hand, in not dismissing simpler language, "unguarded," innocent language. It lies in not devaluing such language because it is based on concepts developed in day-to-day experience, in the world of sensory experience. On the other hand, it also lies in moving away from the concept of "difficult language," impossible language, as development occurs around abstract concepts. This critical way of comprehending and realizing the reading of text and context does not exclude either variety of language, of syntax. It does recognize, however, that writers using scientific, academic language cannot become simplistic even though they must attempt to become more accessible, clearer, simpler, less closed, and less difficult.

No one who reads has the right to abandon the reading of a text because it is difficult, because he or she does not understand the meaning, for example, of a word such as *epistemology*.

Just as bricklayers require a collection of tools and instruments, without which they cannot build up a wall, student-readers also require fundamental instruments, without which they cannot read or write effectively. They require dictionaries,[2] including etymological dictionaries, dictionaries focusing on verbs and those looking at nouns and adjectives, philosophical dictionaries, thesauruses, and encyclopedias. They need comparative readings of texts, readings by different authors who deal with the same topics but with varying degrees of language complexity.

Using these tools is not, as many may think, a waste of time. The time one spends when one reads or writes, or writes and reads, on the use of dictionaries or encyclopedias, on the reading of chapters or fragments of texts that may help a more critical analysis of a topic, is a fundamental component of one's pleasurable task of reading or writing.

When we read, we do not have the right to expect, let alone demand, that writers will perform their task, that of writing, and also ours, that of comprehending the text, by explaining every step of the way, through footnotes, what they meant by this or that statement. Their duty as writers is to simply and *lightly* write, making it easier for the reader to attain understanding but without doing the reader's job.

A reader does not suddenly comprehend what is being read or studied, in a snap, miraculously. Comprehension needs to be worked, forged, by those who read and study; as subjects of the action, they must seek to employ appropriate instruments in order to carry out the task. For this very reason, *reading* and *studying* form a challenging task, one requiring patience and perseverance. It is not a task for those who, excessively hurried or lacking humbleness, transfer their weaknesses to the author, whom they then blame for being impossible to study.

It is important to make clear, also, that there is necessarily a relationship between the level of content in a book and the reader's actual level of development. These levels depend on the intellectual experience of both reader and author. The comprehension of what is read is tied to this relationship. When those levels are too far apart, when one has nothing to do with the other, all efforts toward *comprehension* are fruitless. In such cases, there is no consonance between the author's view of the necessary treatment of the topic and the reader's ability to apprehend the language required for that treatment of the topic. That is why studying is a preparation for knowing; it is a patient and impatient exercise on the part of someone whose intent is not to know it all at once but to struggle to meet the *timing* of knowledge.

The issue of the necessary use of the instruments indispensable to the task of reading and the work of writing raises a concern with the purchasing power of students and teachers, in light of the high costs of basic dictionaries, philosophical dictionaries, and so on. Being able to have access to such resources is a material right of students and teachers alike; this right corresponds to schools' duty to make these materials available by creating and furnishing libraries that are open on realistic schedules. Demanding this access is a right and duty of students and teachers alike.

I would now like to return to something I referred to previously: the relationship between reading and writing, which should be understood as processes that cannot be separated. They should be understood as processes that must be organized in such a way as to create the perception that they are needed for something, a perception, as Lev S. Vygotsky[3] emphasized, of being something that children need and that we too need.

Initially, oral expression precedes writing, but writing has encompassed oral expression ever since the moment humans became able to express themselves through symbols that said something about their dreams, their fears, their social experience, their hopes, and their practices.

When we learn how to *read*, we do it upon the writing of someone who previously learned how to read and write. As we learn how to read, we are preparing to immediately write the talk we socially construct.

In the literate cultures, without reading and writing it is impossible to study, to seek to know, to learn the subjectivity of objects, to critically recognize an object's reason for being.

One of the mistakes we often make is to dichotomize reading and writing and, even from children's earliest steps in the practice of reading and writing, to conceive of these processes as detached from the general process of knowing. This dichotomy between reading and writing follows us forever, as students and as teachers. "I have a tremendously hard time writing my papers. I cannot *write*" is the comment I hear most frequently in the graduate programs I have been involved with. Deep down, this fact reveals the sad fact of how far we are from a critical understanding of what it means to teach and to learn.

It is important that we take critical ownership of the formation of our selves, which socially and gradually, over time, become active and conscious, speaking, reading, and writing, and which are both inherently and socially constructed. In other words, we must not only realize what we are, but we must also fully embrace ourselves as these beings "programmed for learning," as François Jacob[4] put it. Then we must learn how to learn; in other words, we must, among other things, recognize that oral and written language, their use, are equally important objectively.

Those we study, and those we teach and thus study as well, require that we not only read texts but write notes, write book reports, and compose small texts about the things we read. We must read the works of good writers; of good novelists, poets, scientists, and philosophers; of those who do not fear working their language in search of beauty, simplicity, and clarity.[5]

If our schools, from the earliest grades, were to devote themselves to the work of nurturing in students a taste for reading and writing and were to maintain that nurturing throughout their school lives, there would possibly be fewer graduate students who spoke of their inability to write or their insecurity about writing.

If studying were not almost always a *burden* to us, if reading were not a bitter obligation, if, on the contrary, studying and reading were sources of pleasure and happiness as well as sources of the knowledge we need to better move about the world, we would have indexes that were more indicative of the quality of our education.

This is an effort that should be initiated in grammar school, should be intensified during the stages of literacy development, and should continue without ever stopping.

It is undeniably important to read the works of Jean Piaget, of Lev S. Vygotsky, of Emilia Ferreiro, of Madalena F. Weffort, among others, as well as to read the work of specialists who deal, strictly speaking, not with literacy but with the reading process, such as Marisa Lajolo and Ezequiel T. da Silva.

If we think about the intimate relationship between reading, writing, and thinking and about our need to intensely experience this relationship, we might accept the suggestion that at least three times a week we should devote ourselves to the task of writing something. That writing could be notes about something read, a commentary about some event reported in the media, a letter to an unknown person—it doesn't matter what. It is also a good idea to date and keep these writings and, a few months later, critically analyze them.

Nobody can write who never writes, just as one cannot swim who never swims.

Though I underscore here that the use of written language, and thus of reading, is tied to a society's material development, I would like to emphasize that my position is not an *idealistic* one.

Just as I refuse any *mechanistic* interpretation of history, I refuse any *idealistic* one as well. The former reduces conscience to a mere copy of society's material structures; the latter subjects everything to an all-powerful conscience. My position is a different one: I understand that these relationships between conscience and the world are dialectic.[6]

What is not appropriate is for us to wait for material transformations before we begin to face up to the problem of reading and writing correctly.

A critical reading of the texts and of the world has to do with the changes in progress within them.

NOTES

1. About codification, reading of the reading world, of the sense word, exact common knowledge, learning, and teaching, see Paulo Freire, *Education as the Praxis of Freedom* (Rio de Janeiro: Paz e Terra), *Education and Change* (Rio de Janeiro: Paz e Terra), *Cultural Action for Freedom* (Rio de Janeiro:

Paz e Terra), *Pedagogy of the Oppressed* (Rio de Janeiro: Paz e Terra, 1970), *Pedagogy of Hope: A Return to the Pedagogy of the Oppressed* (Rio de Janeiro: Paz e Terra, 1992), and *The Importance of the Reading Act* (São Paulo: Cortez, 1992); Paulo Freire and Sergio Guimaraes, *About Education* (Rio de Janeiro: Paz e Terra, 1987); Paulo Freire and Ira Shor, *Fear and Daring: The Educator's Day-to-Day* (Rio de Janeiro: Paz e Terra); Paulo Freire and Donaldo Macedo, *Literacy, Reading of the World, and Reading of the Word* (Westport, Conn.: Bergin and Garvey, 1987); Paulo Freire and Marcio Campos, "Reading of the World—Reading of the Word," *Courrier de L'UNESCO* (February 1991).

2. See Freire, *Pedagogy of Hope.*

3. Luis C. Moll, ed., *Vygotsky and Education. Instructional Implications and Applications of Sociohistorical Psychology,* 1st paperback ed. (Cambridge and New York: Cambridge University Press, 1992).

4. François Jacob, "Nous sommes programmé mais pour apprendre," *Courrier de L'UNESCO* (February 1991).

5. See Freire, *Pedagogy of Hope.*

6. To this end see Freire, *Pedagogy of Hope.*

5

TEACHING AS POSSIBILITY

A LIGHT IN DARK TIMES

Maxine Greene

BORROWING FROM A BITTER POEM by Bertolt Brecht, Hannah Arendt entitled a book of essays *Men in Dark Times* (1968). The poem, "To Posterity," she explained, spoke of the horrors taking place in the early days of Nazi rule in Germany and of the absence of outrage. Things were covered up, she wrote, by "highly efficient talk and double talk"; and she stressed how important it always is to have a space in which light can be shed on what is happening and what is being said. Granted, our times may not be marked by the kinds of monstrosities associated with the Nazis; but dark times are no rarity, even in American history. In the darkest moments, she wrote, we still "have the right to expect some illumination . . . and such illumination may well come less from theories and concepts than from the uncertain, flickering, and often weak light that some men and women, in their lives and their works, will kindle under all circumstances . . . " (p. ix). I view our times as shadowed by violations and erosions taking place around us: the harm being done to children; the eating away of social support systems; the "savage inequalities" in our schools; the spread of violence; the intergroup hatreds; the power of media; the undermining of arts in the lives of the young. And then I think of the "light that some men and women will kindle under almost all circumstances," and that makes me ponder (and sometimes wonder at) the work that is and might be done by teachers at this problematic moment in our history.

There is doubt, unquestionably, within and outside the schools; and there is dread. The poet Adrienne Rich has written some remarkable poetry about the different kinds of dread experienced by different people. When asked how, in the face of this, she could maintain such an affirmative attitude, she said, "If poetry is forced by the conditions in which it is created to speak of dread and of bitter, bitter conditions, by its very nature, poetry speaks to something different. That's why poetry can bring together those parts of us which exist in dread and those which have the surviving sense of a possible happiness, collectivity, community, a loss of isolation" (Moyers, 1995, p. 342).

Arendt and Rich, each in her distinctive voice, are speaking of the capacity of human beings to reach beyond themselves to what they believe should be, might be in some space they bring into being among and between themselves. The two remind us (by speaking of an uncertain light and of something different) of what it signifies to imagine not what is necessarily probable or predictable, but what may be conceived as possible. All of those who have parented children or taught the young may resonate to this on some level, particularly when they recall the diverse, often unexpected shapes of children's growing and becoming. Many may find a truth in Emily Dickinson's saying that "The Possible's slow fuse is lit / By the Imagination" (1960, pp. 688–689). Imagination, after all, allows people to think of things as if they could be otherwise; it is the capacity that allows a looking through the windows of the actual towards alternative realities.

It is obvious enough that arguments for the values and possibilities of teaching acts (no matter how enlightened) within the presently existing system cannot be expressed through poetry, even as it is clear that the notion of "teaching as possibility" cannot simply be asserted and left to do persuasive work. The contexts have to be held in mind, as does what strikes many of us as a backward leaning, inhumane tendency in our society today. For all the apparent resurgence of Deweyan progressive thinking in the school renewal movement, parent bodies and community representatives in many places are explicitly at odds with what they believe is being proposed. They respond more readily to the media-sustained talk of standards and technology than they do to the idea of multiple patterns of being and knowing, to a regard for cultural differences, to an attentiveness when it comes to voices never listened to before.

Teachers who are consciously and reflectively choosing themselves as participants in school renewal are being challenged to clarify their beliefs and (more and more often) to defend their practices. If the discourse they are developing can be infused with the kinds of metaphor that reorient ordinary common-sense thinking, if they can break through more often what John Dewey called "the crust of conventionalized and routine consciousness" (1954, p. 183) when attention is turned to the school, neighborhood or district discussions may be moved beyond the customary and the self-regarding. If the fears and suffering of local people, some of them feeling themselves to be ignorant and powerless, can be taken into account, what Paulo Freire called a "pedagogy of hope" might even take form (1994), and dialogue of a different sort might take the place of the language of prescription or complaint or demand. If teachers can begin to think of themselves as among those able to kindle the light Arendt described or among those willing to confront the dread and keep alive the sense of "a possible happiness," they might find themselves revisioning their life projects, existing proactively in the world.

Paying heed to the repetitive drumbeat of current concerns—for professional development, standard-setting, authentic assessment, an enriched knowledge base, technological expertise, teachers cannot but occasionally ask themselves "to what end?" There are, of course, the official announcements and prescriptions. There are presumably obvious "goods" linked to each statement of an educational goal. Most often, we realize, the benefits of reform are linked to the nation's welfare, or to market expansion, or to technological dominance in a competitive world. Suppose, however, we were to summon up an articulation of purpose suggested by Rich's "possible happiness, collectivity, community, a loss of isolation." The words imply a reaching out for individual fulfillment among others, in (perhaps) the kind of community in the making John Dewey called democracy. They are, to a degree, abstract, metaphorical; but, speaking indirectly as they do, they respond to some of the evident lacks in our society, to the spaces where people feel solitary and abandoned, to domains of felt powerlessness.

If our purposes were to be framed in such a fashion, they would not exclude the multiple-literacies and the diverse modes of understanding young persons need if they are to act knowledgeably and reflectively within the frameworks of their lived lives. Situatedness; vantage point; the construction of meanings: all can and must be held in mind if teachers are to treat their students with regard, if they are to release them to learn how to learn. Their questions will differ, as their perspectives will differ, along with their memories and their dreams. But if teachers cannot enable them to resist the humdrum, the routine, or what Dewey called the "anesthetic" (1931, p. 40), they will be in danger of miseducative behavior, ending in cul-de-sacs rather than in openings. If situations cannot be created that enable the young to deal with feelings of being manipulated by outside forces, there will be far too little sense of agency among them. Without a sense of agency, young people are unlikely to pose significant questions, the existentially rooted questions in which learning begins. Indeed, it is difficult to picture learner-centered classrooms if students' lived situations are not brought alive, if dread and desire are not both given play. There is too much of a temptation otherwise to concentrate on training rather than teaching, to focus on skills for the work place rather than any "possible happiness" or any real consciousness of self. Drawn to comply, to march in more or less contented lockstep (sneakered, baseball capped, T-shirted), familiar with the same media-derived referents, many youngsters will tacitly agree to enter a community of the competent, to live lives according to "what is." There are, of course, young persons in the inner cities, the ones lashed by "savage inequalities" (Kozol, 1991), the ones whose very schools are made sick by the social problems the young bring in from without (O'Connor, 1996). Here, more frequently than not, are the real tests of "teaching as possibility" in the face of what looks like an impossible social reality at a time when few adults seem to care. There are examples, in Mike Rose's work on "possible lives," for instance, where he expresses his belief that "a defining characteristic of good teaching is a tendency to push on the existing order of things" (1995, p. 428).

In Toni Morrison's *The Bluest Eye,* the child Claudia is explaining her hatred of Shirley Temple dolls, to her the very exemplars of a world of objects, a world in which people yearn for possessions, above all, including white china dolls for Black children. "I did not know why I destroyed those dolls," writes Claudia. "But I did know that nobody ever asked me what I wanted for Christmas. Had any adult with the power to fulfill my desires taken me seriously and asked me what I wanted, they would have known that I did not want anything to own, or to possess any object. I wanted rather to feel something on Christmas day. The real question would have been, 'Dear Claudia, what experience would you like on Christmas?' I could have spoken up, 'I want to sit on the low stool in Big Mama's kitchen with my lap full of lilacs and listen to Big Papa play his violin for me alone.' The lowness of the stool made for my body, the security and warmth of Big Mama's kitchen, the smell of the lilacs, the sound of the music, and, since it would be good to have all of my senses engaged, the taste of a peach, perhaps, afterward" (1970, p. 21). This cannot be attributed to teaching; but it is a "push on the existing order of things"; and it may hold clues to what good teaching can be. Claudia is cared for harshly by her mother; but she is confident of her concern and of her love. She is, at least at that young age, able to resist the existing order of consumable and ownable things and to tap into some deeper need for what she calls "experience." Perhaps this cannot be taught but Claudia's seems to be an insight that underlies the insistences of the culture, that has to do with being sensually alive and within a loving world.

This is not a purely fictional phenomenon. Too many teachers, by now, have read their students' journals and stories and poems; they have exposed themselves to many kinds of dread and many kinds of desire. Much of the suffering, much of the deprivation is due, quite obviously, to economic and social injustices; but there is a sense in which imagination and desire can feed the recognition of the need to transform and, perhaps, the passion to change. To have that sense is to be able to listen to what Wallace Stevens calls "the man with the blue guitar" who "does not play things as they are" (1964, p. 165). Imagination alters the vision of the way things are; it opens spaces in experience where projects can be devised, the kinds of projects that may bring things closer to what ought to be. Without such a capacity, even young people may resemble the inhabitants of the town of Oran Albert Camus described at the start of *The Plague*, "where everyone is bored and devotes himself to cultivating habits." The point is made that you can get through the day without trouble once you have formed habits. In some other places, the narrator says, "People have now and then an inkling of something different" (1948, p. 4). They have had an intimation, and that is so much to the good. He did not necessarily mean an intimation of the end of the plague and a return to normal life. He meant, perhaps, an intimation of mortality, of injustice that has to be struggled against, of silences that have to be acknowledged and at once overcome.

For us, that may imply a recognition, not solely of the human condition, but of the contradictions in what we think of as a democratic society. Even to think about bringing about significant changes within the school is to contest on many levels the behaviorist, stratifying tendencies that still mark the culture as it impinges on the school. To encourage the young to develop visions of what might be and then, against those visions recognize how much is lacking and what is may be to strike against all sorts of easy platitudes that obscure the turmoil of change. Most of us realize that, only when we envisage a better social order, do we find the present one in many ways unendurable and stir ourselves to repair. The sight and description of the new schools at the present time—the Coalition schools, the Charter schools, the New Vision Schools—make it uniquely possible to identify what is wrong with the traditional schools. All we need to do is to take heed of what can happen when a junior high school girl, caught in an overcrowded city school, visits one of the new theme schools. Abruptly, she may notice what is lacking in her own school: a brightly decorated classroom, small groups and family circles, a breaking through of the forty-five minute class period. Without witnessing a better state of things, she could not have realized what was lacking, what was wrong.

Sometimes, introduced to a reflective or a learning community, someone will become aware of the dearth of understanding in her/his own domain, of the blocks to knowing and to questioning. Sometimes, a teacher or a relative or a friend may pay heed, as does the singer Shug Avery in *The Color Purple* (Walker, 1982). She suggests to Miss Celie a way of being without "that old white man" in her head, actually a way of becoming free. Celie writes: "Trying to chase that old white man out of my head. I been so busy thinking bout him I never truly notice nothing God make. Not a blade of corn (how it do that?) not the color purple (where it come from?) Not the little wild flowers. Nothing" (p. 25). She, too, made aware of alternatives, can discover that "she feels like a fool" because of what she was never enabled to notice and about which she had never asked.

Inklings and intimations, of course, are not sufficient, as the townspeople in Oran discovered when they organized sanitary squads to fight the plague, "since they knew it was the only thing to do" (p. 120). Imagination is what imparts a conscious quality to experience and the realization that things do not repeat themselves, that experience should not be expected to be uniform or frictionless. Imagination, moreover, is enriched and stimulated through live encounters with others, through exposure to diverse vantage points and unfamiliar ways of looking at the world. Imagination should not, however, as Dewey warned, be permitted to run loose so that it merely builds "castles in the air" and lets "them be a substitute for an actual achievement which involves the pains of thought" (1916, p. 404). Yes, there are distinctive moments made possible by the poetic imagination; but the social and ethical imagination is concerned for using ideas and aspirations to reorganize the environment or the lived situation.

Paulo Freire had this in mind when he wrote about the shaping of a critical discourse that showed adult learners "the lovelier world to which they aspired was being announced, somehow anticipated, in their imagination. It was not a matter of idealism. Imagination and conjecture about a different world than the one of oppression are as necessary to the praxis of historical 'subjects' (agents in the process of transforming reality as it necessarily belongs to human toil that the worker or artisan first have in his or her head a design a 'conjecture,' of what he or she is about to make" [1994, p. 39]). Freire believes that democratic education requires enabling ordinary people to develop their own language, derived from their readings of their own social realities, their own namings, their own anticipations of a better state of things. We might return to the present use of story-telling, especially contextualized story-telling, by means of which young people explore the influences of social life on their becoming, of race and gender and ethnic membership, of traditions, of the stories told to them.

Dialogue can arise from story-telling in a shared classroom space; and out of dialogue and conjecture can come the making of projects also shared. They may be as simple and concrete as polling the neighborhood mothers on immunization of their babies, as rehabilitating rooms somewhere for homeless classmates, as volunteering for a tutoring program, as organizing street dances or a marching band. There is considerable talk these days of how fair societies may be nurtured in families, schools, work places, and congregations. Modern democracies, says Michael Sandel (1996), can be nourished close to home, in settings where people experience and act upon accepted responsibility. One of his examples is of the civil rights movement, which actually began in small black Baptist churches in the South and extended from there to a national movement. We might be reminded also of Vaclav Havel writing from prison a decade ago. He found hope in small student movements, ecological movements, peace movements, because he believed that "human communality" begins in a "renaissance of elementary human relationships which new projects can at the very most only mediate" (1989, p. 371). This may well ascribe new importance to the school and to teachers willing to foster the values Havel talked about: "love, charity, sympathy, tolerance, understanding, self-control, solidarity, friendship, feelings of belonging, the acceptance of concrete responsibility for those close to one"—all with an eye on the social formations that decide the fate of the world. Freire, also thinking of how to move beyond the small community, the local, spoke about "the invention of citizenship," clearly with imagination in mind once again (p. 39).

The processes of speaking, writing, and reading must be attended to; there must be reflectiveness with regard to the languages in use—the language of images, of technology, of ordinary communication grounded in everyday life. The current interest in narrative and in the landscapes on which people's stories take shape is enabling many learners to explore their own idioms, to create projects by means of which they can identify themselves. To do that is inevitably to take the social setting into account, the social situation without which no self can come to be. We might recall Edward Said saying that no one is purely one thing, that "labels like Indian, or woman, or Muslim, or American are not more than starting points, which if followed into actual experience for only a moment are quickly left behind" (1991, p. 336). We need to listen to other echoes in the garden, he reminds us, to attend to the continuity of old traditions as well as to the connections only now being disclosed. Both require a consciousness of location, an awareness of both contemporaries and predecessors.

We are realizing how much the negotiation of identity today has to do with connectedness and membership; and the notion of participant membership has to feed into our conceptions of democratic citizenship. Visions of public spaces may open, if we allow them to, spaces where all kinds of persons can come together in collaborative concern for what is lacking or what is wrong, what needs to be improved or repaired. The greatest obstacle in the way, as Hannah Arendt saw it, is "thoughtlessness—the heedless recklessness or hopeless confusion or complacent repetition of truths which have become trivial and empty . . . " (1958, p. 5). Clearly, this has pedagogical implications, as did Dewey's warning about a "social pathology" standing in the way of inquiry into social conditions. "It manifests itself in a thousand ways," he wrote, "in querulousness, in impotent drifting, in uneasy snatching at distractions, in idealization of the long established, in a facile optimism assumed as a cloak, in glorification of things 'as they are' . . . " (1954, p. 170). Again, there is the implied demand for attention to a "blue guitar," even as persons are asked to think about their own thinking, their own denials, their own ends in view. Both Dewey and Arendt paid attention to the problem of impersonality and to the empty sociability taking over from community. Both spoke of business, consumerism, and (in time) of bureaucracy. Action and the sense of agency were crucial for both; their writings urged readers to appear before one another, to allow something to take shape between them, a space where diverse beings could reach towards possibility.

Both knew that dialogue and communication were focal and, when conceivable, face-to-face communication, with persons addressing one another as who, not what they were. It was the lack of authentic communication, Dewey wrote, that led to the "eclipse of the public." He pointed out that Americans had at hand "the physical tools of communication as never before, but the thoughts and aspirations congruent with them are not communicated and therefore are not common. Without such communication, the public will remain shadowy and formless, seeking spasmodically for itself, but seizing and holding its shadow rather than its substance" (1954, p. 142). Writing seventy years ago, Dewey may have anticipated the predicaments of a computerized society with a public transmuted into audience or listeners interested in consumption of ideas as well as goods. He might not have been surprised by the crotchety, of insulting telephone calls to the talk shows, by the prayerful heaves at evangelists' meetings, the shouts at rock concerts, the hoots and screams at football games. Certainly, people are entitled to make all sorts of sounds, to express themselves in multiple ways; but when the "thoughts and aspirations" Dewey sought are subsumed under noise and sound bytes, teachers are challenged to pay heed.

Classroom preoccupations with efficacy or technical efficiency or even "world-class standards" will not solve the problem of communication or the "eclipse of the public." Nor will they suffice when it comes to consideration of the arts of practice, much less the arts and mystery of being human. The things covered up by "highly efficient talk and double talk" (Arendt, 1968, p. viii) still call for many kinds of illumination. Teachers may well be among the few in a position to kindle the light that might illuminate the spaces of discourse and events in which young newcomers have some day to find their ways. Dewey wrote that "democracy is a name for a life of free and enriching communion. It had its seer in Walt Whitman" (1954, p. 184). Whitman's "Song of Myself" comes insistently to mind, with its call for liberation and for equity! "Unscrew the locks from the doors," he wrote. "Unscrew the doors themselves from their jambs, / Whoever degrades another degrades me, / And whatever is done or said returns at last to me. / Through me the afflatus surging and surging, through me the current and index. / I speak the pass-word primeval, I give the sign of democracy, / By God, I will accept nothing which all cannot have their counterpart of on the same terms" (1931, p. 53). Dewey knew this was not a definition of democracy, nor a series of slogans nor a sermon nor a lesson in political science. The function of art "has always been," he said, "to break through the conventionalized and routine consciousness." Art is what touches "the deeper levels of life," and when they are touched "they spring up as desire and thought. This process is art." And then: "Artists have always been the real purveyors of the news, for it is not the outward happening in itself which is new, but the kindling by it of emotion, perception and appreciation" (p. 184).

It must be noted that Dewey affirmed the uses of the arts in the midst of a study of the public, and he spoke about the "deeper levels of life" at the end of the chapter called "Search for the Great Community." Not only was he emphasizing the place of art experiences in moving persons beyond what was fixed and stale and taken for granted. He was suggesting once again the importance of informing the state of social affairs with knowledge, intelligence, and the kinds of connections—past and present—that compose the fabric of what we have come to call the common world.

Teachers, often troubled by charges of imposition of white, western culture upon young people arriving from different worlds, are often at a loss when it comes to providing the kinds of shared cultural referents that help weave networks of relationship. There was a time when the Scriptures offered something in common, or the orations of statesmen like Thomas Jefferson and Abraham Lincoln, or certain plays of Shakespeare, or folktales or (beginning in the 19th century) fictions capturing aspects of the American experience at sea, in the woods, on the rivers, on the open roads. It is said today that television shows have replaced such common cultural holdings: "David Letterman," "The Today Show," and "Saturday Night Live" shape the culture's conversation, and the "deeper levels of life" are rolled over or ignored.

Teachers concerned about illumination and possibility know well that there is some profound sense in which a curriculum in the making is very much a part of a community in the making. Many are aware of the call on the part of hitherto marginal groups—ethnic minorities, women, gays and lesbians—for an inclusion of their own traditions in what is sometimes thought of as the "core" of intellectual and artistic life. For all the dissonances and uneasinesses, there is a demand for a kind of historical consciousness on the part of diverse persons within and outside of their associations. That signifies a recognition that the past is like a stream in which all of us in our distinctiveness and diversity participate every time we try to understand. There are, of course, thousands of silenced voices still; there are thousands of beings striving for visibility; there are thousands of interpretations still to be made, thousands of questions to be posed.

The common world we are trying to create may be thought of as a fabric of interpretations of many texts, many images, many sounds. We might think of interpreted experiences with such texts taking the place of a tradition in the old sense of canonical objectivity. When Hannah Arendt wrote about a common world (1958), she put her stress on the innumerable perspectives through which that common world [prevents] itself and for which a common denominator can never be devised. In a classroom, this would mean acknowledgment of and recognition of the different biographical histories that affect the shaping of perspectives. More than in previous times, teachers are asked to confront and honor the differences even as they work for a free and responsible acceptance of the norms marking whatever community is in the making: concrete responsibility for one another; respect for the rights of others; solidarity; regard for reflective habits of thought. At once, there are the ways of thinking and seeing that enable various young persons to decode and interpret what is made available: the ability to distinguish among the discourses in use, to have regard for evidence and experience, to be critically conscious of what is read and heard, to construct meanings in the diverse domains of their lives. "Be it grand or slender," said Toni Morrison in her *Nobel Address,* "burrowing, blasting or refusing to sanctify; whether it laughs out loud or is a cry without an alphabet, the choice word or the chosen silence, unmolested language surges toward knowledge, not its destruction. But who does not know of literature banned because it is interrogative; discredited because it is critical; erased because alternate? And how many are outraged by the thought of a self-ravaged tongue? Word-work is sublime because it is generative; it makes meaning that secures our difference, our human difference—the way in which we are like no other life. We die. That may be the meaning of life. But we do language. That may be the measure of our lives" (March/April 1996, p. 11). This should apply to all the young, whoever they are, if—like Whitman and Morrison as well—we refuse at last to withhold recognition, to degrade or to exclude.

Michael Fischer, an ethnologist also concerned for connectedness, writes about the importance of the present tendency to encourage participation of readers themselves in the production of meaning. The conscious effort to move readers to respond to incompleteness and make connections becomes, he suggests, an ethical device attempting to activate in readers a "desire for communitas with others, while preserving rather than effacing differences" (1986, p. 233). We might visualize interpretive encounters with Hawthorne's Hester Prynne daring to engage in speculative thought while living on the verge of the wilderness; Melville's Bartleby who "preferred not to," compared with "a piece of wreckage in the mid Atlantic"; Edith Wharton's Lily Bart, caught like a cog in the wheel of a material society. Or we might think of the narrator of Ellison's *Invisible Man* saying he has "whipped it all except the mind, the mind. And the mind that has conceived a plan of living must never lose sight of the chaos against which that pattern was conceived." Or the chaos due to nameless pollution and the falsifications of the media in De Lillo's *White Noise,* or Doctorow's cities with their denials and their cover-ups and their violations of children. Or Tillie Olsen's narrator standing behind her ironing board, hoping only that her daughter will be more than a dress beneath the iron. And so many other voices, Hispanic and Asian and Native American, all activating questions whose answers create no "common denominator," but which make each text deeper, richer, more expansive, yes, and more replete with mystery.

That, in part, suggests what is meant by teaching as possibility in dark and constraining times. It is a matter of awakening and empowering today's young people to name, to reflect, to imagine, and to act with more and more concrete responsibility in an increasingly multifarious world. At once, it is a matter of enabling them to remain in touch with dread and desire, with the smell of lilacs and the taste of a peach. The light may be uncertain and flickering; but teachers in their lives and works have the remarkable capacity to make it shine in all sorts of corners and, perhaps, to move newcomers to join with others and transform. Muriel Rukeyser has written:

> Darkness arrives
> splitting the mind open.
> Something again
> Is beginning to be born.
> A dance is dancing me.
> I wake in the dark. (1994, p. 284)

She offers a metaphor and a watchword. It may help us light the fuse.

REFERENCES

Arendt, H. (1958) *The Human Condition*. Chicago: Chicago University Press.

Arendt, H. (1968) *Men in Dark Times*. New York: Harcourt Brace (Harvest Books).

Camus, A. (1948) *The Plague*. New York: Alfred A. Knopf.

Dewey, J. (1931) *Art as Experience*. New York: Minton, Balch, & Co.

Dewey, J. (1954) *The Public and Its Problems*. Athens, O.: The Swallow Press.

Dickinson, E. (1960) "The Gleam of an Heroic Act," in T. H. Johnson, Ed. *The Complete Poems*. Boston: Little Brown.

Fischer, M. M. J. (1986) "Ethnicity and the Arts of Memory," in J. Clifford and G. E. Marcus, *Writing Culture*. Berkeley: University of California Press.

Freire, P. (1994) *Pedagogy of Hope*. New York: Continuum.

Havel, V. (1989) *Letters to Olga*. New York: Henry Holt.

Kozol, J. (1991) *Savage Inequalities*. New York: Crown Publishers.

Morrison, T. (1970) *The Bluest Eye*. New York: Washington Square Press/Pocket Books.

Morrison, T. (1996) "The 1993 Nobel Prize Lecture: Honors in Stockholm," in *Humanities*, March/April 1996, Vol. 17, No. l.

Moyers, B. (1995) *The Language of Life*. New York: Doubleday.

O'Connor, S. (1996) *Will My Name Be Shouted Out?* New York: Simon and Schuster.

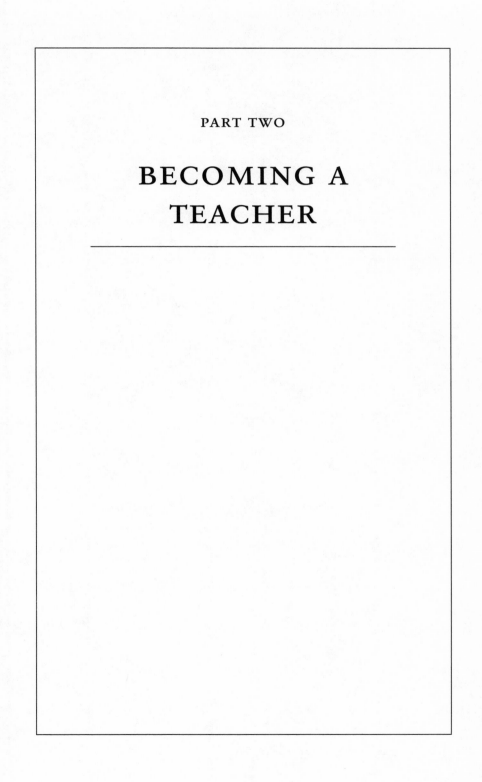

PART TWO

BECOMING A TEACHER

6

LEARNING TO READ

Patrick McWilliams

FROM THE FIRST DAY, I thought I knew what my role as teacher was meant to be. I had spent four years of graduate study learning how to tell the difference between good writing and not-so-good. I had learned a great deal about how to revise my own writing. I had learned that a writer has a responsibility to the reader. Now I was to be a professional "reader." My job was to search out the flaws in my students' writing, to notify them of the many errors of their ways, and to enforce my judgment with a solidly objective grade. "You have got exactly what you deserve," says the arid schoolmaster of Terence Ratigan's *The Browning Version* to a schoolboy who wishes to know if he has passed—"nothing less and certainly nothing more." I could have played that schoolmaster.

In the first semester of my teaching, into my hardened hands fell a narrative essay by Laurie. She was the perfect victim for my exercise of critical acumen. Laurie was wholesome, eager, not at all unread, but more acquainted with Nancy Drew than with *Tess of the D'Urbervilles,* and to all appearances ready to accept advice from her teacher. I think I liked best about Laurie her way of puffing out her cheeks when she was wrestling with a tough question in class. I had seen her puff out her cheeks in the same way in sports contests. It was always a sign of effort with her.

Laurie had given me a paper about a particularly satisfying three-day hike she had taken in the New Hampshire mountains. Her essay had not a flaw that care and diligence could prevent: no misspellings, no grammatical errors, no malapropisms. But it wasn't perfect—it was full of clichés.

The great thing, or so I thought in those days, was to find an essay with faults that happened to be within the range of my rather shortsighted vision. In my glossary of Errors My Students Shall Not Commit, the cliché occupied a large section.

The very subject Laurie had chosen was, to my mind, a cliché. In only three months at my first job in New Hampshire, I had already read something like ten narratives about hiking experiences. I made a note to her about choosing fresh topics even before I had finished the first paragraph. The clichés in Laurie's account of her hike were the usual suspects, and like Claude Rains in *Casablanca* I rounded them up dutifully.

"The breeze," she told her reader, "lifted my hair gently from my cheek." And furthermore, "The sunlight filtered through the pines onto the forest path." And, "The air was crisp and invigorating." Also "The climb up the mountainside was tiring but fun, and the view from the top was panoramic."

When Laurie's foot slipped at the edge of an escarpment, she "could feel the adrenaline flowing" as she righted her balance, and "not a split second too soon," she grabbed for an overhanging branch.

I knew my job: to search out error wherever it occurred and cow my student writers into giving me what I wanted. I had searched for clichés—and I had found them. Now I was ready to cow—er, teach—Laurie.

Of course, I didn't know my job at all. My first lesson in that fact came the day after I had returned Laurie's essay. I had given it a half-hour of my time, not a bad ratio to her six or seven hours of composition. I had written a long paragraph or two explaining the importance of showing, not telling. I had dutifully explained that clichés are substitutes for genuine narration and description. I had discoursed on the writer's responsibility to give the reader a fresh account of experience. And I had given her a generous dose of green-inked underlinings (not red—even I knew better than that) and a large helping of the word *cliché*, possibly ten times in four pages.

The day after I had returned her paper, with a magnanimous B-minus, Laurie showed up in my classroom just after school. I was surprised. She had not struck me as the type to argue over a grade. I was right, at least, about that. She had not come to argue about the grade.

She stood beside my desk, ignoring my offer of a seat. I felt at a disadvantage. Laurie was a strong, athletic girl. And she was looking down at me now, puffing out her cheeks, with probably the same look she gave a soccer ball she was about to propel with a swift kick.

She kicked. She said to me, "How would you feel if someone asked you to write about something you cared deeply about [I had asked just that when I made the assignment], and then they write 'cliché, cliché, cliché' in the margin after every other sentence?"

I didn't have an answer. Or rather, Laurie knew and I knew that the answer was obvious. But I had never asked myself the question she was asking. I had assumed that my job was to judge and that her job was to be judged (and to be at least respectfully chagrined to know that I knew her every sin of writing). I had so little imagination that I hadn't connected how I feel when my own writing is not well received with how my students might feel. I had lured my young writers into thinking they were writing for a friend; then I had pounded on them like the beadle in *Oliver Twist*. I didn't have an answer for Laurie. I hadn't known my job at all.

After seventeen years of teaching I know better. I know that my job has nothing to do with judging the writing of my students. Like anyone else, I have the perfect right to judge the writing of professionals—the people who charge us money to read what they have written. But my students are not professional writers. My job—my duty—as a teacher is to find the best in what my students have done and to help them see for themselves the difference between their best work and their indifferent work. Students don't need critics; they need teachers. They don't need adversaries; they need readers. They aren't miscreants; they are growing writers. We who teach are not meant to search for faults but for possibilities. It took me a while to learn that.

7

ORDER IN THE CLASSROOM

Andrew Dean Mullen

"TO SURVIVE AROUND HERE, you've got to be tough as nails. Show them who's boss right from the start." These words from my supervising teacher stayed with me through my student teaching, but I couldn't seem to put them to use. I sometimes wondered if my fifth-grade students took advantage of the fact that I wasn't a "real teacher" yet and actually sat down together and plotted against me. Just when I'd convinced myself that their crimes must be premeditated, I'd notice that they were very good at spontaneous uprisings, too.

With my student teaching behind me, I started out with a clean slate at a school in another part of town. My former supervisor's words were still with me: I did not intend to face another classroom where I didn't have control.

Day one I read my new charges (fourth grade this time) the longest list of rules and routines they'd ever heard. Yes, we would play games. Yes, we would have activity centers for students whose regular work was complete. Yes, everyone would have a good year, but only if they cooperated with me. I was the teacher. I was running the show. It was the students' job to sit still, listen, and do as they were told. Much to my surprise, they did just that.

After the first day of polite listening, I told myself not to be fooled. Beneath their docile appearance lurked the potential for untold disaster. But days went by without a crisis. Two weeks passed, and still no threatened rebellions. I was in control.

By the end of September the principal, Mr. Williams, was noticing how straight a line we maintained as we walked to the cafeteria. My colleagues praised the class for getting drinks after gym so quietly. Visitors passing by in the hall smiled as they looked in at the straight rows of diligent, orderly students. I was pleased.

It wasn't just the students I controlled. I also had charge of the physical space assigned me. The gray, windowless classroom Mr. Williams had shown me in August was now ablaze with color. Art and science centers beckoned from every corner. Posters lit up the walls. Private reading zones, suitably equipped with pillows, competed with listening centers for students' time and attention.

Best of all, I was fully in command of the curriculum. I filled my plan book with one creative idea after another. Some teachers might make do with commercial worksheets, math drill from the text, and lessons from the basal reader, but I wanted better. Why have students read the science text when I could spend the time conducting some experiments for them? Surely, the skill in the language book could be turned into some kind of game. A few homemade charts might make those concepts in fractions easier to understand.

I might have felt even more successful if I hadn't felt tired all the time. By three o'clock each day the room was a mess and I was a wreck. After an hour of frenzied running around, I'd stop and realize I'd accomplished nothing. I was lucky if I'd rearranged a few piles on my desk. Papers to be graded, charts to be updated, and forms to be sent to the office mushroomed everywhere. Teachers' magazines I'd once devoured eagerly began to gather dust.

Success stories that Mr. Williams trumpeted in faculty meetings—prizes won, grants awarded, commendations received from parents—convinced me I wasn't working hard enough. I gave up Saturdays. Then Sunday afternoons. I stayed in my classroom later and later each day, putting up one more bulletin board, cutting out one more game piece, making just one more set of cards.

The classroom continued to run smoothly, but I was burning out fast. I found myself being resentful of my students, who didn't seem to be living up to their end of the bargain. If I was working so hard, why weren't they? And sometimes I'd look out during my lessons and see unresponsive faces. How dare they just sit there and not fully appreciate everything I was doing for them?

I shared my frustration with Greg, the experienced teacher across the hall. He seemed sympathetic and invited me to observe one of his classes. I didn't want to like his class, and at first I didn't have to. My first impression was of loud voices and of students moving around the room at will. This was a writing class? What was the teacher doing? The talking and the movement didn't seem to ruffle Greg in the least. What was happening here? The longer I stayed, the more I was amazed. Greg wasn't being "tough as nails," and yet this wasn't really chaos at all. Students were writing, critiquing one another's work, collaborating on illustrations, discussing ideas. They didn't seem to need controlling—they were controlling themselves.

"How did you get this to work?" I asked Greg later that day. "If I gave my kids a time like this, half of them would just sit there and do nothing."

"It doesn't always work," he said, "but most kids will cooperate if you give them enough responsibility and enough freedom."

I thought about that long and hard. I thought I had learned that giving a class freedom could only lead to trouble. Responsibility? My students had plenty of that: they were responsible for turning in their homework and for keeping their desks in order. I definitely agreed with Greg about responsibility.

It took me a while to catch on, but the seeds had been planted. The next week I put Amy in charge of straightening books in the classroom library, giving her a stake in running the class. When would she accomplish her task? Well, maybe she could have a little extra free time. Responsibility and freedom seemed to go together.

Matt, my best reader, was always enthralled with the current events articles I cut out of the newspaper for Friday social studies. Why not ask him to bring in some articles himself and share them? Why not extend that invitation to everyone? The novelty of listening to their peers might wake a few of them up.

The bulletin boards that kept me at school so late . . . Mickey and Lanita had asked to help on various occasions, but I had turned them down. I was proud of my room's appearance and was afraid it wouldn't look as nice. But maybe just this once it wouldn't hurt to give them this space in the corner and see what they did with it.

Francis would be glad to use my camera and take pictures for the class scrapbook. Shelley, my gifted writer, would be proud to take care of the weekly report. After all, it was the class's scrapbook, not just the teacher's.

Gloria, who loved to mind everyone else's business, could serve as chief desk inspector, even be allowed to choose her own assistants. Slowly, I realized I wasn't the only person in the world capable of doing all parts of a science demonstration. With a little guidance, everyone could participate.

I was catching on to the fact that what was true for me was true for my students: I worked hard when I felt in control of the situation. And so did they. In a classroom where the teacher did everything, it was only natural that the students stopped working hard. When Andre saw his dinosaurs and ninjas on the classroom walls, his attitude was different. This was now his place, too; he, too, had a stake in running things.

It didn't happen overnight, but the classroom gradually became a happier place for all of us. I wasn't as tired because I wasn't the only one working. My students—most of them, at least—were working much harder. And they were enjoying it.

Four years later I'm still learning. I still want to run the show. It's often more difficult for me to relax, sit back, and watch a student take charge than to bear the entire responsibility myself. This morning I caught myself squirming in my seat when Jessica took two minutes to establish order at the beginning of class. I had to remind myself that the order, the control, when it eventually did come, would be a whole lot easier to live with, easier and happier for all of us.

8

"WELCOME TO THE SIXTH GRADE"

Brad Wilcox

"MEN GET ALL THE BREAKS!" the veteran teacher announced to me. A cold greeting. Her stare stabbed like an icicle.

"Hello," I countered, extending my hand. "I guess we'll be teaching together this year."

"I swear, all you have to do is wear pants and walk into an elementary school and they hire you! It makes me sick!" I would have responded, but she turned her back to me and stomped off down the hall. I exhaled and pocketed my outstretched hand. "Welcome, Mr. Wilcox," I said to myself. "Welcome to the wonderful world of professional education."

Who would have imagined that the biggest challenge I would face during my first year on the job would not be students, but fellow teachers? Fresh from the university, I had heard horror stories about how hard it is to motivate and discipline eleven- and twelve-year-olds. But I had been well trained. I felt confident in my ability to handle children. I knew the latest techniques. I wasn't afraid of any problems that students might cause. Teachers were a different matter.

"You can't put that there!" Another teacher burst into my classroom. "You can't put the teacher's desk at the back of the room!"

"Pardon?"

"If you put your desk way back there, you won't be able to see them cheating!"

"I don't plan to be sitting at my desk a whole lot," I explained as politely as I could.

"Well," she huffed, "you'll soon learn how things are in the real world," and, like the witch in *The Wizard of Oz* who appears to torment Dorothy and then pedals furiously away on her bicycle, she was off. Her visit did little to calm my Scarecrow brain, warm my Tinman heart, or build my Lion courage.

Next I was told I must not arrange student desks into abutting clusters because "the students might talk too much." I must not use yellow backing paper on my bulletin boards because "it'll make the students restless." I must not put real plants in my room because "they make a mess." I must not put anything into the filing cabinet in my room because "the teacher who had this room last year promised to trade it with the third-grade teacher because she needs those extra-wide drawers."

At the opening faculty meeting, I was presented to the group. "Mr. Wilcox will be taking Miss Jackson's place," the principal announced. I smiled my best new-teacher smile.

"You're kidding," said one of the faculty. "She's not coming back? How are we going to do the Christmas program without her?"

After the meeting I waited around to greet my colleagues. Only one came up and spoke. On the heels of the last few days, I lapped up her friendly attention like a lonely puppy. "So . . . ," she concluded, "can I count on you to join the teacher association and pay your dues?"

Where were the kindly mentors who had opened hearts and files for me at other schools during my student teaching? I'd had classes in everything from making bulletin boards to dealing with the severely handicapped. But how to handle professional peers when they were not acting professional?

At home my wife kept assuring me, "You're there for the kids. When you meet your students, things will be different." And she was right. One day the bell rang and there were thirty-five wonderful sixth graders sitting at their desks (still arranged in clusters) and it *was* different. I was happy.

"Welcome to sixth grade." I began the year as I'd rehearsed for months. "My name is Mr. Wilcox." This is what I had wanted to be doing since I myself was a sixth grader. This is what I had trained for through those long university years. "You'll notice," I continued, "my desk is at the back of the room." They chuckled. "I don't want that desk between us. I want to be involved in your learning and involved in your lives."

In the days that followed, I ate with my students at lunch ("Wilcox shouldn't do that!"); I played with my students at recess ("That's unheard of!"); I read with my students in the library ("He's wasting time!"); I even stayed after school with some boys who got in trouble with the principal ("He's undermining the school's entire discipline program!").

My students flourished and I was certain that they were doing innovative things never before done in the history of education.

After one especially successful art lesson, I asked permission to display the work in the hall outside the lunch room. With every tape loop I placed on the back of thirty-five minimasterpieces, I guessed what my self-appointed critics might say: "Who does he think he is? He's trying to hog the best wall space before parent-teacher conferences."

As surely as I predicted the downpour, the next day their reactions came in torrents. Sopping wet, I went home to my wife. "Don't worry," she said. "They're just threatened by you because you're new *and* you're good. New teachers are supposed to be having lots of problems. Let the other teachers know you're not a threat. Just keep being nice to them."

Obediently, I pulled out the Golden Rule, dusted it off, and vowed to start again. As I did with the children, I started looking for specific, positive things I could build upon and reinforce sincerely in my colleagues: "Nice job on the announcements this morning!" "Wow! I like that worksheet you made up." "Man, your kids walked down the hall so quietly." "I heard your class singing great songs. You do a super job with music!"

"I like your bulletin board," I said to Mrs. Icicle Eyes.

"Really?" she asked. "It's just the same old thing I put up every year." She reached out and straightened a sagging border. Then, not unlike one of my students, she added, "Do you really like it?"

"Yes," I answered firmly. As sure as sun beams, the Golden Rule was shining, and things were finally warming up.

That very afternoon, a few parents went to the principal's office asking if their sixth graders could be moved into my class. Of course the students were not transferred, but when the grapevine circulated the request, up went the old barbed wire fence, complete with machine guns.

The principal called me into his office. "I appreciate your enthusiasm. But do you have to be quite so . . . " he fished for the right word, "so energetic?"

"I'm sorry. I don't mean to be a problem. What am I doing wrong?"

He pawed awkwardly through his mental thesaurus. "You're not doing anything wrong. But can't you just tone it down and keep the peace?"

His advice rankled all evening long. Tone it down. Tone it down? Do I have to do less than my best job to keep peace with colleagues in today's educational system? There must be another way. That night I floundered like a goldfish in an empty bowl. Finally, early in the morning, I decided what to do. As a first-year teacher, I was painfully aware of all I had to learn. But I had a few things to teach, too, and not all of them to sixth graders.

I continued to do the best job I could. I worked. I taught. I cared. I waited for a breakthrough moment.

Months passed. It was lunch recess. "Where's Mrs. So-and-So?" I asked the secretary. I was, in fact, searching for Mrs. Icicle Eyes. I needed to consult with her. The secretary shrugged as she continued talking on the phone. I asked the principal. "Check the faculty room," he offered. She wasn't there. Finally, in exasperation, I asked a boy walking down the hall. "Have you seen Mrs. So-and-So?"

Grinning, he came toward me as if sharing a secret. "She's outside shooting baskets with the girls!"

"She's playing basketball with the girls?" I asked incredulously. (Mrs. Icicle Eyes is out there slam-dunking!)

"Yeah," he nodded. I smiled. I didn't say another word. But my smile inside was even bigger than the one on my face.

9

EXCERPT FROM *WHITE TEACHER*

Vivian Gussin Paley

THE FIRST DAY OF SCHOOL IS FILLED with suspense. Here are thirty strangers who will become your intimate family. While you are watching them, they will be cautiously watching you. Nothing can be covered up. They instinctively know what you mean, whether or not you say it.

Each child wants to know immediately if he is a worthy person in your eyes. You cannot pretend, because the child knows all the things about himself that worry him. If you act as if you like him, but ignore the things he is anxious about, it doesn't count. The child is glad you are nice to him, but down deep he figures if you really knew what he was like, you'd hate him. So your liking him without knowing him just makes him feel guilty.

This was the first day of school.

"Mrs. Paley, are you Jewish?"

I looked at the name tag to see who was asking the question. It seemed out of context. Barbara Marcus.

"Yes, Barbara, I'm Jewish."

Barbara spent the first week asking children if they were Jewish. She did not ask black children, but she asked Asian children. She often asked people more than once.

Barbara made me uneasy. Is it healthier when a black child asks if someone is black? Why does that sound good? What was different about Barbara and her question? Maybe I still preferred that Jews not draw attention to themselves. On the other hand, I would have been concerned if a black child kept up this inquisition for a whole week. But a black child usually can see who is black; Barbara could not tell by looking.

Sitting at the table at snack time, Barbara would suddenly say, "Everyone who's Jewish raise your hand." Or, she'd be at the painting table: "If you're Jewish come to my side of the table." Something had to be done, but I kept avoiding the problem. One day Barbara announced she was organizing a Jewish club. She let everyone in who agreed to be Jewish, except black children. She told them only white people were Jewish.

That night, a concerned black parent called me. "Mrs. Paley, Ellen is crying because she's not Jewish. Could you please explain what's going on in your classroom?" I exploded with laughter and explained to Ellen's mother, "Mrs. Loam, we have a girl named Barbara who is having an identity problem. She told Ellen that black people can't be Jewish."

"Did you tell her about Sammy Davis, Jr.?"

"Well, no. I don't really want her to make any converts." I was laughing again.

"Mrs. Paley, what should we do about Ellen?"

I became serious. Ellen's mother saw no humorous aspect to her daughter's dilemma. I told her I wanted to think about the problem and call her back.

"But what should we do about Ellen?"

"Look, don't worry about Ellen wanting to be Jewish. Just treat it lightly. It's no different than if she came home and cried for a new doll her friend has."

I called back in an hour and asked Mrs. Loam if Ellen had a favorite Sunday school song, perhaps an African song. She suggested, "Caney Mi Macaro," which was on our Ella Jenkins record. I told Mrs. Loam I would try out a few ideas and talk to her again soon. I was going to need her help.

At 8:45 the next morning, Barbara was busy making Jewish stars out of construction paper. There were only five Jewish children in the class, but she had already passed out eleven stars, each with masking tape, ready to wear. I called everyone to the piano. "Barbara has been thinking a lot lately about being Jewish. I know a song with Hebrew words that some Jewish children like Barbara learn in Sunday school. 'Shalom Chaverim.' It means 'hello friends.' " We sang it twice and Barbara said, "Sing it again. I love it." So we sang it again.

I asked Ellen to bring the Ella Jenkins record. "Ellen's mother told me about a song they love at Ellen's Sunday school. It's not a Jewish Sunday school, because they're Methodists. Ellen goes to a Methodist Sunday school. This song is from Africa." Ellen jumped up. "My teacher is Mr. Raymond. He used to live in Africa. Can I put on the record?" "Caney Mi Macaro" has a strong beat, perfect for rhythm sticks. We made a lot of noise and a little bit of music.

After music, Barbara finished making her stars. She passed the rest out and gave one to Ellen, who looked very pleased. I was tempted to lift it from Ellen before she took it home, but decided to place some faith in the Loams, hoping they would be more relaxed about it than my parents would have been had I brought home a cross from school.

I began calling parents. Our school has quite an international population. This class had families from Pakistan, India, China, and Panama. In addition there were fairly recent immigrants from France, Germany, Hungary, and Italy.

I explained that we were collecting our own songs and would try to learn each other's music. I asked the parents to write out the song and send it to school. Or better yet, to send the music or a record. Otherwise the children could sing the song for the music teacher, who is skilled in writing down music.

For a while we sang our family songs every morning, intermixed with a lot of American folksongs. When we sang a Hebrew or Yiddish song, Barbara had a chance to tell everyone that she is Jewish. She had stopped asking people to label themselves. A few of the other Jewish children began to talk about themselves. None had ever joined Barbara in her crusade. Andy told us that his grandfather lives in Israel. "In Israel, the ambulance has a Jewish star on it," he said, as if he could not understand how this could be so.

Vasanti, from India, brought a picture of her cousin sitting on an elephant. She also had a song about an elephant named "Chichi" which sounded as if she had made it up. We sang "Chichi" over and over and pretended to be elephants swinging our trunks. Vasanti was delighted. The next day she brought us a book about a baby elephant. She pointed to a girl in the book and said it was her cousin and that the photographer was her uncle. This impressed everyone. Every day children looked up Vasanti's cousin in the book.

I had been caught up in white-black differences and Jewish-gentile differences. My own background made these very real for me. Differences that had no emotional overtones for me, but were real enough to each child, were being neglected.

Carol Shen is Chinese. One day we were looking at a book about how babies are born. There is a page at the end that had a drawing of six babies. The racial origin of the two white and two black babies was clear. The babies intended to portray Asian and "other" were perhaps not so clear. I asked the children to point to the baby that looked like their own baby pictures.

All the white children pointed to white babies. Half of the black children pointed to white babies and half to black babies. The Asian and Middle Eastern children vacillated between all types, but most finally chose white. Carol would not choose. She got up and left the group. She took a book and inched her way into a corner near the piano. I suddenly realized that Carol was not at ease in this class. From the beginning I had been impressed by her reading and writing abilities, and her general maturity. If she had anxieties about her differences, they did not appear on the surface.

David Hoo-Yen was the only other Chinese child in the class. He had told us that his father was teaching him to read Chinese before he learns how to read English so that he wouldn't get mixed up. David and Carol played checkers every day at snack time. I sat at their table and printed the Hebrew word for "boy." "David, do you know how to write 'boy' in Chinese? Here it is in Hebrew."

"Oh, sure. I already know lots of Chinese words." He printed "boy" in such big letters it filled up the page.

"Anyone like to copy a very big Chinese word? David wrote it for us." Barbara was the first to run over. "This is the very first time in my life I'm writing in Chinese," she told us. Barbara always liked to explain what she was doing. Though she was not pasting stars on people any more, she still seemed to be involved in an identity search. Her latest passion was drawing people with brown skin. She made a picture of herself with brown skin.

I wondered if Barbara would reorganize the Jewish club every time she entered a new class. Her chances of getting another Jewish teacher at this school were slim. There were even fewer black teachers, one Asian, and no Middle Eastern or Latino teachers. What if Steven Sherman's first teacher had been black? Wouldn't his kindergarten year have been less traumatic?

Certainly his most serious problems would have existed with any teacher and any class. But Steven's initial confrontation had been, "I don't have to listen to no white lady." A black teacher might have gained his trust sooner.

I had no answers. How much does it matter if a child cannot identify ethnically or racially with a teacher? Does it matter at all? If the teacher accepts him and likes him as he really is, isn't that enough?

How is Carol Shen to be shown that she is accepted? David Hoo-Yen seemed to have no problem being Chinese in a white school. Carol evoked memories of myself as a young girl. She avoided any activity or discussion that had to do with her own people and culture. She was spending more time reading and less time playing. This is a cause for concern. Kindergarten is a time for play. A child's good feelings about himself and others come through play, not reading.

Carol was avoiding us. She was using books and paintings to isolate herself. Her manners were always correct. She helped children when asked, and she cleaned up properly. She smiled, but it was the smile of someone who is afraid to frown, someone who wants to avoid attention.

I asked Dr. and Mrs. Shen to come in for a conference. They were from Taiwan, and both had heavy accents. There were quite a few of Mrs. Shen's words I could not catch. Often Dr. Shen would provide the missing word. They began voicing their concern about Carol. Dr. Shen's mother had come for a prolonged visit from Taiwan, and Carol had begun behaving very poorly at home. She was rude and sulky. She refused to speak Chinese to her grandmother, who spoke no English. Carol, it turned out, spoke Chinese fairly well.

I told the Shens that Carol's behavior was not unusual in an American-born child of immigrants. The cultural differences can be confusing. I had a cousin who never brought PTA notices home in hopes that her mother would not come to school and reveal her foreign accent and peasant clothing to the teacher.

Mrs. Shen's eyes reddened and she said something to her husband in Chinese. Dr. Shen said, "My wife thinks it might have been better if we had not come to America." My grandmother used to say things like this as she saw us growing distant and resentful.

"Mrs. Paley, this is not your problem. It has nothing to do with school," Dr. Shen said.

"But it's part of Carol. It's tied up with everything." I told them what was happening at school. "How about coming for a visit, with your mother-in-law? Let's try it out." Mrs. Shen agreed to come, but with no enthusiasm. That evening Dr. Shen called. "Carol is quite upset. You can probably hear her crying. She does not want her grandmother to come for a visit."

I asked to speak to Carol. "Honey, lots of people don't want visitors in school. If you change your mind, let us know. It's perfectly fine either way."

"Ok, Mrs. Paley," was the tearful reply.

One can move too fast. Sometimes preparation is needed. I had been wanting to involve parents more in our activities but had been too lazy to do anything about it. It does require planning. If you want children to feel comfortable with their parents coming to school, and parents to feel they belong here, you must plan for it.

Cooking is good common ground, I thought. Maybe Carol's mother or grandmother enjoy cooking. But first let some other parents come in. Carol does not want to appear different. Right now she would rather copy others.

I asked Vasanti's mother first because I knew she was writing a cookbook. She showed us how to make little triangular pies filled with chopped meat. Each child filled his own "sandiwich," as Vasanti called them. Mrs. Kanrayyals always wore a sari, and Carol seemed fascinated by it. She kept touching its filmy pastel material. Mrs. Kanrayyals noticed this and said she would show us how she puts on the sari. Vasanti's usually somber face was lit up with smiles and giggles. From time to time she kissed her mother's hand and her mother always returned the kiss on the top of Vasanti's head.

Ellen's grandfather, a baker, came several days later. He is at least 6 foot 6 inches tall and with his tall white hat he looked like a beautiful black giant. He made corn bread and corn pones because Ellen asked him to. This was a professional operation. He had four tables going at the same time. We served everything warm and with jam and margarine.

The following week David's mother, Mrs. Hoo-Yen, made won ton. As she began to roll out the dough, Carol ran over. "My grandmother makes this. My grandmother makes won ton!"

I asked Mrs. Hoo-Yen if she could teach us something in Chinese. She and David, in unison, repeated a saying of his grandmother. "When the Kitchen God sees how good and kind I am, everyone will be happy." The Hoo-Yens say this at the time of the Chinese New Year. David and his mother went over it again, one word at a time, and we all followed. Barbara said, "This is the first time in my whole life I'm speaking Chinese."

The next day Carol brought in a little statue of the Kitchen God. She showed it to me, but then put it in her cubby without showing it to anyone else. Later Carol played in the doll corner with Mimi and Lisa. Her statue was sitting on top of the kitchen cabinet. Barbara came in, insisting, "I'm the mother!" Everyone objected because Lisa was already the mother. Carol said, "You can be the grandmother coming for a visit. You have to bring this to me for a present." She handed her the statue.

Several days later Carol came up and whispered, "My grandmother doesn't speak English." Ah, she told her secret.

"Do you understand when she speaks Chinese?"

"Yes, and I can even talk in Chinese." She ran off to the doll corner to play.

The elder Mrs. Shen returned to Taiwan without a visit to school. But on Carol's birthday her mother came and brought some Chinese candy they had made at home. It's a bit salty and tastes like plums. Carol told everyone at her table, "This is real Chinese candy."

TEACHERS COLLEGE
AND STUDENT TEACHING

Herbert Kohl

AFTER SIX MONTHS AT THE Reece School, I began to think about public school teaching again and about working with so-called normal children. The slow rate of change of my students depressed me. I'd see a tiny positive difference negated by a change in the weather or in the emotional constellation of the class. I saw the children's fear of change overwhelm their desire to grow. I also knew I was beginning to do kind and decent work. But it wasn't enough, was too slow, too removed from the world of lively, articulate children I wanted to work with. I kept thinking of the secretary at the New York City Board of Education and resigned myself to going to Teachers College, Columbia, and taking courses, any courses, that would get me a regular elementary school credential and a job in the public schools.

Every beginning teacher has to face similar questions: What kind of child do you want to spend five hours a day with? How many children do you like to work with at one time? What age do you enjoy being with? The central question teachers have to answer for themselves is: What kind of growth do you want to nurture?

My wife is an excellent teacher of severely disturbed children, takes pleasure in observing small increments of growth, and has the patience to see them disappear and reappear. She likes to work with small groups. I'm different. I like large groups, enjoy noise and defiance, and dramatic change. Teaching friends of mine all have their preferences: Some like to work with adolescents, some with very young children. Some change every three years in order to experience growth on different age levels. Others are subject obsessed and enjoy stimulating scientific, mathematical, literary, or historical understanding. What we all realize, however, is that our most effective teaching arises from being in a situation where the growth we nurture is something we find beautiful to witness.

My time at Teachers College dragged. I spent the summer of 1961 taking classes on the teaching of arithmetic and reading, on curriculum development (which taught us how to make our own Ditto masters), on educational counseling (which told us to be nice to children), and on children's literature (which exposed us to books which, it seemed to me then, were written to avoid exposing children to poetry and fiction that dealt with life in complex and controversial ways). My professors gave the impression that they knew how to mold one into a good teacher. All you had to do was be nice, be organized, fit into the system as it was, follow the methods you learned at Teachers College, and you'd have a long and happy career. None of it seemed right to me and so for that summer and through the fall semester when I took a full course load and did student teaching, I played bad boy and devil's advocate. I brought poet friends of mine to the children's literature course, asked impertinent questions about abstract math during a class on the teaching of times tables, raised the issue of racism in the class on individual counseling. I realized the contradiction between my wanting to be respected as a teacher and my disrespectful attitude toward my professors. Part of my attitude could be attributed to a small doubt about whether indeed a Harvard man should teach in elementary school. But there was another, more serious aspect of my questioning. The content of what was being taught to us was vacuous, the skills and techniques could have been mastered by a high school sophomore and the psychology found in any Miss Lonelyhearts column. The reality of life in the classroom, the complexity and variability of children, the effect of the school and community on the teacher, the role of culture in learning—these were never dealt with and I cannot recollect anything specific about those classes other than that they were boring. The classes I hoped to learn most from, those about the education of disturbed children, were the worst. They talked about categories of disturbance, about interventions and therapeutic strategies, and said nothing pertinent or helpful about John, Fred, or Harry.

If it wasn't for the nurturance, good sense, and eventual protection of my supervisor Dorothy McGeoch, I never would have survived Teachers College and gotten a teaching credential. Throughout my experience I have always been lucky to find one or two teachers who helped me to grow the way I came to help my students. Without those teachers and colleagues, none of us sustain a life of teaching. It makes good sense when going to a new school to take time to look for such a colleague, to find someone whom you want to learn from and share what you know with.

I had two student teacher placements instead of the more usual one. My first placement was at P.S. 140, right opposite Peter Cooper Village, a middle-class development on Manhattan's East Side. I was assigned to a well-ordered, smoothly functioning, traditional sixth-grade classroom. The day opened with reading the headlines and one article from the front page of the *New York Times* and went step by step through group reading, individualized reading, spelling, math, social studies, art—what seemed to me an endless series of disconnected lessons that students had to go through. Here were normal children doing just what my students at the Reece School were doing. At Reece it was clear that the structure and the workbooks existed as much to control behavior as to teach anything. It hadn't occurred to me until I had spent six weeks at P.S. 140 that the same thing was being done to normal students. Every day was the same, every lesson the same, every question like every other. I didn't hear student voices except on the playground and in the lunchroom. The teacher, Mrs. Jay, only spoke to the students about formal matters (absence notes, parents' permission forms, etc.) or when she gave orders or asked questions about a lesson. I wanted to object to what I saw, to try to have conversations with my students and find out what interested them. They looked so lively and alert on the playground. Fortunately Dorothy McGeoch convinced me to keep quiet and do what I was told. She reminded me that my goal in student teaching was to pass the course, not reform the school. I could try that, she said wryly, when I got my credential and was doing real work.

I almost survived 140. However, I made a number of inadvertent mistakes that led to the involuntary termination of my student teaching two weeks before it was to have ended. The first mistake was to treat the principal informally. I had always been able to relate to my professors and colleagues at the Reece School on a first-name basis and didn't realize that formal address was required in exchanges between student teachers and staff and administration.

Another mistake was fraternizing with students. I said hello to every youngster I passed on the street, in the yard, or in the hall. After a while some children began asking me questions about myself or telling me the neighborhood or school gossip. I didn't realize it made the other teachers as well as the administrators around the school angry to see me chatting with the students, and it wasn't until I left the school that another student teacher told me that the principal had held me up as an example of how a teacher should not behave. He informed the other teachers at the school that eating lunch with the students and playing with them on breaks instead of having coffee in the teachers' room was unprofessional behavior that contributed to the breakdown of discipline and respect and could not be allowed in an orderly school.

Mrs. Jay, my supervising teacher, didn't like to have me in the room. I was too arrogant toward her, an attitude that I now see as foolish and one that may well have kept me from learning from her. She contrived to have me work with a small number of her "slower and difficult" students in a small conference room down the hall. I was given four students—Stanley Gold, the biggest and oldest boy in the school, who it turned out was half Jewish and half Puerto Rican; Betty Williams, who was black; Robert Moy, who was Chinese and had recently arrived in the country; and Ana Suarez, who was Puerto Rican. With one exception, they were the only minority children in the class of thirty-five.

When I first heard of the arrangement, it felt like being demoted to the Reece School—one teacher and four deviant youngsters. However, it proved to be a gift. I couldn't have learned more about children, culture, and learning in such a short time than I did from working with those four lively, intelligent, defiant, and thoroughly delightful youngsters.

As soon as we left the classroom the four came alive, chatted about what was going on, asked me about myself, particularly why I wanted to be a teacher. Once I sat down to read with them, some unexpected things began to happen. Betty didn't know the alphabet, or even how to hold a pencil. I asked her how long she'd been in school, since everything about formal learning seemed so foreign to her. She told me that this was her first year, that she had come from a small farm community in the South where the children didn't go to school much. When Betty first came to school in September, there was a suggestion she be put in the first grade, but that was abandoned because she was so tall. She spent her time in the sixth grade in the back of the room, flipping through picture books.

Betty was my first teaching success. I taught her how to hold a pencil, read stories to her and had her copy them, gave her flash cards using words she wanted to know, and watched her learn to read. She wasn't dumb or a failure—just a child who hadn't learned to read and was learning at twelve, not a bad age to begin formal reading instruction.

Working with Betty showed me the futility of trying to teach reading solely through phonics. Betty grew up in the Deep South, and she and I simply didn't pronounce *a, e, i, o* and *u* in the same way. In fact, between my Bronx accent and her Southern accent, there were few words that sounded identical to us. The meaning of sentences and the content of stories, however, made it easy to overcome these differences. Betty and I spoke about books and understood each other perfectly. The more we talked about books, the more interested she became in reading well. Our lessons were planned around questions she raised about reading. I began to realize that she was my best source of information about teaching her to read. As long as she could specify what caused her reading problems, I could help her. If endings like -ion or -ally were a problem, I could simply tell her how they were used and pronounced. If combinations like -oa- or -ae- or -ea- created confusion, it was easy to undo them as long as she could point to them. Through teaching Betty and the other three youngsters that were assigned to me, I learned how to use students' knowledge of their own learning problems as a major source for designing educational programs.

Betty's mother met me one day after school. She told me that Betty was very happy about learning to read and she wondered if I could give her materials so Betty could practice more at home. In her eyes I was a real teacher, though I knew I was only improvising. Nevertheless, I bought six inexpensive simple reading books at a remainder bookstore, six pencils and a pencil sharpener, a notebook and a pack of three-by-five index cards, and packaged them in a plastic box with Betty's name stenciled on it. That was her personalized reading kit and from what I heard several years later from another student, she had used it and taught herself to read.

Robert Moy, another one of my four, also fascinated me. I tried to administer a Gates Reading Test to find out his level and gave up one-fourth of the way through. He couldn't read any English, could hardly pronounce the sounds of the language. There was a math section on the test and I tried that since there was no reason to assume he couldn't do math because he couldn't read English. He scored 100 percent or the equivalent of twelfth-grade level in math. A few days later I gave him an eighth-grade math test and he scored in the ninety-ninth percentile, yet in class he was in a fourth-grade workbook because he couldn't read the verbalized math problems. I remember feeling at the time that the main difference between the Reece School and P.S. 140 was that in 140 the adults were doing crazy things to sane children instead of the other way around.

I noticed some Chinese writing on Robert's book and asked him if he wrote Chinese. Yes, he knew over a thousand characters and would be delighted to teach them to me. I shared my discovery about Robert's writing ability with my supervising teacher and she made a note of it, to use, as she told me, during the China unit she was planning for the second half of the school year. She didn't say anything to Robert. I watched as he systematically went about learning bits and pieces of English. He may not have been well schooled at 140, but somewhere he had been educated well. He just needed to be pointed in the right direction and given a few basic instructions in order to learn to read skillfully.

The students I got closest to in that class were Ana Suarez and Stanley Gold. Neither had a reading or a math problem. Older than the other students, they were leaders in the small ghetto a few blocks from the school, and had no relationship with most of the students in P.S. 140, which was at that time over 80 percent white. The teachers, they claimed, didn't like them and so they "refused to do any work, period," as Stanley said.

I brought Ana romances and gothics, which she loved. After learning that Stanley's father was a woodcarver and Stanley a talented artist, I got him some art instruction books. That was my first reading class—Betty copying Dr. Seuss, Robert teaching me Chinese, Ana reading romances and talking endlessly about the story, while Stanley drew and read about art.

After three weeks Ana's little sister Maria came to me after school and said their mother and father wanted to invite me to lunch on Saturday. I accepted though I had no idea why the invitation was made. It turned out Stanley's mother, Ana's parents, and a few other parents had been watching my work and felt I cared about their children. They knew my tenure at the school would be brief and wanted to pump me about how their children were being treated. The lunch, which stretched through dinner and well into the evening, was wonderful. It was the first Puerto Rican food I'd eaten and was a delicious new cuisine to explore. The more I praised Gertrude's cooking in my broken Spanish (she spoke no English at all, though her children were fully bilingual), the more new dishes appeared on the table. We talked about school for a few hours, then some people joined us, some beer was passed around, musical instruments appeared, there was music, dinner, more talk about schools, and an invitation to return the next Friday for a really special dinner.

I became friends with the Suarez family and with Stanley's mother and remained friends for years. In fact, when I got married three years later, Rafael, Ana's father, was the musician at the wedding. Fraternizing with parents has been one of the joys of my teaching life. It has also given me roots in the communities I serve and makes it easy to ask people to help me teach their children.

My extracurricular relationship with Stanley Gold, however, was what led directly to my being removed from 140. Stanley and I prepared an art project to present to Mrs. Jay's class during the morning I would be expected to run the whole class by myself. Mrs. Jay would evaluate my student teaching on the basis of the math, language, and art lessons presented then. I decided to put math and art together and do a lesson on how cathedrals stand up. I was intoxicated with the cathedrals I'd seen in France, and Stanley had shown me pictures of carved models of churches his father had made. For the lesson, Stanley was going to draw on the chalkboard a schematic of a cathedral with flying buttresses and then do a scale drawing of Chartres that compared it in size with the school and the Empire State Building. The math component of the lesson was an introduction to scale and relative proportion. The whole thing was to take up the first hour of class time. The lesson couldn't have worked, but I didn't know it. The class wasn't prepared for an open-ended discussion about anything, much less about flying buttresses; the math was too sophisticated; I had no experience working with a whole class and no sense of how to maintain control. To make matters worse, that day Mrs. Jay was absent and a sub appeared at the door at eight-forty. Stanley and I had been in the room since eight o'clock, he drawing on the board and I setting up the materials for my other lessons. The sub looked at Mrs. Jay's lesson book and let me take over.

The class came in and settled down. I began talking about the plans for the morning and then asked if anyone knew what a cathedral was. Six hands went up, three people shouted, someone made a strange noise. If Mrs. Jay was there, none of that would have happened, and it might have been possible for me to rescue part of the lesson because of the control her presence exerted. But with a sub in the room, I got more loudness than openness. After fifteen minutes the sub walked to the front of the room, banged a ruler on the desk, and in an experienced voice informed the class that she not only knew how to maintain order but demanded it instantly. She got her silence and then turned to Stanley, then to the buttressed church on the board, and commanded, "Erase that." He refused, she commanded again, and Stanley turned to me and asked if I was going to make him erase it. I saw our whole relationship dissolving, felt the possibility of his withdrawing from me as he did from all his other teachers, and I turned to the sub, saying something like "It stays." She then commanded me to erase the board. I refused and she stormed out of the room.

Somehow I fumbled through what was left of my lesson plans until recess. After my class left the room, the principal came in and told me to take the rest of the day off.

When I returned the next day, there was a note taped to my locker in the student teacher's lounge, informing me to go to the principal's office. The locker was emptied of all my books and materials, which the principal later presented to me in a neatly sealed box while instructing me that I was never to return to P.S. 140 again, for any reason. I had violated the sacred law of the teaching profession: Never under any circumstances support a student against another teacher in the presence of students. I was not even allowed to say good-bye to the class.

Halfway out of the building, I started crying quietly. It felt as if I was being sent away from home, from what I loved more than anything else. The place, the children, the energy, the best and the worst of that school, all of a sudden were precious, and now I would never get my credential and be part of it.

Dorothy McGeoch rescued me. She somehow managed to bury the principal's report and get me assigned to Walden School, a small progressive private school on Central Park West. However, every moment I could manage was spent with Stanley or the Suarez family and their friends in the neighborhood of P.S. 140.

A number of things impressed me during my brief stay at Walden. Children can be self-governing at an early age and can learn well without being pushed, manipulated, or controlled. The Walden primary school was beautiful. I had never seen Cuisinaire rods or Montessori and other manipulative materials before. Play and learning weren't separate in my life, but Walden showed me how the two could work together in a school setting.

The upper grades, however, seemed as dismal to me as the primary grades seemed wonderful. The setting was informal. There was no physical punishment or reward system. Teachers and students were on a first-name basis. Yet I sensed that the students were being psychologically manipulated and often punished by their teachers. I remember a particular case where a boy didn't want to participate in a quiet activity. He wanted to run around, talk, perhaps sing or dance. His teacher came over to him and said, "You don't want to run around, do you?" The boy's answer was "Yes," to which the teacher responded, "What's troubling you today?" I began to witness a minitherapy session which seemed all wrong to me. The youngster wanted to do something loud but positive and was being treated as a neurotic who had to be brought into line. It seemed to me that it would have been sounder for the teacher simply to admit (as was the case) that the staff insisted upon an hour's quiet work during the day instead of trying to manipulate the student into accepting something he was opposed to. I believe in being direct and clear about your intentions and reasons, and letting children know why you're acting the way you are. In the Walden case, the problem was that the teachers wanted to coerce the students into an hour of silence but their philosophy was opposed to coercion. The only way they found to overcome that contradiction was to resort to psychological manipulation. Fortunately my student teaching ended before I had a chance to express my feelings about this to the staff, or else I probably never would have gotten through Teachers College.

CHANGE, RESISTANCE, AND REFLECTION

Seymour B. Sarason

I HAVE SAID THAT YOU CAN count on death, taxes, and being wrong about something you were convinced was right, natural, and proper. Now I must add to the list that beginning at the time of your entry into a teacher preparatory program, you can count on feeling the need to change, either because something inside you says you should change or because the pressure comes from an outside source. You can truly count on that, which means that when you experience those internal or external pressures—and sometimes they occur at the same time—you should not be all that surprised. People differ markedly in response to such pressure. In the case of internal pressure, there are people who will view it as a sign of a personal inadequacy, a kind of defect symptomatic of a lack of wisdom and maturity, as if they had a view of themselves as paragons of perfection. There are those who will rationalize away or downplay the validity of that internal pressure, as if it is a kind of temporary aberration that one puts in the file-and-forget category. And then there are those who accept the significance of the internal pressure but who conclude that external circumstances work against pursuing change. There are other reactions I need not list. The point is that these internal pressures are predictable, important, and consequential. They are signs that you are struggling with the dynamics of growth. I deliberately put it in positive terms to emphasize that personal-intellectual-professional growth is a struggle, an opportunity to test and justify one's beliefs and practices. If at this point in your life you were asked if you expected to experience changes in your beliefs, ideas, and ways of acting, you would unhesitatingly answer, "Of course." If you were then asked whether those changes would be associated with struggle, conflict, guilt, and turmoil, would your answer be another unhesitating "Of course"? I have asked both questions of scores of young people in the process of making a career choice (in and out of education), and I have to predict that your answer to the second one would not be an unhesitating "Of course." It is quite likely—I will bet and give you attractive odds—you will be nonplussed, become reflective and even inarticulate! What I ask you to accept as a fact is that when we in our mind's eye project ourselves into "our" future, we do not envision ourselves as struggling with more or less frequent internal pressures to change in some important ways. And yet those pressures are predictable, even if their substance, strength, occasions, and consequences are not.

What are examples of internal pressures experienced by some teachers? Here are a few:

1. "Why do I have so much trouble managing children who are aggressive with other children? Why do the teachers who previously taught them report they had no special difficulty? I must be doing something wrong. What should I do differently? How should I change?"

2. "Why is there so little laughter in my classroom? Why do other teachers say that I take myself too seriously, that I do not give them the impression I am enjoying my work? What does that say about me and how I understand myself? How can I learn to be different?"

3. "Why is it that I no longer come to school with the eagerness and anticipation I used to have? What does that mean? Does it mean that I have changed but I was unaware of it? What can I do to change this state of affairs?"

4. "Why is it that when I come away from a meeting with my principal or one of the curriculum supervisors, I am angry with myself because it is so hard for me to tell them what I really feel? They probably think we see eye to eye, but that is not the case, and for the rest of that day I feel angry, depressed, and terribly lonely. I had to change whether I like it or not."

5. "I have five math classes a day. If God is on my side, I may have one student in each class who catches on quickly and is a joy to have. The others are uninterested or dense or both. Something, that

still, small voice, tells me that I am wrong in blaming the students, that I am copping out, that I have to change the way I am teaching."

6. "I have taught in this school for fifteen years. The children we get today are the opposite of the eager beavers that used to live in this neighborhood. When things changed, I vowed *I* was going to change what and how I taught. And I haven't. Was that a mistake? Should I have changed in some ways? I know I should have made more of an effort to get to know the children and their parents. Is it possible that a part of me has rejected them because they are so different from what I am and from what children and their parents used to be? Should I change? Can I change? Do I really want to change? *Something* has to change."

The type, strength, seriousness, and frequency of internal pressures will vary from teacher to teacher. These and other internal pressures are very difficult for teachers to verbalize. Verbalizing such internal pressures is hard for any person in any profession in which sustained, intimate relationships are an obvious feature. It is my opinion—substantiated by research studies—that these pressures are inherent in the nature of such work, albeit they can be exacerbated by differences among teachers in temperament, sense of security, and capacity for self-scrutiny. If they are inherent in the nature of such work, they are not necessarily negative but can be viewed as internal conflicts that can stimulate change and growth. They can have untoward effects if they are unheeded, if they do not stimulate reflection, if they lead the person to wallow in self-depreciation or apathy. Developing as a person and professional is rough stuff, especially in a world like ours, where it is too easy to feel that one is a snowflake in a storm.

Undoubtedly there will be people who will conclude that I am doing a pretty good job dissuading young people from choosing teaching as a career. To such people I can only say that in my experience what I have been saying is no more or less true than for most people in the human service professions. And leaving aside those professions, everything I have said is true in spades for the "profession of parenthood." It is no way my intention to dissuade anyone from choosing teaching as a career. It is my intention to alert such people to the predictable realities of life in that profession. To suggest that growing up in the profession means traversing a well-paved, well-lit, pothole-free highway containing no barriers, detours, or dangers is insulting to and derogating of the capacity of young people to handle truths fateful for their lives. And if it is not insulting and derogating, it comes perilously close to asking them to renew their belief in Santa Claus.

Let us turn to examples of external pressures.

1. Undoubtedly you will hear your instructors say something about how you should think and act in response to a particular problem or event in the classroom, and your spontaneous, internal response is that you disagree; that is, it does not square with your personal experience or values. Or it may be that what the instructor is suggesting is inimical to your personal style of relating to people.

2. It will also happen in the course of your professional education that you will be observed interacting with students in the classroom and the observer (supervisor) is critical of how you handle situations. That will certainly happen when you do your practice teaching and your supervising "master" teacher presents you with a list of "don'ts and should nots," some of which you agree with and some of which you clearly do not.

3. In your first year of teaching, you will be told—formally and informally, directly or indirectly—that "this is the way we do things in this school." This may be told to you simply as information but not infrequently as a response to something you did that you thought appropriate but that "others" obviously did not.

4. Your principal or curriculum supervisor observes you in the classroom and is critical of how you handle teaching this or that subject matter. Or it may be that they disapprove of how you have organized the classroom; that is, the physical arrangement, atmosphere, "noise level." These criticisms may or may not be presented to you graciously. The important point is that you disagree with the basis of the criticism, which you regard as counterproductive or even antieducational.

5. It has been decided by the administration of the school system or the school principal that your school will be a university research site to improve the educational outcomes of the students in your school. This will require you to participate in workshops aimed at changing the substance and mode of classroom teaching, which, of course, includes *you*. You not only resent not having had a voice in the decision, but when you are in the first workshop, it is clear that you will be expected to change your accustomed ways of teaching,

and these are changes about which you have a good deal of reservation.

Please note that in regard to neither internal nor external pressures have I indicated whether you or anyone else was "right or wrong."* My goal was to indicate that there will be frequent sources of pressure to change how you think and act. And implied in that goal is what I consider to be a fact: none of us takes kindly to change, because to conclude that you should change indicates something faulty in your previous thinking and action.

There was a period in my life when I spent hours working psychotherapeutically with people with personal problems. With few exceptions, they came because of habits, thoughts, feelings, and actions that produced conflicts within themselves or with others or (almost always) both. They concluded they needed help to change. It is in no way to deny the sincerity of that need to say what every psychotherapist learns (usually the hard way): at the same time that we seek change there is a part of us that mightily resists change. It makes no difference whether the need derives from internal or external pressures or both. We resist change. If that is true for people who seek change, it is even more true for people who do not seek change but are pressured by external circumstances to change.

By what criteria should we judge whether to accept or reject pressure for change? That question should be preceded by another question: To what extent do you believe that you have cornered the market on truth about how to think and act? (That, I should hasten to add, is no less relevant for those pressuring you to change than it is for you.) Have you "bought" the unverbalized invalid assumption that for any one problem or task, there is only *one* way to think and act in regard to it? Relevant here is a famous study by Dr. Max Wertheimer, who was one of the great

---

*There is one exception (point 5 in external pressures), and that concerns resenting not having been consulted about being selected as a research site. I am of the conviction, as I think you should be, that you should have a voice in any decision that will affect you, your students, and the school. Let us assume that the research effort is virtuous and/or justified in every respect. The fact remains that that in no way justifies ignoring the political principle that if you are to be affected by an educational decision, *you* should have *some* role in the decision-making process. *That is no less true for your relationship with your students.* Unilaterally made decisions have a way of engendering self-defeating consequences.

psychologists of this century. He observed the teaching of geometry in a classroom; more specifically, how to solve the parallelogram problem. After he finished his observations, he endeavored to demonstrate to the students a different way of arriving at a solution. The students not only resisted his mode of proof but asserted that he was "wrong" because the teacher had demonstrated the "right" way of proceeding. We can assume that it was not the intention of the teacher to persuade the students that for any problem in geometry there was one and only one way of demonstrating a proof. But there is no question that the students had "learned" to resist possibilities no less valid than the one they had been taught.

Nothing in what I have said was intended in any way to suggest that because you are confronted with internal or external pressure to change, you should embrace that change. What I have been implying and now make explicit is that you regard such pressure in two ways. The first is that you regard your emotional reaction, your resistance, as both an opportunity and a trap: an opportunity because the pressure may be a basis for new, productive experience, and a trap because you may too easily conclude that you do not need such an experience. You are familiar with the saying of that great American philosopher, Pogo, that "we have met the enemy and it is us." The pressure to change brings out the best and the worst in us. The second way you should regard such pressure for change is to steel yourself to ask and reflect on this question: *Independent* of my feelings, what are the pros and cons of the *substance* of the pressure; that is, what are the pedagogical pros and cons? There are always pros and cons, there are always intended and unintended consequences. Someone once said that it is hard to be completely wrong, and so if you find yourself quickly dismissing the change because it is wrong, completely wrong, it should be a warning that your resistance to change is swamping your ability dispassionately to analyze pros and cons.

In the course of your professional education and career, you will, you should, experience strong pressure to change. That is a given, whether you are an educator, a physician, a psychologist, or anyone else. It is also a given that such pressures are unsettling, sources of fear, inadequacy, and even anger. So what else is new?

What do we mean when we say "you should be true to yourself"? What that question assumes is that indeed we know ourselves: what we believe, what we stand for, what we think is and should be the relationship between our goals and the means we employ to achieve those goals. What we learn, and have repeatedly to learn, is that the pressure to change causes us to question how well we know ourselves; the pressure challenges the way we have viewed ourselves. There is no easy way out, unless you believe that how you think and act is the only way you should think and act. To be true to yourself means many things, but at its core it means being true *with* yourself; that is, accepting the fact that like every other human being your obligation to yourself is to try to make sense about *whether* you should resolve the struggle between what you are and have been, on the one hand, and what pressures for change ask you to become, on the other hand.

I would be both irresponsible and unfair if I did not indicate that the pressure for change too frequently is in an atmosphere defeating of the goals of change. Let me illustrate that point by recounting what happened in the late fifties and sixties when reformers introduced the "new math" into our schools. What you need to know is that introducing the new math was preceded by and associated with severe criticism of how teachers taught math. The pressure on teachers to change was enormous. And those pressures were external, not internal, to teachers. I ask you to perform an act of faith and accept the position that there was much to criticize. What you should not accept is the implication that what was wrong about the teaching of math was "willed" by teachers; that is, they knew better but chose not to act otherwise. No one needed to tell teachers that teaching math was not a rewarding, productive experience for them or their students. Teachers taught the way they had been taught in their school years and in their preparatory programs.

So we had an atmosphere that, if it was not intended to be unsympathetic to teachers, nevertheless produced an atmosphere not calculated to reduce the resistance of teachers to change. The new math was new, very different from the old math. That meant that teachers had to learn the new math. So what happened in many school districts is that teachers were required to attend a one- or two-week workshop in the summer before school opened when the new curriculum was to be used. I sat in on several of those workshops. It was quite an upsetting experience for me, the teachers, and those running the workshops. What became immediately apparent was that there were two sources of pressure. The first I already have mentioned: throughout the society, there was articulated criticism of our schools, especially of teachers. The second pressure that pervaded the workshops was *the pressure of time.* Teachers *had* to learn the new math *quickly;* that is, according to a time perspective I can only characterize as unforgivably stupid. *Teachers not only had to learn a new way of thinking, but they had to unlearn old ways, and to do that learning and unlearning—and with all the struggle that implies—quickly.* The frustration, fear, and resentment of the teachers were visible and almost palpable. I think it fair to say that most teachers came to these workshops with a relatively open mind, curious and even eager for new experience. Predictably, the introduction of the new math was one of this century's major educational disasters.

This brief anecdote illustrates several themes. The first is that when teachers were teaching the old math, they were ignoring *their* experiences with math when they were in school. Put more generally, they (the usual exceptions aside) were not using personal experience that would allow them to distinguish between productive and rote learning. The second theme is that teachers had passively resigned themselves to a role not connected at all to educational decision making that would affect them and their students. Teachers permitted themselves to be *objects* of change, not *participants* in decisions about change. And the third theme is that there was a lack of collegiality among teachers that would have permitted them to be whistleblowers; that is, to say about the workshops, "This is crazy, unfair, and self-defeating. We are not and cannot be ready by the opening of the new school year."

In the abstract, the rationale for the new math had many virtues. It was very far from being completely wrong! It was the rationale for implementation that was very close to being completely wrong. It was a rationale that not only created an atmosphere inimical to change but also led to workshop sessions in which the teachers of the teachers seemed to make every pedagogical-psychological mistake for which teachers have ever been criticized. One of the unfortunate consequences of this is that teachers ended up in strong disagreement with *all* of the rationale for the new math rather than distinguishing between the rationale and the mode of implementation. It was a case of throwing the baby out with the bath water.

The pressure for change, whether internal or external in source, should never be seen apart from the atmosphere for change. In my experience, teachers too readily blame "atmosphere," which becomes an excuse for not changing. But it is also my experience that when a teacher or group of teachers comes to the conclusion that change is necessary, action is required, they can alter the atmosphere for change. Yes, the atmosphere conducive to change can be a mammoth obstacle, but that does not necessarily mean that you are without means to change it in some way. I have witnessed such change not only in schools but in a variety of complicated organizations, public and private. That is a point deserving of emphasis, because what I have said about teachers in schools is *not* peculiar to schools. I urge you to disabuse yourself of the belief that schools are unique in their social, organizational, hierarchical, decision-making features. Schools *are* different. They are *not* unique.

IS PASSIONATE TEACHING
FOR NEW TEACHERS, TOO?

Robert L. Fried

> *I decided to do a unit on astronomy with my sixth graders. I
> know the barest minimum about astronomy, and I told them so.
> One of my kids retorted, "So now you're gonna teach us some-
> thing you know nothing about?" and I said, "You bet I am! Any
> homework that I assign to you, I'm going to do, myself. We're
> going to have a blast learning this together—so, anyway, what's
> your sign, baby? What's in your night sky?"*

—Mark Knapp, science teacher

DURING THE PAST SEVERAL YEARS, I have been teaching college students
who are about to enter the teaching profession. I've also supervised student teachers who are trying out their wings in elementary-school classrooms, and I've worked alongside middle-school teachers in their first year
or two of classroom teaching. [People] often ask, "Is passionate teaching
really for new teachers like me, or should I get my feet firmly planted in
'the way things are' before trying such a radical departure from 'business
as usual' in schools?"

There are a lot of things I'm uncertain about when it comes to teaching, but not this one. *Passionate teaching is the best way to begin your
career as a teacher.* You don't have to earn your right to be a passionate
teacher by spending years proving that you can teach in conventional

ways. You may, though, have to be courageous, take some risks, antici-
pate making some mistakes, and commit yourself to the pleasure and pain
of intensive learning. You will certainly have to learn a lot about human
relationships and something, too, about the politics of schools as complex
organizations.

A large percentage of teachers—a third, at least—leave teaching during their first few years, due to frustration, exhaustion, or disillusionment.
Had these people consciously begun as passionate teachers, their careers
might have continued. Few people can suffer the abandonment of their
ideals without serious consequences. Some become hardened to a culture
that disrespects teachers and students, and they often adopt insensitive
ways of running a classroom. Alas, society might be better off if they had
left the profession early rather than becoming inured to the status quo and
(as we used to say in the sixties) becoming "part of the problem."

Age has no monopoly on resistance to the idea of passionate teaching
and learning. When I talk with principals and head teachers, I am as likely
to hear the complaint that "some of our youngest teachers are the ones
most afraid of trying new approaches" as that "it's our older staff who
want to keep things they way they are."

Your life as a beginning teacher may well be more challenging and
more frustrating than anything you've imagined. As Deborah Meier says,
"the only cure for inexperience is experience," and nobody can rush that
process for you. But try not to abandon your idealism as you adjust to the
often painful realities of your first teaching job.

Melissa Parent, Mark Knapp, and Kimberly Frazier-Booth are first-year
teachers, although each has had some previous experience in working
with kids. Melissa Parent teaches third grade at the Walker Elementary
School, in Concord, New Hampshire, which serves a mostly white,
working-class neighborhood; Mark Knapp teaches science to sixth and
seventh graders at the Josiah Quincy Upper School, in Boston's China-
town, with a mixed population of mostly Asian-American and African-
American children; Kimberly Frazier-Booth, who was a journalist for ten
years, teaches English in the City on a Hill public charter school, also in
Boston, where her ninth- and eleventh-grade students are largely
Caribbean and African-American.

All three have faced a number of problems in their first year, and yet
all three seem to have begun—and remained—passionate about their
teaching. I've invited them to collaborate with me on this chapter.

"It's really tough if you're not in a school that welcomes and supports
new teachers," Melissa Parent commented. "A classmate of mine faces
that in the school she's teaching in. She feels all alone; but even worse, all

she seems to be getting are these little negative messages—'You should be focusing more on teaching reading . . . ' or 'You should pay more attention to math . . . ' I don't think she's going to stay with teaching past this year. And she could be a really good teacher, if she were getting a bit of support."

Mark Knapp recalls substitute teaching in public schools in western New York, where "too many of the teachers seemed to be in it only for themselves, not caring about the goals of the school as a whole. Here, at Quincy Upper School, there's much more openness and discussion. If there's a problem, such as scarcity of lab equipment or VCRs, we talk about it, we compromise, and we lend a hand instead of hoarding for ourselves. There, whenever teachers were asked to cover another teacher's class for a period, they would throw a tantrum in the faculty room. People here want the entire school to work well. It's a 'big picture' approach."

Kimberly Frazier-Booth has found a somewhat different challenge.

> In my school, we have so many young and newer teachers that there are few seasoned teachers to turn to for long-range perspective and experience. I've gotten feedback from my supervisors, who are younger than I am, that "I'm not quite sure how to assess you—you don't *look* like a first-year teacher." My principal has been principal for two years; my lead teacher is in her first year in that role. So, I need to be vigilant in my *own* reflections, because the feedback I get doesn't go deep enough.
>
> I spent the first two-thirds of the year being frustrated about this. Then I sort of kicked myself and said, Hello—there's an opportunity here to do my own assessment, to look at myself first, and also turn to my students for advice on what works and doesn't work for them. When you ask kids those questions, they are brutally honest. It's more focused than what I might expect from a supervisor. The kids know that what's at stake is *their education.* And that's when you become a better teacher.

New teachers face lots of challenges and obstacles to their ideals. In this chapter we will examine three really big ones that every new teacher has to cope with:

- fitting into your school's culture—"the way things work around here";
- having to teach curriculum material you're not familiar with;
- gaining control of the class, including dealing with the misbehavior of at least some of your students.

Another issue has emerged from these interviews—the exhaustion and overwork that new teachers face as they try to learn their new profession. I'm not sure passionate teaching has the answer for that one, but the answer may lie in a new "law of physics about teaching" that I'd like to propose. And all teachers face the question of how to find a balance between their own views on teaching and the constraints of having to cope with state- or district-sponsored standardized testing.

How you respond to these major challenges will greatly affect the degree of optimism, energy, and joy that you are able to bring to the advent of your teaching career. It may even determine whether or not you remain a teacher. The stakes are high.

Let's take a look at each of these three challenges in more detail, with the benefit of advice from first-year teachers Melissa Parent, Mark Knapp, and Kimberly Frazier-Booth.

Fitting In

You arrive at school and pretty soon you are enveloped by that school's particular climate or atmosphere. A certain feeling in the air tells you, "This is a great place for kids and adults to be." Or it says, "Some of these people like to be here, but some of them clearly don't," or even, "Most of the folk here are pretty cynical and burned out, and the kids show it, too." You sense the degree of staff friendliness and collegiality and the stance that most staff members take toward the students. Do they view them as "a great group of kids who need to be challenged," as "a bunch of rascals who would try the patience of a saint," or as a collection of "good kids" and "bad kids"? You should prepare for the possibility that your initial response to the culture may make fitting in more difficult than you have anticipated.

To a greater or lesser degree, you will feel that this culture—particularly how the people around you seem to feel about the kids and their learning potential—challenges your own assumptions and dreams. You may well feel tempted to hide your feelings, to shove your ideals into the background and quietly find your place within the status quo. *Don't do it! Now, at the start of your teaching career, is when you must reaffirm your high expectations and values, if only to yourself, to a few close friends, and—most important—to your students.* Of course, you must present yourself as a friendly, cooperative, respectful professional, as somebody who acknowledges that she or he has lots to learn. But it's more than a question of how to survive. It's also a matter of deciding if the culture of the school you're in makes it the right place or the wrong place for you to earn your wings as a teacher.

In these days of teacher shortages, district officials and school principals now see the importance of devoting resources and attention to welcoming new teachers into the profession and helping them survive their first few years.

It was not always thus. My mother, who re-entered the teaching profession in the 1950s after the last of my brothers entered first grade, faced the typical initiation of beginning teachers. The district put her in the least desirable school, with the toughest and most unruly kids, in the noisiest or most cramped classroom, with the oldest set of textbooks. She was bullied by a principal famous for driving her teachers to tears.

My mom barely survived her first year and then transferred. It was not a nice experience, but she was buoyed by her fierce determination to make a success of teaching and by her down payment, with her first paycheck, on a brand-new dishwasher, a symbol to her of liberation from enforced domesticity. She developed into a wonderful teacher and served for many years.

Just last year, a beginning teacher told me that her first job was to replace a teacher who had decided not to return after Christmas, due to illness. That woman got up out of her sickbed to guard her old room from being stripped bare by her colleagues of all her furniture, books, and materials, which she wanted to leave for this new teacher.

The idea that a new teacher has to earn her stripes by having to deal with the toughest kids is still alive. It's a product of teachers' having been disrespected and patronized by administrators for decades. Unempowered teachers tend to treat beginners as the new kids on the block who have to pay their dues in order to join the club. For Kimberly Frazier-Booth, this notion is unacceptable. "I'm thirty-three years old. I've already *paid* my dues in one profession; I don't want to fall into that same ridiculous mentality. You have to keep reminding yourself of why you've become a teacher. It's all about the kids, and not the politics of the teachers' room."

Mark Knapp remembers, "In the school I substitute taught in, back in western New York, there were teacher cliques where people would only talk to others within that clique. People held grudges over room assignments that amounted to mutual hatred." If you have to deal with a school culture that is unpleasant, demeaning, or hostile to new teachers, you might think of it as something akin to racial or gender discrimination—a vestige of practices that once were commonly and openly practiced throughout society. Your best defense may be to hold on to your self-respect, try to create a sense of mutual respect in your own classroom, stick close to your friends, and start looking for a better school to transfer to.

Even in a pretty good school, there will be a lot that is unfamiliar. There may be age, style, and cultural differences between you and colleagues old enough to have been your elementary-school teachers. You may find yourself calling them "Mrs. McIvey" or "Mr. Flood" even when they call you "Karen" or "Bill." Your way of relating to the kids may reflect differences between how you were treated at home and what older teachers experienced growing up in the 1950s. There may be times when you identify more with the kids than with the grown-ups, such as when recess is canceled because of rain or cold but most of the kids still want to go outside. Attitudes toward authority figures may also be different, particularly if your colleagues have had years of kowtowing to administrators (while mouthing off at them behind their backs).

There are the nitty-gritty aspects of fitting in—everything from when it's okay to send disruptive kids to the office, to where and with whom you eat your lunch, to whether or not you can go to the bathroom without calling in somebody to baby-sit your classroom. Details like what to do when you run out of pencils, how many pages you can photocopy for your class, how to respond to an upset parent, or how to leave your classroom drapes at the end of the day may also color how you and your first school relate. The way your colleagues and administrators respond to your inevitable gaffes or foibles will indicate much about how the school's culture treats newcomers.

But the most vital aspect of any school's culture, in my opinion, has to do with *stance*—how teachers and other staff think about the kids. Melissa Parent, who is happy as a clam with the way adults relate to students in her school, is well aware that things could be much different.

> When I was still in college, I interned in a school that had kids very much like the mix of kids here, many from complicated families or disadvantaged backgrounds. When I arrived there, I wasn't introduced to anyone. Everybody seemed to assume that I was only there for a short while, so I wasn't worth getting to know. And when I did talk to anyone, the first thing they would tell me is that I was brave for coming to work with such kids.
>
> There was a sense of hopelessness about the place. Teachers were always trying to outdo each other in complaining about individual kids: "You think Joey gave *you* a hard time today? That's *nothing!* Wait till I tell you about Andrew . . . " I felt that the kids were *branded*—their family life was always brought up; every bad thing

they had ever done was repeated; and all their academic difficulties were blamed on the "lousy attitudes" of their parents.

Here, in the school I'm in now, I got welcoming hugs from all the teachers on my first day—even though they thought I was only here to fill in for a sick teacher. Here, teachers give high fives to kids from other classes as they pass them in the halls, and everybody seems to know each of the three hundred kids by name. Instead of blaming the parents, I hear compassion: "Well, you know, his mother's trying really hard" or "His father tries to be there for his kid, even though the couple is getting divorced." Of course, teachers complain if they're having a hard time, but they're always ready to talk about the good things kids do, the funny things that have taken place. They'll say to me, "Wait till you get Dana next year—he's *such* a good kid."

As I write this chapter, the tides of the marketplace have turned. There is now a teacher shortage in many places, and that should keep the balance in your favor as you adjust to your school. It's a lot tougher when you are in a position where you must hold on to a job, however alien or alienating you find the culture of the place. Trust your instincts. Focus most of your attention on your students. You will soon know if this is the right school for you. Don't try to be somebody else. Don't let the culture change how you look at teaching kids.

Teaching Stuff You Don't Know

Inevitably, you will face others' expectations about what to teach or even when and how to teach it. Such expectations have increased dramatically, for many teachers, due to the demands of standardized testing and the pressures to "teach to the test." Some curricular material will be familiar to you, based on your training and experience. But a lot will be new. Even the familiar stuff will seem strange, at times, since you will have little advance warning of how receptive your students are to it. Not only are you expected to cover subject matter that you are unfamiliar with, but you'll have to devise new strategies to get across the stuff you think you already know.

You will be tempted to hide your ignorance and unfamiliarity and to lean on the text or the teacher's manual or even a colleague's old notes and lesson plans while you try to figure out how to present this material to your students. *Don't do it! Now, at the start of your teaching career, is the time to define yourself as a learner, as someone with the curiosity and skills to investigate the unknown or unfamiliar. Here is when you begin your career as a model to your students of how people learn.*

In a graduate course on curriculum that I taught a few years ago, I learned a lesson: *If I want more than a few students to participate actively, I'd better pose interesting questions that students* know *I don't have the answers to.* While we were discussing a new magnet elementary school for the university, the issue of cursive writing came up, and I asked them, "As we enter the twenty-first century, do you think that we should still be teaching cursive writing to kids?" The discussion was so much more spirited than anything else we had talked about that I had to ask myself what was the critical factor that prompted almost everyone to jump in.

I'm convinced it was because I had no position on the issue; there was no "right answer" that I was looking for. The normal caution that many students feel about responding to a teacher's inquiry, the fear of getting it wrong, of failing to guess what's on the teacher's mind, was missing. I now try to build such questions into every class session.

Posing such questions is also a good way to deal with unfamiliar material. From my experience observing new teachers, it's often the least utilized approach. I believe that the most effective way to teach subjects or skills that you are not proficient in is to be both honest and curious about your areas of ignorance. *You should be a role model of a teacher who is first and foremost a questioner and a learner.* When in doubt, be curious.

It's what most passionate teachers do. Yvonne Griffin in sex education; Dan Bisaccio in biology; David Ervin in music and theater; and so on. *They lead with their curiosity, rather than just with their wisdom.* Granted, all of them are experienced, master teachers with command of their field. They are convinced that in order to truly engage their students they have to be, first and foremost, *learners,* even if that has meant throwing away their old lesson plans and starting anew. As passionate teachers, they did not wait until they had full command of their subject before inviting their students into a learning partnership.

You can do it, too. All growth involves taking risks. The risks you take now, early in your career, on behalf of passionate teaching are likely to help you gain more experience and more confidence in less time than if you try to limit your vulnerability by teaching only what you're certain about (or what's in the teacher's edition of the text).

Melissa Parent showed me a newsprint sheet on which she had documented her own attempt to write a paragraph. It had lots of corrections, arrows, new words inserted. It looked like anybody's messy working draft. She explained,

> When I first started teaching writing to them—they're preparing for the state test on paragraph writing—I would try to show them the

"right way" by presenting a perfectly composed example. But now, with support from a writing specialist, I'm trying the "writer's notebook" approach, which emphasizes that the only way to get a great piece of work is to start with great ideas that don't come out right at first. But you go back to it, again and again, to build a better piece. And I do that, too, as you can see from this newsprint, I show the kids that my writing starts out as a mess (I even purposely make some mistakes, and the kids love pointing them out).

Kids naturally think that teachers know everything, but when they see me struggling to rewrite, they realize that you don't have to be perfect at the beginning. If we teachers focus too much on getting it right the first time, the kids end up writing these little babyish sentences. They get afraid to take risks, and all the really good ideas are lost.

In exploring new subject areas, Melissa has adapted the old KWL approach—"What do we already KNOW? What do we WANT to know? And what have we LEARNED?" She uses it to build her curriculum:

For example, in science, with the topic of sound, I tell the kids, "We're going to study sound because we're supposed to, but you get to decide what we actually *learn* about." This helps me because it allows me to key my own lesson prep to aspects of sound the kids have identified as most interesting. For them, it was questions like, "How do we hear?" or "What makes a sound loud or soft? What makes some things sound good and others sound really bad?" I tell them, "*You* are the designers of this unit. We will learn the things that you are interested in." And I often remind them that I am a first-year teacher and I have a lot to learn. They think it's more fun, because then I'm not teaching it to them, we're learning it *together.*"

Mark Knapp gave me another example. "I decided to do a unit on astronomy with my sixth graders. I know the barest minimum about astronomy, and I told them so. One of my kids retorted, 'So now you're gonna teach us something you know nothing about?' and I said, 'You bet I am! Any homework that I assign to you, I'm going to do, myself. We're going to have a blast learning this together—so, anyway, what's your sign, baby? What's in *your* night sky?'"

None of this is an excuse for ignorance or unpreparedness on your part. You can't fake your way through teaching. As veteran fifth-grade teacher Alphonse Litz told my class at Northeastern, "There's a world of difference between coming into class with lots of questions about what you want to teach, and being disorganized or unprepared. The one builds curiosity; the other can result in chaos." As a professional, you owe it to yourself to keep learning about the subjects you teach, and with experience you will learn better ways to teach them and how to keep old topics fresh and interesting to you, so that you will continue to model how learners act. For now, rather than hide your inexperience or lack of knowledge and run the risk of turning off your students by dragging them and yourself through the textbook, try using your energy and enthusiasm as a *teacher-learner* to lead them by example toward critical inquiry and understanding.

Sometimes such an approach pays off in unexpected ways. Ironically, it may not always be your enthusiasm that motivates your students but rather your exhaustion. Even the best-prepared teachers have days when things don't work out as expected. Kimberly Frazier-Booth faced "the blank wall of the classroom" after knocking herself out completing a term paper for a graduate course. But in this case, her lack of being fully prepared—and her ability to take risks—took an unusual turn:

> I finished my paper last night. I ate dinner and I couldn't even think about preparing a lesson plan on *I Know Why the Caged Bird Sings* for my ninth graders. Five minutes before class starts, I'm staring at the "agenda" list on my blackboard with not nearly enough activities planned to fill an eighty-minute class. So I was just honest with the kids. I told them, "Look, I was just too tired after finishing *my* paper to make up the test I was supposed to give you, today. And I'm *still* tired. So I need you to help out. I need some volunteers to present your oral projects on the Black National Anthem, 'Lift Every Voice and Sing,' which you have connected to a scene in the Maya Angelou book."
>
> The tone of the class changed. I didn't have to plead or cajole anybody to present. Every kid—I mean *every kid*—rose to the occasion. It was the first time I saw passion from all of my students, not just one or two. One girl who had been struggling since her transfer to the school, and who had never been willing to stand up and present her work to the class before, did a great job. To have the kids come forward and do their best on the day that I was, arguably, at my worst, was amazing to me. I had to blink back the tears. What it said was that they trust me, that something in my stance is right, because they're not wanting to take advantage of my weakness. Because they see me as a teacher-learner, as someone who is learning with them, they see me as someone they can help out when I need them to.

Was she just lucky this time? Perhaps. But I think Kimberly Frazier-Booth was cashing in on an investment she had been building all year with these kids. I think that there's a key, here, to the third big issue new teachers face.

Gaining Control of Your Classroom

Many new or aspiring teachers tell me that what holds them back in their desire to begin as passionate teachers is this: "How can I be an enthusiastic, idealistic teacher for *all* children," they ask, "so long as there are a few kids, or more than a few, who seem not to want to learn, or who insist on disrupting the learning of others? How can I be the kind of teacher I want to be and yet maintain enough control so that the kids don't walk all over me?"

Everyone knows of some new teacher who naively entered a classroom anticipating an eager bunch of learners, only to be overcome by a degree of student resistance that went beyond anything she had anticipated or planned for. The response is anger, sadness, tears of frustration, plus a grim determination to "get control of those kids before they get control of me."

You may well feel tempted to hide your true personality behind a mask of sternness and authority, to make sure the students know that you are in charge, right off the bat. There will be teachers who will tell you, straight out: "You'd better come down hard on the kids—at least at the beginning—to show them who's boss. Then, once you have established control, you can relax a little—but not before!"

Don't go down that path without thinking clearly about what that means for you and your kids! What worked for those teachers may not work for you. I'm not even sure it does work for each of them. Look at the students in those "well-controlled" classrooms. Are they excited about learning? Are they taking responsibility for themselves and for their behavior as learners? Or are they held in check in a manner that suggests that as soon as things loosen up—such as with a substitute—all hell will break loose?

There are some teachers whose strictness comes from a deep-seated sense of dignity and respect for one's elders, teachers who grew up in a culture that revered authority figures who were unmistakably committed to the well-being of those they led. Such teachers are able to convey compassion and high idealism as part of being strict, and the kids seem to know and respect this. But that is quite different from merely trying to let them know who's boss as a management technique.

There will be other teachers who will try to give you other friendly advice: "Look, honey, my first year of teaching was hell. I cried every night for the first month, and only by April did I realize I would make it as a teacher. Keep your back to the wall, keep your chin up, and plow ahead. You'll survive." *Don't follow their advice, however kindly or well meaning. Now, at the start of your teaching career, is the time to quietly, firmly, with humor, pride, or however it feels most natural, begin to create the kind of respectful community that will allow you and your students to do their best work.* It will take a while for your students to get used to you and you to them. Your skill with various approaches to working with students will improve with time. Don't begin by imprisoning yourself in a fortress mentality.

There may even be college professors who will say to you: "Well, you know your subject and you have the right ideas on multiculturalism, constructivism, gender equity, parent involvement, and full inclusion of kids with special needs. You'll do just fine in the classroom." *Don't trust that they know what they're talking about.* Having the right ideas is important, but it's not enough. You're the one who has to put them into practice five days a week.

The problem with all this friendly advice is that it either assumes as inevitable a struggle between your students and yourself or it pretends that ideology alone will carry you through. It won't.

The Physics of Teaching

There must be some law of physics-in-teaching that goes: If your energy and the kids' energy are moving in the same direction, without major conflicts and continually reinforcing one another, lots of great things can get accomplished. You put a lot into it, you get tired, but it doesn't deplete your energy. When it's going right, teacher and students gain new energy from the pride they feel as they work hard and learn together. They keep surprising themselves and each other. It's exhilarating, renewing. It takes a lot out of you, but it gives you something wonderful in return.

But when your energy and the kids' energy are at cross-purposes—when you try to get them to behave, or do their work, or speak up in class at a time when they have other things on their minds; when something upsetting has happened; when they don't know why you are making them do stuff; or when there's little sense of community and shared enterprise within the classroom and kids are busy teasing or putting each other down—then the opposing forces will soon deplete and demoralize you, even as it convinces some kids that they are "dumb," that you are "mean," or that "school sucks."

The critical moment comes when you first encounter the resistance. Do you push hard against it and try to overcome it by raising your voice or issuing threats? Too many of us do this. Feeling challenged and vulnerable, we reach for those old weapons of threats and sanctions, when what we should do is stop, point out the potential conflict, and move into a problem-solving mode, so that we and our students can try to work it out. It's hard to think straight when we're challenged like that. But that is exactly what's required.

The standard solution is supposed to lie in the area of teaching called behavior management. But this well-worn phrase deserves scrutiny.

Just listen to those two words, "behavior management." Doesn't this tell you that something's not quite right with the philosophy behind it? Are you a person who takes kindly to somebody *else* figuring out how to manage *your* behavior? Why should your students feel differently?

Nobody wants to be "managed" by anybody else. It undermines one's dignity. It is disrespectful. It says, in effect, "Since I don't believe you see it in your interest to behave well, it's up to me to manipulate you so that you behave well *without* having to do so on your own initiative. You need a bribe, or the threat of a punishment." Whether we're talking about gold stars or pizza parties; extra free time or balloons; time-outs, detentions, or phone calls home, if we try to control or manage our students' behavior other than by working with them to make what they are learning about interesting and meaningful, we undermine our power as role models. In *Punished by Rewards,* Alfie Kohn has some very interesting things to say about this issue.

You want to be in control of your classroom. Not being in control isn't an option. But you need something more fundamental than behavior management. You need *relationships*.

The Centrality of Relationships

Here's the mantra. It may sound a bit simplistic, but I'm hoping you won't be offended:

It's the *kids*. Teaching is about the kids. It's about *you* and the *kids*. Teaching is about you helping the kids to become powerful as learners. For you, a beginning teacher, nothing matters more than your relationship with your students. Nothing else even comes close.

You know your subject matter? Fine! You've organized your lesson plans for the whole first month of school? Good for you! You've set up the room so that it's pleasing, friendly, cheerful? Splendid! You're philosophically committed to seeing each child as an individual, with individual strengths and potential? Terrific! But if you stop there, you may find yourself in big trouble. Because, what it's really all about is you and the kids and the kind of learning community you are able to create for and with them.

One of my current graduate students, Tania Stathoulopoulos, has been an assistant kindergarten teacher for three years. After reading a draft of this chapter, she commented,

> It's important to remember that it *is* "about the kids." I find myself forgetting this, and I have to think back to how I felt right out of college, when I believed children could actually enjoy school and love learning. Although many of the teachers in my school have been very helpful to me, they seem to have forgotten that it is all about kids. They are buried with concerns over preparing for the standardized tests and covering all the state-mandated material, and they don't realize they may be ruining their students' view on education.

This is, by far, the toughest challenge in teaching. There may be a few teachers who start off with a class of eager, confident learners who are at or above their grade-level expectations in reading, writing, and math. For everyone else, some or most of the kids will have self-images as learners that have been damaged by prior experiences in school or at home. This is not to blame teachers or parents; it is to remind us that what we see in pre-school and kindergarten and maybe first or second grade—those eager hands raised, those kids ready to do anything and everything their teacher asks—we see much less of in the years that follow. I devote most of my second book, *The Passionate Learner,* to the dimensions of and responses to the plight of the child whose natural desire to learn has been blighted by school experiences.

For you, as a beginning teacher, the critical task is to *build a learning community with your students.* You can do that best by gaining your students' trust that *you really are there for them* and that your goal is to *help them become more powerful and more capable learners.* Neither you nor your students are starting from scratch. Everyone has had lots of experience being a learner, in good and bad situations. A number of students, especially those who have experienced unloving, inconsistent, or untrustworthy adults at home or in school, may not at first see you as someone worthy of trust. They don't know yet that you are on their side.

A number of these students may have been tracked into low-level or remedial classes, or called "disruptive," "immature," "ADHD," or any of the other labels that schools tend to apply to problem students, particularly when they don't come from middle-class, well-educated families. Such students may see you at first as just another in the line of teachers who will soon get frustrated with them and end up harping on their mistakes, failures, and "poor attitudes." The antidote, for many new teachers, requires a certain openness, a willingness to engage with them on a personal level, as young people who are not solely defined by their in-school behaviors.

Kimberly Frazier-Booth has found that "the valued relationships are often forged outside the classroom. You've got to be there, hanging around the lockers in the hallway, going to a basketball game, leading an extra-curricular activity. They have to see you as a person, outside of the classroom environment."

An undergraduate student of mine spent six months working in a middle school, where she was assigned to teach literacy to a bunch of "special needs" boys.

> They hated me, at first. They wanted nothing to do with me or with the reading and writing I was trying to get across. They were angry, mean-spirited, down on themselves and on everything about school— everything, that is, except football (they were the core of their school's football team, the one place where their toughness was appreciated). At my wit's end, I persuaded my roommate to go with me to one of their Saturday football games. We dressed in jeans and sweatshirts, and we waved to them from the stands.
>
> They couldn't *believe* I had come to watch them play! Some of them had never had a parent attend their games, and they all came over to me during halftime. I took notes on what each of them did that helped their team, and when I showed them my notes—on the computer—in class next week, they were really impressed. We spent that whole week doing literacy based on football—a subject they were sure they knew something about. We did sentences, paragraphs, vocabulary, everything. They corrected me on the stuff about football that I hadn't understood, but there was no gloating or sarcasm about it; they just wanted to get it right. Our working relationship was completely transformed. They were ready to work with me—that is, until the lead teacher got jealous and told me not to "waste time on topics that aren't in the curriculum." I was furious, and I eventually quit working there—but these "unteachable" kids had showed me how to teach them. I had first to care enough to show up at the place where they felt proud.

Before we leave our discussion of behavior management, there is another category of advice on how to handle kids' behavior that's a lot harder to ignore than those who counsel "Don't smile till Christmas" or "Have the right philosophy and all will be well." This advice points away from any particular philosophy and toward specific *techniques* for handling discipline. A popular approach in working with kids in grades 4–12, for example, is to announce, "*The first time I have to speak to you about your behavior, I give you a warning. The second time, your name goes up on the board. If you continue to misbehave, I put a check next to your name . . . *" and you proceed to describe the consequences for various levels of disruption (missing recess, detention, letters or phone calls home, conferences with parents).

Another technique, appropriate for younger kids, involves using cards—one green, one yellow, one red (like traffic lights)—for each child, such that anyone who is out of line is asked to move his or her card from green to yellow ("warning") and then to red, if the misbehavior continues (again, with "consequences"). The idea is to minimize the teacher's having to interrupt the lesson to chastise a student while, at the same time, emphasizing student self-responsibility. I have recently observed this technique in a well-run second-grade class, and it seems to work like magic.

But in discussing these approaches with my class of preservice teachers, we realized that a technique is only as good as the relationship already in place between student and teacher. Techniques may *enhance* the creation of a trusting and affirming classroom climate but cannot *substitute* for it. No technique can replace a teacher's role in relating to each student from the heart, and in respectfully conveying one's hopes and confidence that everyone is part of the learning community.

Melissa Parent characterizes herself as "very strict," but it was apparent to me that she carries it with a smile and a genuine openness to power sharing with her third graders.

> I tell them, "There are school rules which all of us have to follow, but we don't have any rules in this class—that is, until we make them up." During the first week of classes, we talked a lot about "rules" and what would happen if we didn't have any.
>
> At first, when we brainstormed our class rules, everything they came up with was "Don't . . . Don't . . . Don't." But then I looked them in the eye and asked: "What do you feel like when you see a sign that says 'Don't'—like when it says 'Don't pee in the swimming pool'?" And they said, "I want to DO it!" So we figured we had to have other kinds of rules, ones that are easy to follow and that you mostly want to do, anyway. We came up with what I call "The Sacred Five": 1. Please keep your hands and feet to yourself. 2. Please be respectful. 3. Listen carefully and follow directions the first time. 4. Always try your best. 5. Please be safe. [She pointed to them, up above the blackboard.]

> On days when things are not going smoothly—lots of disruptions, teasing, everyone seeming to have a tough time—I'll stop everything and say, "Look up at our Sacred 5 and see where we're going wrong." Then we talk about that. It helps that the kids know that these are my rules, too. When I stood up on a chair to reach something, the kids warned, "Ms. Parent, you're not being safe!"

It's unlikely that any teacher walking into a new classroom will be able to avoid some disciplinary tricks of the trade—raising one's voice, sending a kid out into the hall or to the principal's office, threatening to call the parents. It may happen once in a while, or every day, as we attempt to establish an effective working atmosphere in our classes. Kids will test us; they will push us to see where or if we will set limits. It's how we respond that makes the difference. And, once again, our own experiences as learners are often our greatest source of influence.

The conventional warning to new teachers, "Remember, they don't have to *like* you; just make sure they *respect* you," is eloquently wrong. Children *don't* respect people they don't like, although they may, indeed, learn to fear them. There's a difference between a teacher "acting like a kid" to curry favor and one who strives to create a climate where students can like you *and* respect you. Our own experience as learners often helps us identify with students without our having to act as though we are not the adults that we are.

For Mark Knapp, the breakthrough happened when the kids noticed, and commented on, the large scar on his forehead.

> I told them that when I was in junior high school, I dived into a lake, in early spring, and hit my head on a rock. I came out bleeding and almost died while my dad drove me the forty-five minutes to the hospital. It was a real stupid thing—I was showing off. In fact that's what one of the kids said—"You were *so* stupid!"—but I could tell she said it with affection, imagining me with my head split open. And I could tell them, then, "That happens to *all* of us, one time or another. Making stupid mistakes doesn't make you a *bad* person. It's just a poor decision. And hopefully you recover and learn from it. But you have to avoid judging yourself or others too harshly. So, you don't have to say, 'Oh, I didn't do well on that test. I'm too stupid to go to college.' You just learn how to do better next time."

Kimberly Frazier-Booth tells me it was her ability to acknowledge her own mistakes, in her teaching, that has gained her the trust of her students.

I've been honest when I've screwed up on something, like when I tried to teach my eleventh graders how to write essays for the schoolwide writing competency. I had never been through the process before, and I focused on the wrong thing. I spent hours teaching them how to write a good thesis statement, but not how to pinpoint and answer the question posed. A third of them failed because they didn't respond directly to the written prompt.

I took responsibility. I told them, "I have to share at least some of the blame with you for what happened." The funny thing was, none of them blamed me. But what was more important, none of them looked at themselves as failures. They knew it wasn't just about them. They were learners who hadn't mastered something yet. In my sharing the blame, they were able to look to *why* they had failed, instead of *that* they had failed.

We are not operating in a war zone. The kids are not the enemy, not even the disruptive ones. Ignorance, inequality, prejudice, denial of opportunity, insensitivity to someone's culture or someone's suffering, are the true enemies. The kids are who they are. As psychologist Mary Montle Bacon says, "You *got* what you *got*." The challenge for every teacher is to take what you got and, by the example of your own passions, to help the students learn. You may not be able to transform an entire school through your own teaching practices, but you surely can make a difference for the kids in your classroom.

Part of the answer, Mark Knapp believes, lies in the other kind of "discipline," which, for him, is biology.

Middle-school kids are really into all kinds of gross stuff, when it comes to the human body. So we begin at the *end,* so to speak, with methane from people or animals, and we work backward up the GI tract. It's by far the best way to get them interested in nutrition—rather than to harangue them with what they're *supposed* to eat, you know, the food pyramid. Putting issues that they are concerned about—sex, drugs, bodily functions—out in the open is one of the best ways to get and hold their attention. I tell them they can bring up *any* legitimate question about their bodies. And they are *always* asking me what I was like at their age.

Ten Tips for an Aspiring Passionate Teacher

As someone who helps prepare people for teaching, I believe there are things that may help you hold on to your enthusiasm while gaining the necessary experience that comes only with time. It is crucial that these challenges strengthen rather than overwhelm your ideals and values. Here is my list of critical factors in coping with the challenges every new teacher faces.

1. **Stay alive as an active learner.** Keep reading books and journals that contain both philosophical and practical responses to the issues that you face. Nothing, for example, is more useful in helping you deal with the pressures of standardized testing on your approach to teaching than to see how other educators are wrestling with this challenge to teacher autonomy and school-based decision making.

2. **Remember that you are not your kids' first teacher—you're not responsible for how they come to you.** Remind yourself that the kids in your class have had other teachers before you (even if you teach kindergarten) and that the attitudes they bring to class—both positive and negative—have been nurtured elsewhere. Don't blame yourself for any bad habits or poor attitudes they display, or the fact that they don't rush to join you in your enthusiasm.

   But neither should you feel compelled to accept the norms that previous teachers have enforced, such as yelling or using threats or bribes to keep the kids "on task" and "in line." Don't knock yourself out trying to change every dysfunctional aspect of every kid. Let your students know, both as a group and individually, that you are concerned about aspects of their attitudes or behavior and that you will work with them to improve as learners. In time, you'll earn your share of the credit (or blame). Right now is your chance to begin to create with them the kind of work environment you think will help them succeed.

3. **Be aware that all schools are not alike.** Take stock of positive and negative aspects of your school's culture (e.g., morale issues, levels of staff cooperation, administrative practices, policies that may discriminate against students or staff, attitudes toward parents). Your teaching is greatly affected by the climate and culture of the school you are working in *now*. Your teaching effectiveness will change— for better or worse—should you decide (or be obliged) to teach elsewhere. Do your best where you are, but keep looking for the right school.

4. **Visit other classrooms and invite other teachers to visit yours.** Now that you are yourself a teacher, you should remain a scholar of good teaching. Use a free period, staff development day, or other excuse to visit classrooms in your own and other schools where teachers

with more experience have worked out effective and engaging approaches to their work with students.

Even if you end up learning what *not* to do, by watching the effect of other teachers' practices on their students, you will have improved your own teaching. The same is true for inviting other teachers in to see your work. Many schools have mentoring programs for new teachers, and these are often very useful. Good mentors respect the individuality of the people they are working with.

5. **Build a network for yourself as a person and a professional.** Don't try to go it alone. And don't wait for things to get bad before you reach out for support. Create a network *before* you set foot in the school—including other new teachers in the district, college classmates who are also new teachers, and/or colleagues at your grade level or in your discipline whose work you admire.

   As a new teacher you will, of course, feel vulnerable. That's unavoidable. But having a network of support—e.g., a group of fellow teachers who meet for coffee every other Wednesday—can help keep your vulnerability at a tolerable level.

6. **Build strong positive relationships with the parents of your students** (especially in elementary and middle school, but also in high school). Reach out to parents, even if there is not much parental involvement in your school. The earlier you contact parents—do it during the months before school begins and in the first few days of the school year—the more cooperation you will have. Send home a one-page weekly newsletter to tell parents what's happening and how they can help. Let your students help write it.

7. **Think more about *procedures* and less about *rules*.** Students of all ages like to think of themselves as grown up. Once they know how to operate independently, as members of a classroom community, your job as disciplinarian is much reduced. As Harry and Rosemary Wong point out in *The First Days of School,* the less your students depend on you to get things moving each day of class, the more they will develop positive and productive work habits. I have visited elementary-school classes where students calmly and quietly place the tongue depressor with their name on it in the "restroom" slot before leaving the room without disturbing anyone; classes where students come in, take their writing folders, and set to revising their work while their teacher is still conferring with a colleague in the hall.

8. **Keep "respect" at the forefront of your attitudes and expectations—but aim higher, for "excellence."** As long as you and your students

are still finding your way with one another, a focus on mutual respect is likely to be the best philosophy for building a good working relationship. Respect, in this sense, is more than just treating people fairly and being polite. It should also include *respect for the learning potential in every student.*

As you get to know your students better, you want to be able to use respect as a foundation for your work with them. But, as important as it is, respect is not *the* goal—it's a prerequisite for something better, namely, *true partnership in learning,* and *excellence in student performance.*

9. **Avoid the most common traps in grading student work.** More teachers get in trouble with their students—unnecessarily—about grading than about almost anything else (except, perhaps, how they handle disruptive student behavior). I have written about this in *The Passionate Learner* as well as elsewhere. . . . The gist of my argument is that if we believe that students are individuals who learn in differing ways, we need to be flexible in how we grade them, so that we don't rely too heavily on a one-size-fits-all assessment.

   Of course, this approach may be seen to conflict with the ideals of fairness, objectivity, and consistency that teachers are supposed to adhere to. The solution is to train our students to be largely self-correcting and self-assessing in their work, so that we become their coaches, not their judges. We want them to feel free to come to us for suggestions on how to improve their work, rather than to complain about a grade that reflects a judgment already made. As coaches, we place ourselves *on their side* in the challenge to perform well as learners. It's another example of our stance.

10. **Know that student excitement about learning is your best protection against whatever the culture of the school throws at you.** Hollywood understands this: every inspirational movie about kids and teachers, from *Stand and Deliver* to *Mr. Holland's Opus* to *Dead Poets Society,* echoes this theme—the power of the enthusiasm of kids as learners. Of course, it's never as easy as in the movies. But finding a way to generate such excitement is at the heart of passionate teaching.

So here you are: you've handed in your last term paper; you've completed your student teaching and received hugs from the kids. You've received your diploma and been showered with congratulations from those who love you. You've passed that dreaded "teacher test" and received your first certification.

And you've landed your first teaching job—perhaps not at the school you'd hoped for, but at a school that you feel has the potential to be a good place to work. You have, at most, a month or two to try to get your life together and prepare for your new assignment. How will you ever be ready?

Remember, *it's about you and the kids*. Better to start with blank walls (that soon get filled with kids' drawings and written work) and to have a good plan in your head of how you will build a learning community than to put all your time into decorating your classroom without creating a strategy for you and your students to learn happily together.

Think about what procedures you want to start them off with, so that they begin to develop and practice good habits of thinking and working. Think about the little rituals you want to use, each day or week or month, to help your students feel safe, comfortable, included. Think about the questions you want to pose, and the groups you want them to form to talk about and respond to those questions, so that your students can become active players in the intellectual work and not a fidgety audience for your nonstop talking.

Hold in your imagination the elements of passionate teaching—love of knowledge, fascination with kids, devotion to ideals and issues of the world—and make a commitment to engage your students as partners-in-learning. They will respond.

PART THREE

DEVELOPING YOUR SKILLS

13

GROUPS

James Nehring

8:42 A.M. SECOND PERIOD HAS just begun. I round the last turn to my hallway and my classroom. The corridor is clear of students, who at this moment are seated in columns and rows behind closed doors amid much throat clearing, shuffling of books, and sharpening of pencils in anticipation of lessons in math and English and biology and American history and Spanish and French and . . .

I notice a great clot of students—my second-period students—midway down the hall; ninth-graders pacing and spinning and hovering and buzzing like a swarm of bees dancing their cryptic bee-body language around the mouth of the hive. Ninth-graders speak a cryptic body language to which anyone older has no entrée. All memory of it is lost somewhere in the summer between ninth and tenth grades.

"He's coming," says a voice on the edge of the swarm, and the motion at mid-hall visibly picks up.

Dave Bigg, chief ward of the writing center and my next-door neighbor here on the ninth-grade hall, stands in his doorway and eyes me like I was a truant schoolboy treading remorsefully toward the school door. And thus I feel, but Billy Abrams, owner of the boom box and caster of aspersions, had to be shown that rules can be enforced and that abuse is not always tolerated, and I was the only one there to do it, and so I escorted him to George Handelman's office, and so we waited awkwardly, silently, outside George's door because George was with another student, and so in the fullness of time it was our turn, and so I explained to George what was what, and Billy interrupted me, and so there were raised voices and gnashing of teeth, and so I left Billy with George, and so I hastened to my classroom, full on the other side of the building, and so I did arrive late to my classroom, and so I was remiss in one duty in order to serve another, but now I am here, composed and ready, so now you may go about your own business, Dave. Dave disappears into his room. I turn to my students.

"Yes, I am here. No, I did not have a heart attack. No, there was no death in the family. No, I didn't walk through the glass doors. No, you don't get a sub. You get me." I insert the key, turn it, and push the door open.

"Where's your pass, Mr. Nehring?"

"Wise guy." I bop Aaron Hughes on the head playfully as students scatter toward their chairs.

Hurrying toward my desk, I hope to seize this moment of settling to glance over my lesson plan. What *am* I teaching these kids today? Usually I am able to rehearse my second-period lesson on my way back to the classroom from hall duty. Today, though, I have been preoccupied with Billy's bravado and my consequent lateness to class. I strain to recall the plan, even the topic, but I cannot. My mind is elsewhere. I must find my plan written on the back of an old quiz. I thought it was on my blotter. Not there. Top drawer? Not there. Filing cabinet? Which one? South Asia. Yes, that's it, I'm teaching about South Asia. That's my topic. I look in the filing cabinet. Not there. Students are pretty well settled in their seats. As I look around the room there is relative quiet. Some students even have pencil in hand, as if ready to take notes. Why can't they be this way every other day when I know where my lesson plan is? I start to go through my other desk drawers. Silence falls. They know something is wrong. I'll be better off admitting it.

"I'll be happy to teach you all today if I can find my notes." I move back to the filing cabinet.

"That's okay, Mr. Nehring. We don't mind just hangin' out."

"I'm sure."

"Can we talk?"

"As long as you talk about social studies." I slide another drawer open.

"Oh, yeah. That's all we ever talk about."

"It is? Well, my goodness, then why don't you tell me about the history of British colonialism in India?"

"Sure."

"Well . . . I'm waiting."

"Okay. The British, see, wanted these spices. And so they went to India."

"How did they know how to get there?" I ask.

"Well, I guess they looked at a map."

"True enough. Whose map did they look at?" I find the plan on top of the filing cabinet, lying among papers to be corrected.

"Vasco da Gama's!" cries a voice from the back row. It is David Genovese. Gallantly he has come to the rescue of Molly McNulty, who has been chirping precociously from the front row until the last question, which seems to have exhausted her knowledge of Indian history.

"Very good, David. Tell me more about old Vasco."

"Well, like, he's this guy . . . from Portugal, who sailed around Africa . . . in 1498 . . . "

"*Ooh aah,*" goes the class.

" . . . and he went on to India . . . and then he came back and told everybody all about it and made a map and made like photocopies for all his friends."

"Photocopies?"

"Yeah, that's what you told us yesterday."

"Oh . . . well, I was kidding. You couldn't make photocopies in 1498, because there was no place to plug in the photocopy machines because people didn't know yet how to use electricity. So they didn't have wall outlets. In fact, they didn't have photocopy machines, either. But I am truly impressed, class. Next time you tell me you talk about social studies in your spare time, I'll believe you. Now I have an important announcement. You have good luck today. I've found my notes. History may proceed."

The class groans in unison. They are good kids. And they are now ready to get down to work. I couldn't have *planned* a better opener than the one that emerged spontaneously from the loss of my notes and Molly McNulty's good-natured truculence. Serendipity has a place in teaching.

Today's lesson, which happily I now remember as I glance over my notes, is about Mohandas Gandhi's nonviolent methods of political reform.

"I have a question for you today. How do you win a war without putting up a fight?" Blank stares. "I mean, is it possible to win a war when your enemy is firing at you without shooting back?"

"No way," says Andy Newcomb.

Randy Emon's hand goes up.

"Yes, Randy."

"I s'pose if you run away."

"Okay, let's suppose you run away. What may happen to you?"

"You get shot in the back," says Andy.

"That's one possibility," I say.

"Or you get away and don't get shot," says Tom Conners, who sits on Andy's left.

"Yeah," says Andy, "but even if you get away, you still didn't win. You might get caught later and be a prisoner of war or get shot or something."

"Which means you haven't won the war," I add, to round off Andy's thought.

"Right," says Andy.

"Well, then," I say, "that brings us back to our original question. Do you think it's possible to win a war without fighting back?"

Scattered nos around the room.

"Well, today we're going to begin to learn about somebody who tried to do just that, a person in India who decided he was going to try to get the British out of India without starting a war, even though the British were armed and had no intention of leaving."

"You mean we're gonna talk about Gandhi?" says Esther Cole from the middle of the room.

"Yes, ma'am. Mohandas K. Gandhi," I say dramatically.

"I saw the movie," says Esther. "It was dumb."

"How many of you saw the movie?" I ask. About a third of the class raises their hands.

"It was really long," says Ed.

"And boring," adds another critic.

"Hey, maybe we could go on a field trip." It's Molly McNulty, always quick with a good idea.

"Yeah. We could all go see Gandhi. It would be educational," says Ed.

"But I thought Gandhi was dumb and long and boring," I say.

"That's okay. It wasn't really so bad."

"Well, I tell you what. If you do a good job with the work I've planned for you, we'll see about watching part of Gandhi on video."

"Oh, cool," they answer.

"I have a handout for you that is going to help us get started."

Leading an educational discussion with ninth-graders requires deft helmsmanship. The crew has a natural tendency to steer left or right when the destination is straight ahead. Mutiny may result if the helmsman pushes too hard on the rudder to get back on course, but disaster will strike the ship if the crew steers alone. What's needed is constant, gentle vigilance. A little push this way. A little that way. So far today our ship is more or less on course.

I pass out the paper.

I have decided in advance that I will allow students to complete the handout in small groups. We will then reassemble as a class, they will offer their answers, and I will explain civil disobedience, passive resistance, boycott, and strike in the context of Gandhi's nonviolent movement.

Groups. I often have my students spend class time working in groups. I think it's good for them in a lot of ways. One of my goals as a teacher is to get my students to take seriously and talk seriously about important ideas—with each other. Having them discuss civil disobedience and the like in a controlled classroom setting, i.e. where I get to say, "No you can't talk about that, but yes, you should talk about this," is good practice. Also, talk has a way of multiplying creative ideas—two heads are better than one because of the happy possibilities of randomly combined ideas— serendipity again. Groups are also a stimulus to action and engagement. Being faced with two or three peers at a distance of two or three feet is just threatening enough, and just exciting enough, to get most kids doing something. I offer directions hopefully to see that what they do is the something I want them to do. Finally, experience tells me that only in the rarest of circumstances (e.g., test, parent conference) can ninth-graders sustain calm, silence, and concentration for more than a few minutes before breaking into oral or physical activity.

So I do a lot of groups. And there is much talk. And most of the talk is what it's supposed to be about, but sometimes it's not, which means I need to rethink how I make the groups.

Figuring out how to group students for a small group activity is an interesting teacher problem. It involves so many of those things about which teachers learn in teacher-education courses and claim they never use but which they use all the time: adolescent psychology, group dynamics, communication theory, teaching methodology. Let's suppose I say to my students, "Okay, kids, work with anybody you want for the next ten minutes and get this done." I sometimes do just that. The ensuing events in my classroom will probably be very different than if I say, "Okay, kids, get with all the people in your row for the next ten minutes and get this done." And things will probably be different again if I decide in advance what the groups will be and arrange them so that each group has one very able student, one slow student, and one in between. Or suppose I put all the bright kids in one group, all the slow kids in another, and everybody else in another. Or all the kids who work hard together and all the goof-offs together. Or all the shy kids together and the outgoing kids together. Or, dare I say, boys against girls? How about the black kids against the white kids?

Sorry, I got carried away.

Each way of organizing the class produces its own set of effects. I made a big mistake my first year of teaching. In the first week of school I let my slow class make their own groups without considering what I was doing. Everybody was with his or her friends. All the rowdy boys were together, all the chatty girls, all the quiet and serious boys, all the quiet and serious girls. And several individuals who felt uncomfortable joining any of their classmates' unofficial fraternal societies remained at their desks, marking the column and row, now vanished, as students steered their desks together and apart, crashing against walls and other desks in bumper-car fashion. The groups, such as they were, eventually coalesced, except that like electrons changing orbitals, an occasional student suddenly would spin away from one group and join another. I gave my students their task. I went from group to group offering advice, making directions clear, explaining difficult vocabulary words. And despite my best, albeit novice, efforts to carry on with the lesson, the lesson became overwhelmed by the group dynamics.

"Yo, Cindy. Jeff says he likes you."

"Well, tell Jeff I don't like him."

"Well, then, how come I saw you sittin' together outside the mall on Friday?"

"Did not."

"Did too."

"Did not. You're stupid."

"Hey, Angie."

"What?"

"How come John's hangin' around with Ann Marie?"

"I don't know and I don't care."

"I bet ya don't."

"That's right, I don't."

Given the climate, even my quiet and serious types lost interest.

"You hear about the trout that Mulrooney pulled out of Lower Valley Creek?"

"Yeah, it ain't true. He's always sayin' stuff."

"I saw a picture—him and the trout."

"It's prob'ly a fake."

Thus were antagonisms deepened, rumors dispatched, and tall tales told, but little did the planned lesson impress the hearts and minds of my class that day. In fact, having fostered some volatile alliances, I spent much of the remaining school year undoing the effect of one day's innocent attempt at groups.

Anyway, in planning today's lesson Gandhi, I consider my past mistakes and victories with groups. And wishing to create a climate more reasoned than impassioned, I decide to arrange today's groups according to the one method that is blind to friendship and enmity, gender and race. I have my students count off by fives. Thus are created five groups of five. And my students are off to work.

"Mr. Nehring?"

"Yes, Christine."

"I don't get it."

"Well, what don't you get?"

"The whole thing."

"Hmm . . . well, do you know what you're supposed to be doing with the other people in this group?"

"We're supposed to do this." She holds up the handout.

"Right. Have you read the directions?"

"Yeah."

"And what do the directions tell you to do?"

"That's what I don't get."

"I see. Well, let me see if I can put it in different words. This handout describes four situations that the Indian people faced all the time back in the days when the British were running their country."

"Uh-huh."

"Now, I want you to imagine that you are an Indian living back in those days and you don't like the fact that the British are always telling you what to do in your own country."

"Uh-huh."

"So you want to get rid of the British. Problem is, you don't like violence and bloodshed. So you have to try to figure out some way of getting back at the British in each of these situations without resorting to violence and bloodshed."

"So, like, I can't shoot anybody?"

"Like, you can't shoot anybody, right."

"Oh, I get it."

"Good. Why don't you try the first one on your own, and then I'll come back and see how you're doing."

"Okay."

Especially with slower kids, their frustration at not being able to figure out what's going on is made worse by their inability to explain where they got lost.

"What don't you get?"

"I don't get the whole thing."

So Teacher has two jobs. First, Teacher must find out where student got lost—which sometimes takes a long time—then Teacher must set student straight. Teacher must nurture special skill, which I will call backward thinking. Here is a situation that requires backward thinking.

Michael Summer raises his hand on the far side of the room. I leave Christine to help Michael.

"Yes, Michael. What can I do for you?"

"I'm lost."

At this point I decide not to ask where he got lost, because chances are he will say, "I don't know. If I knew, then I wouldn't be lost," and because that little exchange will irritate both sides, it is better left out. I'm not quite sure, however, how to set Michael back on course, but I need to say something and not just stand there looking stupid because, after all, I'm the teacher.

So I say, "Well, Michael. Worry not. We will find you and set you back on course."

What I must do is locate a probable point at which Michael became lost, describe this point to him, and find out whether he recognizes it. So what are some probable points? Thinking backward, they are one of the four exercises described on the handout; the directions that appear at the top of the handout; the existence of Michael's group; the directions I gave to students to form groups; the introduction I gave to the lesson; the topic of study, namely Indian nationalism; the unit of study, namely South Asia; or the course of study, namely Global Studies. I have learned not to exclude distant points, such as the beginning of the course, in my exercises in backward thinking because, indeed, sometimes that is where the student became lost. For example, if a student says, "Why do we gotta do this stuff, anyway?" it most likely means that he got lost at the beginning of the course, and in that case I must go back to the introductory lesson for the course and rehearse with the student all of the reasons why we gotta do this stuff, anyway. If that is where the student got lost, then a recap of the introductory lesson may work, and the student will go back on task, but very often there are other intervening wrong turns that the student has made since the beginning of the course, so that all of the ground covered between the beginning and the present is utterly unrecognizable. And that's a big problem because it means that really what this student needs is to repeat the course.

However, I don't think Michael became lost at the beginning of the course. After all, he did not say, "Why do we gotta do this stuff?" He said, "I'm lost." When a student says, "I'm lost," it usually means that he left the trail somewhere during the day's lesson. That puts some helpful limits on how far back my backward thinking must reach. Time to ask Michael a question.

"Do you understand the directions on the handout?"

"Yeah, and I got some ideas for number one, but what I mean is, I don't get what this has to do with anything."

This is a very helpful exchange. From it I learn that Michael understands the immediate task. Adding this knowledge to my earlier assumption that Michael was not lost at the beginning of the course, I figure he became lost somewhere at the beginning of today's lesson. Time for another question.

"Do you know who Mohandas Gandhi is?"

"Who?"

Bingo. Alas, while I and some students were discussing the Gandhi movie, Michael was engaged in some distraction—staring at clock, reading note from friend, writing note to friend, etching in desk, reading desk, looking at girl next to him, looking out window, or whatever—and completely missed what I thought was such a marvelously spontaneous introduction to today's lesson.

"Mohandas Gandhi is the person who led the Indian people to independence from Great Britain. He believed that the Indians could make the British leave by using nonviolent means. And, believe it or not, he and three hundred and fifty million Indians did just that. Now, what you are doing here is imagining you are in the kinds of situations that Indian people often faced when they were ruled by the British, and I want you to try to figure out how you could in some way oppose the British in each of these situations in some nonviolent manner. Then I'm going to tell you how Gandhi, himself, did it in each of these situations."

"So I can't shoot anybody, like Gandhi?"

"As with Gandhi, you do not want to harm anyone, right."

"Okay, I get it."

Sweet music to my ears. Pat on the back, Mr. Nehring. Of course, it doesn't always work out that way.

"Yo, dude," Jared calls from the other side of the room. I walk over.

"The name is Nehring, Mr. Nehring."

"Oh, Mr. Nehring."

"Yes, Jared. How may I be of assistance?"

"I am, like, totally lost."

"I see. Well—"

"Will you stop it, Jared!" interrupts Amy, who is sitting next to Jared.

"What? Wha' did I do?" says Jared.

"You kicked me. Mr. Nehring, will you tell Jared to quit kicking me?"

"Jared, stop kicking Amy," I say.

"I didn't touch her. She just wants to get me in trouble."

"Well, I'll tell you what. So that both of you stay out of trouble, why don't we see if we can figure out what you're supposed to be doing with this handout."

"I don't get it," says Amy.

"Why do we gotta do this stuff, anyway?" says Jared.

In my first year of teaching I would have regarded this question as profanity. In my inexperienced teacher's mind I would have interpreted the question to mean, "This stuff is bogus, it's a waste of time," and for anybody to suggest that the lesson I spent three hours preparing the night before, laboring with care to create as an exemplar of instructional technique, is "bogus," and for anyone to suggest that what I spent six years in college and graduate school studying, and which the adult world recognizes without question as important and meaningful, is "a waste of time," well, it just shows what an idiot that person is. Of course, what I did not appreciate in that first year was that it was my job to cure kids of their idiocy, i.e., their self-absorption, by showing them the world has a bearing on their lives.

Anyway, I now take "Why do we gotta learn this stuff, anyway" at face value because it is, after all, a forthright question.

"Jared, what is your ethnic background?"

"My what?"

"Think back to the beginning of the year when I had you do a family tree."

"Oh, yeah. Germany."

"Duh!" says Amy.

"Jared, don't kick Amy. Amy, don't insult Jared. In fact, Amy, do you remember the lesson we did back at the beginning of the year with the family tree?"

"Uh-huh."

"Could you explain to us what Jared's family tree has to do with why we gotta do this stuff?"

"Yes. Back at the beginning of the year we all looked up our family tree. Then we drew a big map at the front of the room and put an X where everybody in the class was from. And then we said that the reason that we study other cultures is because everybody in America, except for American Indians, came from other cultures. And if we don't know anything about other cultures, it really means we don't know anything about *our* culture because that's where we're all from, anyway."

"Perfect. I couldn't have said it better. Now, Jared, do you see why we gotta do this stuff?"

"It's boring. I really don't care about all that stuff."

"Jared, do you care about passing this course?"

"Is that a threat?"

"Jared, when I was in high school, I had a teacher who said that there are only two things in life that are required."

"School is one of them, right?"

"No. Death and taxes. You gotta die, and you gotta pay taxes. Everything else is optional."

"So you mean I don't gotta do this stuff?"

"You don't gotta do this stuff. You don't gotta read the paper and know what's going on in the world. You don't gotta pass this course. You don't gotta graduate from high school. You don't gotta get a job."

"Brother . . . "

"I'll be happy to help you if you want help," I say.

"I get it. I'll do it."

If I cannot win their hearts and minds, I may at least win their compliance.

"Who needs help?" Nobody answers. I walk toward Chris, Chrissy, Andrew, Peter, and Naomi, who appear to be hard at work. Andrew and Peter are arguing.

"That's not what Mrs. Hardenburg says."

"Well, maybe Mrs. Hardenburg is wrong."

"Mr. Nehring."

"Yes, Andrew."

"Have you read much Shakespeare?"

"Well, some. And I see a performance now and then."

"Do you think the spirits, elves, fairies, and all are meant to be taken seriously by the audience, or does Shakespeare intend them only as part of the fantasy of the play in general?"

(O goodly students who are thus heterogeneous in thy groups . . .)

"Well, I'm not really sure."

"Mrs. Hardenburg says that spirits and elves were part of the medieval worldview, and that Shakespeare probably believed in them and meant them to be taken seriously by the audience."

"Well," I say, "I guess I'm not so sure. Shakespeare was writing in the late 1500s, early 1600s, well into the Renaissance, and given the circles that he would have traveled in, he probably would have been guided by the more rational worldview of Renaissance thinking."

"See," says Peter, "Mrs. Hardenburg is wrong. Any writer living in 1600 who's any good does not go around believing in elves and fairies."

"Of course, I could be all wrong, and maybe Mrs. Hardenburg is right. But tell me, guys, what does this have to do with Mohandas Gandhi?"

"Well . . . " Andrew looks at Peter. Peter looks at Andrew. Andrew says, "We already finished it."

"Let's see." I look over Andrew's handout. It is completely filled out. The answers are creative and show some prior knowledge of the subject. If my slower, less motivated students challenge my skill in backward thinking, students like Andrew and Peter keep me always breathlessly trying to keep astride of a fast-forward pace.

Andrew and Peter are not atypical. There are plenty of intellectually voracious kids who thrive on academia and who challenge their teachers' ability to nurture high-powered, highly motivated intellect. Though they may not be apparent in the chaos of the hallway, they are there between the Walkmans, striding by the huddles of disaffected teenagers, reading quietly in an out-of-the-way alcove, or exploring the library stacks. For them, the system works. They feel challenged in a way that excites them, and they are rewarded with high grades, academic awards, and the approval of their teachers.

Now, having said that Andrew and Peter are not atypical, I am obliged to typify them, but I am not sure I can beyond the fact of their intellectual interests aligning with their academic subjects. And having said that they may be found sequestered in a quiet alcove, I am not sure I want to characterize "them" as out of the mainstream. And having set them apart from a kind of category of intellectual drones who occupy the same heterogeneously grouped class, I want to shatter my all-too-simple categorization and offer what I hope is a more realistic picture.

Andrew's group offers something like a cross section of my ninth-grade class. I'll say what I know about these five students without having done any special research into their family lives or school history.

Here goes: teacher's perceptions of five kids in second-period Global Studies.

Andrew is about five foot four with a head of short, neatly combed light brown hair. His teeth are straight and his fair skin is free of blemishes. His face is still rounded in a childlike way but is fast taking on a mature, hard edge. Andrew's voice is still alto but cracks occasionally. Today Andrew is wearing a blue oxford shirt with button-down collar and a maroon pullover. He has on clean, not-quite-new Levi's jeans and a silver-and-blue pair of Nike running shoes. He carries his books in a yellow Dacron backpack and uses just one strap.

Andrew speaks confidently. His pal, Peter (only the luck of the count-off put them in the same group today), takes his cue from Andrew. Andrew offers a thesis and Peter serves as friendly antagonist in a gentle, egoistic drama that Andrew usually wins or generously concedes to his admiring buddy.

Andrew becomes visibly irritated when his classmates misbehave in class so as to disrupt the lesson. But he does not show irritation at classmates who do not catch on as fast as he does. When someone like Michael asks a "dumb" question, prompting the class to sigh, roll eyes upward, whisper insults, Andrew looks to me with knit brow, as if to say, "My classmates are cruel; I am not cruel." He then looks sympathetically at the student and may even offer a helpful comment.

Andrew serves as a ninth-grade representative to the student senate and is a member of the school swim team.

In class discussions, he usually waits to hear what his classmates have to say, then offers his position—usually moderate and conciliatory—which often becomes a rallying point for further comments by his classmates. His average in my class right now is 94, and I have strong indications that his grades in other classes are equally high.

Peter and Andrew are pals and have been, they tell me, since elementary school. As I've said, Peter takes his cue from Andrew in my class, but I'm not sure that is true elsewhere. Peter is a freer spirit than Andrew, a quality that I think Andrew envies. Today he has on a T-shirt with a silkscreened print of a tuxedo with bow tie. This he complements with a pair of green Army fatigues and well-worn once-white sneakers. Whereas Andrew's thinking is synthetic and conciliatory, Peter's is divergent, antagonistic. Unlike Andrew, Peter is not a clearly recognizable personality in the class. He speaks up only occasionally and is happy to express a divergent point, then let others carry on the discussion without fighting for the supremacy of his idea. He is confident in his views but not compelled to force them on others.

Peter is close to six feet and seems awkward with his tall, gawky frame. His posture is a little hunched, and though confident in his thinking, he is not the leader or organizer that Andrew is.

Peter collects comic books and writes his own cartoon strip, which is unpublished but which he adds to almost every day. I've shown an interest in his cartooning, so he keeps me up-to-date with his main character, a not so mild-mannered punk rocker with orange hair and green teeth who, when called to action over his Walkman headset, races to the nearest hamburger restaurant and is transformed into a classic American superhero with brilliant white teeth, strong chin, erect posture, and Boy Scout virtue. More than once I've had to gently reproach Peter for cartooning in class. His average in my class is 88. I have a strong feeling that

Peter does not work hard to get good grades, and the relatively high scores he does earn come without much effort. But he is by no means docile. He shows intellectual feistiness; it's just that the possibility of high grades does not entice him as it does someone like Chrissy Duncan.

Chrissy's average in this class is currently 98. I mention that first because for Chrissy, high grades and her efforts toward them say much about who she is. She keeps close watch over her average. I've watched her on days that I return a test or assignment. No sooner is the paper in her hand than she has added the grade to a column of numbers and computed its effect on the running score. Like some Wall Street investor reading down the financial page, Chrissy's whole face tenses in anxious anticipation of today's values, as if, like the investor, her net worth should be measured by the daily rise and fall of numerical values.

Chrissy speaks up at least once during each class. She knows I reward class participation. Her comments, though intelligent, are stock. They are lucid, sophisticated, and bland. Her assignments are perfectly done, usually typed on a word processor and printed out in flawless grammar and thorough, clearly organized prose. Her Number-two Eberhardt-Faber is always sharp.

Today Chrissy wears a white sweater over a baby-blue turtleneck. She has on tight designer jeans, baby-blue socks to match her top, and clean white tennis shoes. She is a little over five feet with clear fair skin and long blond hair pulled tightly back in a single braid. At fifteen, her tidy frame stands momentarily between girlish and womanly.

Next is Chris James. Chris is a neat dresser, hard worker, and frequent asker of questions. He wants always to be sure that he's following along and doing the right thing. Problem is, he's often not following along, and he's often not doing the right thing—or at least not doing it correctly. Chris has weak comprehension skills and is only marginally literate. His composed appearance and apparent self-confidence are deceptive. He attends remedial classes in addition to his regular academic load and struggles just for passing grades. His current average in social studies is 60. Not passing.

I admire Chris for his unflagging effort despite continual disappointment. But I am concerned that continued frustration in school eventually is going to have to manifest itself somewhere in his life. I tend to think that for Chris this heterogeneously grouped class is not a good idea. In it he sees kids like Andrew and Peter doing well and feeling rewarded. Naturally he compares himself to them and aspires to a level of achievement that is probably beyond his reach.

Finally, Naomi. At the moment Naomi has on her desk Chrissy's paper, which she is copying onto hers. This is group work, they tell me. Naomi has a petite frame and could be mistaken for a boy if not for her hair, which is long, straight, brown, and neatly kept. It is difficult for me to say much about Naomi because, I confess, I don't know much about her. I have not until this moment observed her closely. I think, as a male teacher, I sometimes tend to overlook the girls in my class.

Naomi stands out neither for high grades nor low. She remains inconspicuous by speaking up just often enough to keep me from noting her silence. Her average right now is 75. Average. If she has close friends, they are not in this class because she keeps pretty well to herself. But she's not antisocial. She'll talk and laugh with her classmates if there is a conversation nearby. As with most of my students who earn less than superior grades, I believe Naomi lacks only motivation. (Chris James is an exception to this rule.) But I don't know, or have not yet figured out how to induce excitement for social studies in a slightly immature fifteen-year-old girl—beyond my usual tricks and stunts.

I wonder about the effect of this heterogeneous group on Naomi. It is probably good for her to observe peers who are turned on to the class if, as I assume, what she lacks is motivation. Their motivation may rub off since peer behavior has a strong influence. On the other hand, if Chrissy just gives Naomi the answers, as she did when she handed her the Gandhi handout all filled out, then she's being influenced by the wrong kind of peer behavior.

Anyway, that's Andrew, Peter, Chrissy, Chris, and Naomi. I am trying hard to not typify them, but having described them as individuals, I am prone to circumscribe them as identifiable types of students. My mind is immediately ready with a lot of linear scales along which I can place these individuals. Dull to bright, shy to outgoing, unmotivated to motivated, synthetic to divergent, antagonistic to suppliant, socially immature to mature, and so on. Having observed thousands of students over the years, I find it hard not to make comparisons and arrange categories.

I make one more round of the classroom. Almost everybody is done with the handout—either having written out answers for all of the exercises, run out of ideas, or lost patience and interest. Time to reassemble as a class.

"Please move your chair back to its row," I announce over the din. Slowly some students respond. Michael's group and one other do not. I cup my hands to my mouth, aiming in their direction. "And the teacher said, 'Please move your chair back to its row.'" With some sliding and bumping, a few territorial squabbles, and scattered laughter, the class reassembles approximately in the columns and rows to which they are accustomed.

Looking around the room, I see that everyone has either completed the handout or has gotten about as far as he or she could, which means we're ready to pool our ideas as a class.

"Remember, the purpose of this activity is to introduce you to the non-violent methods of social change that Mohandas Gandhi used in India. After we've had a chance to discuss the ideas that you came up with for your handout, I will tell you about Gandhi's ideas and some of the situations in which he used them."

This is what teacherdom calls a structuring/directing comment. It tells kids what they're going to do and why they're going to do it. I make a lot of structuring/directing comments because kids need a lot of structuring and directing. Without it the lesson goes haywire; witness my first-year attempt at groups. That went haywire in a big way. Even today I see places in the lesson where a little more structure would have helped. For instance, I did not intend for Naomi to copy Chrissy's work, but given the loose way the groups were set up, it was very easy.

Finding the right balance between not enough structure and too much is in one sense what teaching is all about. Time for one more first-year story. Same low-track class as the other story, only now it's a few weeks later after a classroom ambience of antagonistic chaos has been firmly established. There are regular disturbances—nonstop chatter, verbal assaults, school-kid pranks, and once a fistfight—and I am feeling unable to calm the waters. Truth be told, I am feeling battered by a stormy surf and unable to right myself in the undertow.

So I come up with an idea how to restore control. First I check the supply cabinet in the main office for twenty file folders. Next I write up a list of guidelines for classroom behavior and academic work. The list goes onto a typed sheet, which I staple inside each folder. With my new system students receive two grades each day: behavior and academic. The behavior grade is either 100 or 0—either the kid follows rules and is rewarded or screws up and gets a 0. At the end of class all academic work goes into the folder and is graded.

Day one of new program: Students behave and do work according to plan. Everybody gets 100. I envision my forthcoming article in *Social Education*: "How to Reinforce Positive Behavior and Increase Academic Success in the Low-Track Class" by James Nehring, Master Teacher in the Amesley Central School District.

By day five the program has gone to hell.

"Yo, Mr. Nehring, do I still have my hundred for today?"

"Not after that little stunt, Jack. I just wrote your name in the zero column."

"Are you sure?"

"Yes, I'm afraid it's too late."

"Are you like absolutely positive?"

"Yes, Jack."

"Good. Now I can like totally fuck up for the rest of the period and you can't do nothin' about it!"

14

CREATIVE TEACHING

Sylvia Ashton-Warner

Organic Reading Is Not New

ORGANIC READING IS NOT NEW. The Egyptian hieroglyphics were one-word sentences. Helen Keller's first word, "water," was a one-word book. Tolstoy found his way to it in his peasant school, while, out in the field of UNESCO today, it is used automatically as the only reasonable way of introducing reading to primitive people: in a famine area the teachers wouldn't think of beginning with any words other than "crop," "soil," "hunger," "manure," and the like.

Not that organic reading is exclusively necessary to the illiterate of a primitive race. True, it is indispensable in conducting a young child from one culture to another, especially in New Zealand where the Maori is obliged to make the transition at so tender an age; but actually it is universal. First words are different from first drawings only in medium, and first drawings vary from country to country. In New Zealand a boy's first drawing is anything that is mobile; trucks, trains and planes, if he lives in a populated area, and if he doesn't, it's horses. New Zealand girls, however, draw houses first wherever they live. I once made a set of first readers on these two themes. But Tongan children's first drawings are of trees, Samoan five-year-olds draw churches and Chinese draw flowers. What a fascinating story this makes!

How can anyone begin any child on any arranged book, however good the book, when you know this? And how good is any child's book, anyway, compared with the ones they write themselves? Of course, as I'm always saying, it's not the only reading; it's no more than the *first* reading. The bridge.

It's the bridge from the known to the unknown; from a native culture to a new; and, universally speaking, from the inner man out.

Organic reading is not new: first words have ever meant first wants. "Before a nation can be formed," says Voltaire, "it is necessary that some language should be established. People must doubtless have begun by sounds, which must have expressed their first wants. . . . Idioms in the first state must have consisted of monosyllables. . . .

"We really find that the most ancient nations who have preserved anything of their primitive tongue still express by monosyllables the most familiar things which most immediately strike the senses. Chinese to this very hour is founded upon monosyllables.

"The Chaldeans for a long time engraved their observations and laws upon bricks in hieroglyphics: these were speaking characters. . . . They therefore, at first, painted what they wanted to communicate. . . . In time they invented symbolic figures: darts represented war; an eye signified divinity."

In July, 1857, Tolstoy wrote in his diary:

" . . . and the most important of all: clearly and forcibly the thought came to me to open a school for the entire county."

Only two years later, in the fall of 1859, he came close to realising his dreams. With the same passion with which he did everything, he gave himself to teaching. Almost to the exclusion of all other interests, he gave three years of his life to the peasant children. His work had nothing in common with the standard, well-regulated school systems. Tolstoy wrote that he had a passionate affection for his school. Under his guidance other young people who helped him in his work developed a similar "passionate affection."

As usual he began by discarding all existing traditions and by refusing to follow any method of teaching already in use. First he must fathom the mind of the peasant child, and by doing away with punishments, let his pupils teach him the art of teaching. In his school his pupils were free to choose their own subjects, and to take as much work as they desired. The teacher considered it his duty to assist the children in their search for knowledge by adjusting his method of approach to the individual child, and by finding the best way of proffering assistance in each case.

These free Tolstoy schools, without programmes, without punishments, without rules, without forcing the will of a child, were remarkably successful. The children spent entire days at their studies and were reluctant to leave the schoolhouse.

Fifty years later, Basil Borosov, one of the peasants, said, "Hours passed like minutes. If life were always as gay no one would ever notice it go by. . . . In our pleasures, in our gaiety, in our rapid progress, we soon became as thick as thieves with the Count. We were unhappy without the Count and the Count was unhappy without us. We were inseparable, and only night drew us apart. . . . There was no end to our conversations. We told him a lot of things; about sorcerers, about forest devils. . . . "

And one of the international volunteers in Kabylia in the mountains of Algeria writes:

"About twenty children were sitting in front of the teacher under an ash tree and reading in chorus the name of their village which she had written on a big sheet of paper. They were enormously proud; time and time again they read us the word.

"But the next evening three of the adults came to ask us to teach them to write their names.

" 'Why do you want to write your name?'

"One of them explained: 'To sign at the Post Office. If I can sign my name to collect a registered letter I shall not need to pay the witnesses.'

" 'And do you often get letters like that?'

" 'Sometimes. From my son in France.'

"We went steadily on; but in the evening, instead of resting under the mosquito net, we were all caught up in the fever of fundamental education."

Organic reading for beginners is not new; it's our rejection of it that's new.

The Key Vocabulary

The method of teaching any subject in a Maori infant room may be seen as a plank in a bridge from one culture to another, and to the extent that this bridge is strengthened may a Maori in later life succeed.

This transition made by Maori children is often unsuccessful. At a tender age a wrench occurs from one culture to another, from which, either manifestly or subconsciously, not all recover. And I think that this circumstance has some little bearing on the number of Maoris who, although well educated, seem neurotic, and on the number who retreat to the mat.

Another more obvious cause of the social failure of Maoris is the delay in the infant room. Owing to this delay, which is due to language as well as to the imposition of a culture, many children arrive at the secondary school stage too old to fit in with the European group and they lose heart to continue. From here, being too young and unskilled to do a competent job, some fall in and out of trouble, become failures by European standards, and by the time they have grown up have lost the last and most precious of their inheritances—their social stability.

With this in mind, therefore, I see any subject whatever in a Maori infant room as a plank in the bridge from the Maori to the European. In particular, reading.

So, in preparing reading for a Maori infant room, a teacher tries to bridge the division between the races and to jettison the excess time.

Children have two visions, the inner and the outer. Of the two the inner vision is brighter.

I hear that in other infant rooms widespread illustration is used to introduce the reading vocabulary to a five-year-old, a vocabulary chosen by adult educationists. I use pictures, too, to introduce the reading vocabulary, but they are pictures of the inner vision and the captions are chosen by the children themselves. True, the picture of the outer, adult-chosen pictures can be meaningful and delightful to children; but it is the captions of the mind pictures that have the power and the light. For whereas the illustrations perceived by the outer eye cannot be other than interesting, the illustrations seen by the inner eye are organic, and it is the captioning of these that I call the "Key Vocabulary."

I see the mind of a five-year-old as a volcano with two vents; destructiveness and creativeness. And I see that to the extent that we widen the creative channel, we atrophy the destructive one. And it seems to me that since these words of the key vocabulary are no less than the captions of the dynamic life itself, they course out through the creative channel, making their contribution to the drying up of the destructive vent. From all of which I am constrained to see it as creative reading and to count it among the arts.

First words must mean something to a child.

First words must have intense meaning for a child. They must be part of his being.

How much hangs on the love of reading, the instinctive inclination to hold a book! *Instinctive.* That's what it must be. The reaching out for a book needs to become an organic action, which can happen at this yet formative age. Pleasant words won't do. Respectable words won't do. They must be words organically tied up, organically born from the dynamic life itself. They must be words that are already part of the child's being. "A child," reads a recent publication on the approach of the American books, "can be led to feel that Janet and John are friends." *Can be led to feel.* Why lead him to feel or try to lead him to feel that these strangers are friends? What about the passionate feeling he has already for his own friends? To me it is inorganic to overlook this step. To me it is an offence against art. I see it as an interruption in the natural expansion of life of which Erich Fromm speaks. How would New Zealand children get on if all their reading material were built from the life of African blacks? It's little enough to ask that a Maori child should begin his reading from a book of his own colour and culture. This is the formative age where habits are born and established. An aversion to the written word is a habit I have seen born under my own eyes in my own infant room on occasion.

It's not beauty to abruptly halt the growth of a young mind and to overlay it with the frame of an imposed culture. There are ways of training and grafting young growth. The true conception of beauty is the shape of organic life and that is the very thing at stake in the transition from one culture to another. If this transition took place at a later age when the security of a person was already established there would not be the same need for care. But in this country it happens that the transition takes place at a tender and vulnerable age, which is the reason why we all try to work delicately.

Back to these first words. To these first books. They must be made out of the stuff of the child itself. I reach a hand into the mind of the child, bring out a handful of the stuff I find there, and use that as our first working material. Whether it is good or bad stuff, violent or placid stuff, coloured or dun. To effect an unbroken beginning. And in this dynamic material, within the familiarity and security of it, the Maori finds that words have intense meaning to him, from which cannot help but arise a love of reading. For it's here, right in this first word, that the love of reading is born, and the longer his reading is organic the stronger it becomes, until by the time he arrives at the books of the new culture, he receives them as another joy rather than as a labour. I know all this because I've done it.

> *First words must have an intense meaning.*
>
> *First words must be already part of the dynamic life.*
>
> *First books must be made of the stuff of the child himself, whatever and wherever the child.*

The words, which I write on large tough cards and give to the children to read, prove to be one-look words if they are accurately enough chosen. And they are plain enough in conversation. It's the conversation that has to be got. However, if it can't be, I find that whatever a child chooses to make in the creative period may quite likely be such a word. But if the vocabulary of a child is still inaccessible, one can always begin him on the general Key Vocabulary, common to any child in any race, a set of words bound up with security that experiments, and later on their creative writing, show to be organically associated with the inner world: "Mummy," "Daddy," "kiss," "frightened," "ghost."

"Mohi," I ask a new five, an undisciplined Maori, "what word do you want?"

"Jet!"

I smile and write it on a strong little card and give it to him. "What is it again?"

"Jet!"

"You can bring it back in the morning. What do you want, Gay?"

Gay is the classic overdisciplined, bullied victim of the respectable mother.

"House," she whispers. So I write that, too, and give it into her eager hand.

"What do you want, Seven?" Seven is a violent Maori.

"Bomb! Bomb! I want bomb!"

So Seven gets his word "bomb" and challenges anyone to take it from him.

And so on through the rest of them. They ask for a new word each morning and never have I to repeat to them what it is. And if you saw the condition of these tough little cards the next morning you'd know why they need to be of tough cardboard or heavy drawing paper rather than thin paper.

When each has the nucleus of a reading vocabulary and I know they are at peace with me I show them the word "frightened" and at once all together they burst out with what they are frightened of. Nearly all the Maoris say "the ghost!" a matter which has a racial and cultural origin, while the Europeans name some animal they have never seen, "tiger" or "alligator," using it symbolically for the unnameable fear that we all have.

"I not frightened of anysing!" shouts my future murderer, Seven.

"Aren't you?"

"No, I stick my knife into it all!"

"What will you stick your knife into?"

"I stick my knife into the tigers!"

"Tigers" is usually a word from the European children but here is a Maori with it. So I give him "tigers" and never have I to repeat this word to him, and in the morning the little card shows the dirt and disrepair of passionate usage.

"Come in," cry the children to a knock at the door, but as no one does come in we all go out. And here we find in the porch, humble with natural dignity, a barefooted, tattooed Maori woman.

"I see my little Seven?" she says.

"Is Seven your little boy?"

"I bring him up. Now he five. I bring him home to his real family for school eh. I see my little boy?"

The children willingly produce Seven, and here we have in the porch, within a ring of sympathetic brown and blue eyes, a reunion.

"Where did you bring him up?" I ask over the many heads.

"Way back on those hill. All by heeself. You remember your ol' Mummy?" she begs Seven.

I see.

Later, standing watching Seven grinding his chalk to dust on his blackboard as usual, I do see. "Whom do you want, Seven? Your old Mummy or your new Mummy?"

"My old Mummy."

"What do your brothers do?"

"They all hits me."

"Old Mummy" and "new Mummy" and "hit" and "brothers" are all one-look words added to his vocabulary, and now and again I see some shape breaking through the chalk-ravage. And I wish I could make a good story of it and say he is no longer violent. . . .

"Who's that crying!" I accuse, lifting my nose like an old war horse.

"Seven he breaking Gay's neck."

So the good story, I say to my junior, must stand by for a while. But I can say he is picking up his words now. Fast.

Dennis is a victim of a respectable, money-making, well-dressed mother who thrashes him, and at five he has already had his first nervous breakdown. "I'm not frightened of anything!" he cries.

"Is Dennis afraid of anything?" I asked his young pretty mother in her big car.

"Dennis? He won't even let the chickens come near him."

"Did you have a dream?" I asked Dennis after his afternoon rest.

"Yes I did."

"Well then . . . where's some chalk and a blackboard?"

Later when I walked that way there was a dreadful brown ghost with purple eyes facing a red alligator on a roadway. I know I have failed with Dennis. I've never had his fear words. His mother has defeated me. During the morning output period—when everyone else is painting, claying, dancing, quarrelling, singing, drawing, talking, writing or building—Dennis is picking up my things from the floor and straightening the mats, and the picture I have of his life waiting for him, another neurotic, pursued by the fear unnameable, is not one of comfort.

Mare resisted any kind of reading vocabulary until one morning when the Little Ones were all talking at once about what they were frightened of he let go, "I shoot the bulldog!" Gay's fear was a dog too. Do we realise just how afraid small children are of dogs?

But I have some dirty, thoroughly spoilt children next door who are never held up with fear. Their Key Vocabulary runs from "Daddy," and "kiss" through words like "truck," "hill," and "Mummy" to "love" and "train." How glorious are the dirty spoilt children.

Out press these words, grouping themselves in their own wild order. All boys wanting words of locomotion, aeroplane, tractor, jet, and the girls the words of domesticity, house, Mummy, doll. Then the fear words, ghost, tiger, skellington, alligator, bulldog, wild piggy, police. The sex words, kiss, love, touch, *haka.** The key words carrying their own illustrations in the mind, vivid and powerful pictures which none of us could possibly draw for them—since in the first place we can't see them and in the second because they are so alive with an organic life that the external pictorial representation of them is beyond the frontier of possibility. We can do no more than supply the captions.

Out push these words. The tendency is for them to gather force once the fears are said, but there are so many variations on character. Even more so in this span of life where personality has not yet been moulded into the general New Zealand pattern by the one imposed vocabulary for all. They are more than captions. They are even more than sentences. They are whole stories at times. They are actually schematic drawing. I know because they tell them to me.

Out flow these captions. It's a lovely flowing. I see the creative channel swelling and undulating like an artery with blood pumping through. And as it settles, just like any other organic arrangement of nature it spreads out into an harmonious pattern; the fear words dominating the design, a few sex words, the person interest, and the temper of the century. Daddy, Mummy, ghost, bomb, kiss, brothers, butcher knife, gaol, love, dance, cry, fight, hat, bulldog, touch, wild piggy . . . if you were a child, which vocabulary would you prefer? Your own or the one at present in the New Zealand infant rooms? Come John come. Look John look. Come and look. See the boats? The vocabulary of the English upper middle class, two-dimensional and respectable?

---

* *haka:* Maori war dance

Out pelt these captions, these one-word accounts of the pictures within. Is it art? Is it creation? Is it reading? I know that it is integral. It is organic. And it is the most vital and the most sure reading vocabulary a child can build. It is the key that unlocks the mind and releases the tongue. It is the key that opens the door upon a love of reading. It is the organic foundation of a lifetime of books. It is the key that I use daily with my fives, along with the clay and the paint and amid the singing and quarrelling.

It is the key whose turning preserves intact for a little longer the true personality. It is the Key Vocabulary.

MAXIMS

in the preparation of
Maori Infant Reading

The Key Vocabulary centers round the two main instincts, fear and sex.

The Key Vocabulary varies from one locality to another and from one race to another.

Backward readers have a private Key Vocabulary which once found launches them into reading.

The power content of a word can be determined better from a backward reader than from an average reader.

In the presentation of key words to five-year-olds, illustrations are to be shunned rather than coveted.

The length of a word has no relation to its power content.

In all matters in a Maori infant room there is a Maori standard as well as a European one.

Private Key Vocabularies

I said earlier that the illustrations chosen by adults to introduce the reading vocabulary could be meaningful and delightful, but that it was the picture of the inner vision and the captions chosen by the children themselves that had the power and the light. However, there is still the odd child who is too emotionally disturbed to caption the inner picture at all.

Rangi, a backward Maori, after learning to recognize eight Maori nouns, stalled on the words "come," "look," "and" for weeks until it occurred to me to ask him what he was frightened of. He said he was frightened of the police. Asked why, he replied that the police would take him to gaol in the fire engine, cut him up with a butcher knife, kill him and hang up what was left of him. When I told the Head about this, he said that Rangi's father ran a gambling den down at the hotel to keep the home going and himself in beer and that the whole family lived in the shadow of the police and that the children had probably been threatened in order not to tell.

When I gave these words to Rangi—police, butcher knife, kill, gaol, hand and fire engine—they proved themselves to be one-look words. Whereas he had spent four months on "come," "look," "and," he spent four minutes on these. So from these I made him reading cards, and at last Rangi was a reader.

Puki, who comes from a clever family, and whose mother and father fight bitterly and physically and often, breaking out in the night and alarming the children who wake and scream (I've heard all this myself), after learning two words in six months burst into reading on Daddy, Mummy, Puki, fight, yell, hit, crack, frightened, broom.

It is an opportune moment to observe the emotional distance of these private key vocabularies from the opening words of the "Janet and John" book: Janet John come look and see the boats little dog run here down up . . .

There are always these special cases on the handling of which depends the child's start in school. No time is too long spent talking to a child to find out his key words, the key that unlocks himself, for in them is the secret of reading, the realisation that words can have intense meaning. Words having no emotional significance to him, no instinctive meaning, could be an imposition, doing him more harm than not teaching him at all. They may teach him that words mean nothing and that reading is undesirable.

The fact that certain words can be surmounted by the average reader does not prove them. That's the red herring. The weight of a word is proved by the backward reader. And there are many backward Maori readers. And to begin them on such bloodless words as "come," "look," "and" provokes one to experiment.

The Key Vocabulary of a Maori infant room, outside the common vocabulary of fear and sex, changes all the time like anything else alive, but here is the current Key Vocabulary running through the infant room this week, from the newcomers. All Maoris.

MOHI: ghost jet jeep skellington bike aeroplane sausage porridge egg car beer jersey kiss . . .

JOE JOE: King of the Rocket Men Indian Phantom Superman . . .

GILBERT: frog walnut truck King of the Rocket Men jet jeep beer tractor bomb horse . . .

MOREEN: Mummy Daddy Tape [dog] lambie *Kuia* kiss . . .

PENNY: Daddy Mummy house plane car . . .

RONGO: peanut cake ghost bed kiss socks . . .

PHILLIP: train boxing truck pea rifle . . .

PHYLLIS: beer pudding bus darling kiss ghost . . .

The words when I print them on big cards fill them with smiles and excitement.

Words over the past two years, however, from the Maori newcomers group themselves as follows, all one-look words to the particular child:

> Fear (the strongest): Mummy Daddy ghost frightened skellington wild piggy police spider dog gaol bull kill butcher knife yell hit crack fight thunder alligator cry . . .
>
> Sex: kiss love haka dance darling together me-and-you sing . . .
>
> Locomotion: jet jeep aeroplane train car truck trailer bus . . .
>
> Others: house school socks frog walnut peanut porridge pictures beer . . .

Emerging from two years of observation, however, are the two most powerful words in the infant-room vocabulary under any circumstances: ghost, kiss, representing in their own way, possibly, the two main instincts. Any child, brown or white, on the first day, remembers these words from one look.

Yet do I include them in a first reading book? There's no end to courage but there is an end to the strength required to swim against the current. For here again is the opening vocabulary of the "Janet and John":

Janet John come look and see the boats little dog run here down up aeroplane my one kitten one two three play jump can go horse ride.

Between these and the Key Vocabulary is there any emotional difference? There is all the difference between something that comes through the creative vent and something that approaches from the outside. Which is the difference between the organic and the inorganic vocabulary.

The Mechanics of Teaching the Key Vocabulary

I take the Key Vocabulary in the morning output period when the energy is at its highest, since it is a creative activity, and I believe that the creative activities are more important than anything else. It's where I place all the mediums of creativeness, between nine and ten-thirty.

I take it the minute they come in before they touch any other medium, because I don't like to interrupt them later when they are deep in blocks of clay. Also I want to catch the first freshness.

The preparation is modest enough. A number of cards at hand, about a foot long and five inches wide, of cheap drawing-paper quality, and a big black crayon. And a cardboard cover a size or two larger than the cards. And their old cards tipped out on the mat.

I call a child to me and ask her what she wants. She may ask for "socks" and I print it large on a card with her name written quickly in the corner for my own use. She watches me print the word and says it as I print, then I give it to her to take back to the mat and trace the characters with her finger and finally replace it in the cover nearby. I call them one by one until each child has a new word.

These self-chosen words mount up and are kept in a box. Each morning before the children come in I tip the cards out on the mat so that when they run in from assembly they make straight for them to find their own, not without quarrelling and concentration and satisfaction. When they have collected their own they choose a partner and sit together and hear each other, their own and the other's words. All this, of course, takes time and involves noise and movement and personal relations and actual reading, and above all communication, one with another: the vital thing so often cut off in a schoolroom. And it is while they are teaching each other, far more effectively than I could teach them myself, that I call each one to me separately to get his new word for the day.

The girl who said "socks," perhaps, comes to me with her old words and says them as she puts them back in the box; but the ones she doesn't remember I take from her and destroy because the word has failed as a one-look word and cannot have been of much importance to her. And it is the words that are important to her that I am after. For it is from these words that she first realizes that reading can be of intense meaning to herself. So the only words she keeps are those that have come from deep within herself and have to be told only once.

It is at this stage that I say, "What are you going to have?" Sometimes she will have it all bubbling hot, "Toast!" and sometimes she will twist her foot and think, and then I suspect the validity of it when she looks about and says, "Windows." And as often as not, later in the day when these words are checked she won't recognize it. So I engage her in conversation until I find out that she sleeps with Maude, or that Daddy has gone to the shearing shed. And I ask her again and may get "shed" or "Maude," which might well prove valid. But they're not often like this and I print the asked-for word on the card while she watches me and says it while I print. Then I give it to her to take back to the mat and trace it with her finger before putting it back in the cover.

I make mistakes over the choice of these words on occasion. It takes me a little while to assess the character of each newcomer. For the variety of character on the five-year-old level is as legion as nature itself. And there are pitfalls like copying, mood, repression and crippling fears which block the organic expulsion of a word. But you get to know all these after a while and there comes in time, sometimes at once and sometimes later on, a regular flow of organic words which are captions to the pictures in the mind.

It may sound hard, but it's the easiest way I have ever begun reading. There's no driving to it. I don't teach at all. There is no work to put up on the blackboard, no charts to make and no force to marshal the children into a teachable and attentive group. The teaching is done among themselves, mixed up with all the natural concomitants of relationship. I just make sure of my cards nearby and my big black crayon and look forward to the game with myself of seeing how nearly I hit the mark. And the revelation of character is a thing that no one can ever find boring.

After the morning interval, during what I call my intake period the new words of the morning come out of the cover and I check to see which are remembered. They mostly are, but the ones that are not are taken away and old ones take their place, so that when the children attempt to write them they are writing words that carry with them an inner picture and are of organic origin.

Then the words go back in the box to be tipped out on the mat the next morning. When there is a small group of beginners, the number of known words mounting up in the box need have no limit, but in direct ratio to the growing size of the group the number of words kept per child diminishes until with a group of twelve to twenty it is not feasible to keep more than the last few for each child.

Note

A minimum of forty personal words is desirable before passing on into the next group. But promotion with me depends not on the amount of intake but the rate of intake.

If a child copies a word of another, he won't remember it the next time he meets it.

A new word every week, however shy or speechless or dull the newcomer. In time he will see that the differing marks on this paper mean important different things.

What I call teaching each other: One holds up the card with "socks" to the other and says: "What's that?" If the other doesn't know, the first one tells him.

15

THE SILENCED DIALOGUE

POWER AND PEDAGOGY IN EDUCATING
OTHER PEOPLE'S CHILDREN

Lisa Delpit

A BLACK MALE GRADUATE STUDENT who is also a special education teacher in a predominantly black community is talking about his experiences in predominantly white university classes:

> There comes a moment in every class where we have to discuss "The Black Issue" and what's appropriate education for black children. I tell you, I'm tired of arguing with those white people, because they won't listen. Well, I don't know if they really don't listen or if they just don't believe you. It seems like if you can't quote Vygotsky or something, then you don't have any validity to speak about your *own* kids. Anyway, I'm not bothering with it anymore, now I'm just in it for a grade.

A black woman teacher in a multicultural urban elementary school is talking about her experiences in discussions with her predominantly white fellow teachers about how they should organize reading instruction to best serve students of color:

> When you're talking to white people they still want it to be their way. You can try to talk to them and give them examples, but they're so headstrong, they think they know what's best for *everybody*, for *everybody's* children. They won't listen; white folks are going to do what they want to do *anyway*.

It's really hard. They just don't listen well. No, they listen, but they don't *hear*—you know how your mama used to say you listen to the radio, but you *hear* your mother? Well they don't *hear* me.

So I just try to shut them out so I can hold my temper. You can only beat your head against a brick wall for so long before you draw blood. If I try to stop arguing with them I can't help myself from getting angry. Then I end up walking around praying all day "Please Lord, remove the bile I feel for these people so I can sleep tonight." It's funny, but it can become a cancer, a sore.

So, I shut them out. I go back to my own little cubby, my classroom, and I try to teach the way I know will work, no matter what those folk say. And when I get black kids, I just try to undo the damage they did.

I'm not going to let any man, woman, or child drive me crazy—white folks will try to do that to you if you let them. You just have to stop talking to them, that's what I do. I just keep smiling, but I won't talk to them.

A soft-spoken Native Alaskan woman in her forties is a student in the Education Department of the University of Alaska. One day she storms into a black professor's office and very uncharacteristically slams the door. She plops down in a chair and, still fuming, says, "Please tell those people, just don't help us anymore! I give up. I won't talk to them again!"

And finally, a black woman principal who is also a doctoral student at a well-known university on the West Coast is talking about her university experiences, particularly about when a professor lectures on issues concerning educating black children:

If you try to suggest that's not quite the way it is, they get defensive, then you get defensive, then they'll start reciting research.

I try to give them my experiences, to explain. They just look and nod. The more I try to explain, they just look and nod, just keep looking and nodding. They don't really hear me.

Then, when it's time for class to be over, the professor tells me to come to his office to talk more. So I go. He asks for more examples of what I'm talking about, and he looks and nods while I give them. Then he says that that's just *my* experience. It doesn't really apply to most black people.

It becomes futile because they think they know everything about everybody. What you have to say about your life, your children, doesn't mean anything. They don't really want to hear what you have to say. They wear blinders and earplugs. They only want to go on research they've read that other white people have written.

It just doesn't make any sense to keep talking to them.

Thus was the first half of the title of this text born: "The Silenced Dialogue." One of the tragedies in this field of education is that scenarios such as these are enacted daily around the country. The saddest element is that the individuals that the black and Native Alaskan educators speak of in these statements are seldom aware that the dialogue *has* been silenced. Most likely the white educators believe that their colleagues of color did, in the end, agree with their logic. After all, they stopped disagreeing, didn't they?

I have collected these statements since completing a recently published article, a somewhat autobiographical account entitled "Skills and Other Dilemmas of a Progressive Black Educator," in which I discuss my perspective as a product of a skills-oriented approach to writing and as a teacher of process-oriented approaches. I described the estrangement that I and many teachers of color feel from the progressive movement when writing process advocates dismiss us as too "skills oriented." I ended the article suggesting that it was incumbent upon writing process advocates, or indeed, advocates of any progressive movement, to enter into dialogue with teachers of color, who may not share their enthusiasm about so-called new, liberal, or progressive ideas.

In response to this article, which presented no research data and did not even cite a reference, I received numerous calls and letters from teachers, professors, and even state school personnel from around the country, both black and white. All of the white respondents, except one, have wished to talk more about the question of skills versus process approaches—to support or reject what they perceive to be my position. On the other hand, *all* of the nonwhite respondents have spoken passionately on being left out of the dialogue about how best to educate children of color.

How can such complete communication blocks exist when both parties truly believe they have the same aims? How can the bitterness and resentment expressed by the educators of color be drained so that the sores can heal? What can be done?

I believe the answer to these questions lies in ethnographic analysis, that is, in identifying and giving voice to alternative worldviews. Thus, I will attempt to address the concerns raised by white and black respondents to my article "Skills and Other Dilemmas." My charge here is not to determine the best instructional methodology; I believe that the actual practice of good teachers of all colors typically incorporates a range of pedagogical orientations. Rather, I suggest that the differing perspectives on the debate over "skills" versus "process" approaches can lead to an understanding of the alienation and miscommunication, and thereby to an understanding of the "silenced dialogue."

In thinking through these issues, I have found what I believe to be a connecting and complex theme: what I have come to call "the culture of power." There are five aspects of power I would like to propose as given for this presentation:

1. Issues of power are enacted in classrooms.
2. There are codes or rules for participating in power; that is, there is a "culture of power."
3. The rules of the culture of power are a reflection of the rules of the culture of those who have power.
4. If you are not already a participant in the culture of power, being told explicitly the rules of that culture makes acquiring power easier.
5. Those with power are frequently least aware of—or least willing to acknowledge—its existence. Those with less power are often most aware of its existence.

The first three are by now basic tenets in the literature of the sociology of education, but the last two have seldom been addressed. The following discussion will explicate these aspects of power and their relevance to the schism between liberal educational movements and that of non-white, non-middle-class teachers and communities.[1]

1. Issues of power are enacted in classrooms.

These issues include: the power of the teacher over the students; the power of the publishers of textbooks and of the developers of the curriculum to determine the view of the world presented; the power of the state in enforcing compulsory schooling; and the power of an individual or group to determine another's intelligence or "normalcy." Finally, if schooling prepares people for jobs, and the kind of job a person has determines her or his economic status and, therefore, power, then schooling is intimately related to that power.

2. There are codes or rules for participating in power; that is, there is a "culture of power."

The codes or rules I'm speaking of relate to linguistic forms, communicative strategies, and presentation of self; that is, ways of talking, ways of writing, ways of dressing, and ways of interacting.

3. The rules of the culture of power are a reflection of the rules of the culture of those who have power.

This means that success in institutions—schools, workplaces, and so on— is predicated upon acquisition of the culture of those who are in power. Children from middle-class homes tend to do better in school than those from non-middle-class homes because the culture of the school is based on the culture of the upper and middle classes—of those in power. The upper and middle classes send their children to school with all the accou- trements of the culture of power; children from other kinds of families operate within perfectly wonderful and viable cultures but not cultures that carry the codes or rules of power.

4. If you are not already a participant in the culture of power, being told explicitly the rules of that culture makes acquiring power easier.

In my work within and between diverse cultures, I have come to conclude that members of any culture transmit information implicitly to co-members. However, when implicit codes are attempted across cultures, communi- cation frequently breaks down. Each cultural group is left saying, "Why don't those people say what they mean?" as well as, "What's wrong with them, why don't they understand?"

Anyone who has had to enter new cultures, especially to accomplish a specific task, will know of what I speak. When I lived in several Papua New Guinea villages for extended periods to collect data, and when I go to Alaskan villages for work with Native Alaskan communities, I have found it unquestionably easier, psychologically and pragmatically, when some kind soul has directly informed me about such matters as appropriate dress, interactional styles, embedded meanings, and taboo words or actions. I con- tend that it is much the same for anyone seeking to learn the rules of the culture of power. Unless one has the leisure of a lifetime of "immersion" to learn them, explicit presentation makes learning immeasurably easier.

And now, to the fifth and last premise:

5. Those with power are frequently least aware of—or least willing to acknowledge—its existence. Those with less power are often most aware of its existence.

For many who consider themselves members of liberal or radical camps, acknowledging personal power and admitting participation in the culture of power is distinctly uncomfortable. On the other hand, those who are less powerful in any situation are most likely to recognize the power variable most acutely. My guess is that the white colleagues and instructors of those previously quoted did not perceive themselves to have power over the nonwhite speakers. However, either by virtue of their position, their numbers, or their access to that particular code of power of calling upon research to validate one's position, the white educators had the authority to establish what was to be considered "truth" regardless of the opinions of the people of color, and the latter were well aware of that fact.

A related phenomenon is that liberals (and here I am using the term "liberal" to refer to those whose beliefs include striving for a society based upon maximum individual freedom and autonomy) seem to act under the assumption that to make any rules or expectations explicit is to act against liberal principles, to limit the freedom and autonomy of those subjected to the explicitness.

I thank Fred Erickson for a comment that led me to look again at a tape by John Gumperz on cultural dissonance in cross-cultural interactions.[2] One of the episodes showed an East Indian interviewing for a job with an all-white committee. The interview was a complete failure, even though several of the interviewers appeared to really want to help the applicant. As the interview rolled steadily downhill, these "helpers" became more and more indirect in their questioning, which exacerbated the problems the applicant had in performing appropriately. Operating from a different cultural perspective, he got fewer and fewer clear clues as to what was expected of him, which ultimately resulted in his failure to secure the position.

I contend that as the applicant showed less and less aptitude for handling the interview, the power differential became ever more evident to the interviewers. The "helpful" interviewers, unwilling to acknowledge themselves as having power over the applicant, became more and more uncomfortable. Their indirectness was an attempt to lessen the power differential and their discomfort by lessening the power-revealing explicitness of their questions and comments.

When acknowledging and expressing power, one tends towards explicitness (as in yelling at your ten-year-old, "Turn that radio down!"). When deemphasizing power, there is a move toward indirect communication. Therefore, in the interview setting, those who sought to help, to express their egalitarianism with the East Indian applicant, became more and more indirect—and less and less helpful—in their questions and comments.

In literacy instruction, explicitness might be equated with direct instruction. Perhaps the ultimate expression of explicitness and direct instruction in the primary classroom is Distar. This reading program is based on a behaviorist model in which reading is taught through the direct instruction of phonics generalizations and blending. The teacher's role is to maintain the full attention of the group by continuous questioning, eye contact, finger snaps, hand claps, and other gestures, and by eliciting choral responses and initiating some sort of award system.

When the program was introduced, it arrived with a flurry of research data that "proved" that all children—even those who were "culturally deprived"—could learn to read using this method. Soon there was a strong response, first from academics and later from many classroom teachers, stating that the program was terrible. What I find particularly interesting, however, is that the primary issue of the conflict over Distar has not been over its instructional efficacy—usually the students did learn to read—but the expression of explicit power in the classroom. The liberal educators opposed the methods—the direct instruction, the explicit control exhibited by the teacher. As a matter of fact, it was not unusual (even now) to hear of the program spoken of as "fascist."

I am not an advocate of Distar, but I will return to some of the issues that the program, and direct instruction in general, raises in understanding the differences between progressive white educators and educators of color.

To explore those differences, I would like to present several statements typical of those made with the best of intentions by middle-class liberal educators. To the surprise of the speakers, it is not unusual for such content to be met by vocal opposition or stony silence from people of color. My attempt here is to examine the underlying assumptions of both camps.

"I want the same thing for everyone else's children as I want for mine."

To provide schooling for everyone's children that reflects liberal, middle-class values and aspirations is to ensure the maintenance of the status quo, to ensure that power, the culture of power, remains in the hands of those who already have it. Some children come to school with more accoutrements of the culture of power already in place—"cultural capital," as some critical theorists refer to it[3]—some with less. Many liberal educators hold that the primary goal for education is for children to become autonomous, to develop fully who they are in the classroom setting without having arbitrary, outside standards forced upon them. This is a very reasonable goal for people whose children are already participants in the culture of power and who have already internalized its codes.

But parents who don't function within that culture often want something else. It's not that they disagree with the former aim, it's just that they want something more. They want to ensure that the school provides their children with discourse patterns, interactional styles, and spoken and written language codes that will allow them success in the larger society.

It was the lack of attention to this concern that created such a negative outcry in the black community when well-intentioned white liberal educators introduced "dialect readers." These were seen as a plot to prevent the schools from teaching the linguistic aspects of the culture of power, thus dooming black children to a permanent outsider caste. As one parent demanded, "My kids know how to be black—you all teach them how to be successful in the white man's world."

Several black teachers have said to me recently that as much as they'd like to believe otherwise, they cannot help but conclude that many of the "progressive" educational strategies imposed by liberals upon black and poor children could only be based on a desire to ensure that the liberals' children get sole access to the dwindling pool of American jobs. Some have added that the liberal educators believe themselves to be operating with good intentions, but that these good intentions are only conscious delusions about their unconscious true motives. One of the black anthropologist John Gwaltney's informants in *Drylongso* reflects this perspective with her tongue-in-cheek observation that the biggest difference between black folks and white folks is that black folks *know* when they're lying!

Let me try to clarify how this might work in literacy instruction. A few years ago I worked on an analysis of two popular reading programs, Distar and a progressive program that focused on higher-level critical thinking skills. In one of the first lessons of the progressive program, the children are introduced to the names of the letters *m* and *e*. In the same lesson they are then taught the sound made by each of the letters, how to write each of the letters, and that when the two are blended together they produce the word *me*.

As an experienced first-grade teacher, I am convinced that a child needs to be familiar with a significant number of these concepts to be able to assimilate so much new knowledge in one sitting. By contrast, Distar presents the same information in about forty lessons.

I would not argue for the pace of Distar lessons—such a slow pace would only bore most kids—but what happened in the other lesson is that it merely provided an opportunity for those who already knew the content to exhibit that they knew it, or at most perhaps to build one new concept onto what was already known. This meant that the child who did not come to school already primed with what was to be presented would be labeled as needing "remedial" instruction from day one; indeed, this determination would be made before he or she was ever taught. In fact, Distar was "successful" because it actually *taught* new information to children who had not already acquired it at home. Although the more progressive system was ideal for some children, for others it was a disaster.

I do not advocate a simplistic "basic skills" approach for children outside of the culture of power. It would be (and has been) tragic to operate as if these children were incapable of critical and higher-order thinking and reasoning. Rather, I suggest that schools must provide these children the content that other families from a different cultural orientation provide at home. This does not mean separating children according to family background, but instead, ensuring that each classroom incorporate strategies appropriate for all the children in its confines.

And I do not advocate that it is the school's job to attempt to change the homes of poor and nonwhite children to match the homes of those in the culture of power. That may indeed be a form of cultural genocide. I have frequently heard schools call poor parents "uncaring" when parents respond to the school's urging, saying, "But that's the school's job." What the school personnel fail to understand is that if the parents were members of the culture of power and lived by its rules and codes, then they would transmit those codes to their children. In fact, they transmit another culture that children must learn at home in order to survive in their communities.

"Child-centered, whole language, and process approaches are needed in order to allow a democratic state of free, autonomous, empowered adults, and because research has shown that children learn best through these methods."

People of color are, in general, skeptical of research as a determiner of our fates. Academic research has, after all, found us genetically inferior, culturally deprived, and verbally deficient. But beyond that general caveat, and despite my or others' personal preferences, there is little research data supporting the major tenets of process approaches over other forms of literacy instruction, and virtually no evidence that such approaches are more efficacious for children of color.[4]

Although the problem is not necessarily inherent in the method, in some instances adherents of process approaches to writing create situations in which students ultimately find themselves held accountable for knowing a set of rules about which no one has ever directly informed them. Teachers do students no service to suggest, even implicitly, that "product" is not important. In this country, students will be judged on their product regardless of the process they utilized to achieve it. And that product, based as it is on the specific codes of a particular culture, is more readily produced when the directives of how to produce it are made explicit.

If such explicitness is not provided to students, what it feels like to people who are old enough to judge is that there are secrets being kept, that time is being wasted, that the teacher is abdicating his or her duty to teach. A doctoral student of my acquaintance was assigned to a writing class to hone his writing skills. The student was placed in the section led by a white professor who utilized a process approach, consisting primarily of having the students write essays and then assemble into groups to edit each other's papers. That procedure infuriated this particular student. He had many angry encounters with the teacher about what she was doing. In his words:

> I didn't feel she was teaching us anything. She wanted us to correct each other's papers and we were there to learn from her. She didn't teach anything, absolutely nothing.
>
> Maybe they're trying to learn what black folks knew all the time. We understand how to improvise, how to express ourselves creatively. When I'm in a classroom, I'm not looking for that, I'm looking for structure, the more formal language.
>
> Now my buddy was in [a] black teacher's class. And that lady was very good. She went through and explained and defined each part of the structure. This [white] teacher didn't get along with that black teacher. She said that she didn't agree with her methods. But *I* don't think that white teacher *had* any methods.

When I told this gentleman that what the teacher was doing was called a process method of teaching writing, his response was, "Well, at least now I know that she *thought* she was doing *something*. I thought she was just a fool who couldn't teach and didn't want to try."

This sense of being cheated can be so strong that the student may be completely turned off to the educational system. Amanda Branscombe, an accomplished white teacher, recently wrote a letter discussing her work with working-class black and white students at a community college in Alabama. She had given these students my "Skills and Other Dilemmas" article to read and discuss, and wrote that her students really understood and identified with what I was saying. To quote her letter:

> One young man said that he had dropped out of high school because he failed the exit exam. He noted that he had then passed the GED without a problem after three weeks of prep. He said that his high school English teacher claimed to use a process approach, but what she really did was hide behind fancy words to give herself permission to do nothing in the classroom.

The students I have spoken of seem to be saying that the teacher has denied them access to herself as the source of knowledge necessary to learn the forms they need to succeed. Again, I tentatively attribute the problem to teachers' resistance to exhibiting power in the classroom. Somehow, to exhibit one's personal power as expert source is viewed as disempowering one's students.

Two qualifiers are necessary, however. The teacher cannot be the only expert in the classroom. To deny students their own expert knowledge *is* to disempower them. Amanda Branscombe, when she was working with black high school students classified as "slow learners," had the students analyze rap songs to discover their underlying patterns. The students became the experts in explaining to the teacher the rules for creating a new rap song. The teacher then used the patterns the students identified as a base to begin an explanation of the structure of grammar, and then of Shakespeare's plays. Both student and teacher are expert at what they know best.

The second qualifier is that merely adopting direct instruction is not the answer. Actual writing for real audiences and real purposes is a vital element in helping students to understand that they have an important voice in their own learning processes. E. V. Siddle examines the results of various kinds of interventions in a primarily process-oriented writing class for black students.[5] Based on readers' blind assessments, she found that the intervention that produced the most positive changes in the students' writing was a "mini-lesson" consisting of direct instruction about some standard writing convention. But what produced the *second* highest number of positive changes was a subsequent student-centered conference with the teacher. (Peer conferencing in this group of black students who were not members of the culture of power produced the least number of changes in students' writing. However, the classroom teacher maintained—and I concur—that such activities are necessary to introduce the elements of "real audience" into the task, along with more teacher-directed strategies.)

"It's really a shame but she (that black teacher upstairs) seems to be so authoritarian, so focused on skills and so teacher directed. Those poor kids never seem to be allowed to really express their creativity. (And she even yells at them.)"

This statement directly concerns the display of power and authority in the classroom. One way to understand the difference in perspective between black teachers and their progressive colleagues on this issue is to explore culturally influenced oral interactions.

In *Ways with Words,* Shirley Brice Heath quotes the verbal directives given by the middle-class "townspeople" teachers:[6]

- o "Is this where the scissors belong?"
- o "You want to do your best work today."

By contrast, many black teachers are more likely to say:

- o "Put those scissors on that shelf."
- o "Put your name on the papers and make sure to get the right answer for each question."

Is one oral style more authoritarian than another?

Other researchers have identified differences in middle-class and working-class speech to children. Snow and others, for example, report that working-class mothers use more directives to their children than do middle- and upper-class parents.[7] Middle-class parents are likely to give the directive to a child to take his bath as, "Isn't it time for your bath?" Even though the utterance is couched as a question, both child and adult understand it as a directive. The child may respond with "Aw, Mom, can't I wait until . . . ," but whether or not negotiation is attempted, both conversants understand the intent of the utterance.

By contrast, a black mother, in whose house I was recently a guest, said to her eight-year-old son, "Boy, get your rusty behind in that bathtub." Now, I happen to know that this woman loves her son as much as any mother, but she would never have posed the directive to her son to take a bath in the form of a question. Were she to ask, "Would you like to take your bath now?" she would not have been issuing a directive but offering a true alternative. Consequently, as Heath suggests, upon entering school the child from such a family may not understand the indirect statement of the teacher as a direct command. Both white and black working-class children in the communities Heath studied "had difficulty interpreting these indirect requests for adherence to an unstated set of rules."[8]

But those veiled commands are commands nonetheless, representing true power, and with true consequences for disobedience. If veiled commands are ignored, the child will be labeled a behavior problem and possibly officially classified as behavior disordered. In other words, the attempt by the teacher to reduce an exhibition of power by expressing herself in indirect terms may remove the very explicitness that the child needs to understand the rules of the new classroom culture.

A black elementary school principal in Fairbanks, Alaska, reported to me that she has a lot of difficulty with black children who are placed in some white teachers' classrooms. The teachers often send the children to the office for disobeying teacher directives. Their parents are frequently called in for conferences. The parents' response to the teacher is usually the same. "They do what I say; if you just *tell* them what to do, they'll do it. I tell them at home that they have to listen to what you say." And so, does not the power still exist? Its veiled nature only makes it more difficult for some children to respond appropriately, but that in no way mitigates its existence.

I don't mean to imply, however, that the only time the black child disobeys the teacher is when he or she misunderstands the request for certain behavior. There are other factors that may produce such behavior. Black children expect an authority figure to act with authority. When the teacher instead acts as a "chum," the message sent is that this adult has no authority, and the children react accordingly. One reason that is so, is that black people often view issues of power and authority differently than people from mainstream middle-class backgrounds.[9] Many people of color expect authority to be earned by personal efforts and exhibited by personal characteristics. In other words, "the authoritative person gets to be a teacher because she is authoritative." Some members of middle-class cultures, by contrast, expect one to achieve authority by the acquisition of an authoritative role. That is, "the teacher is the authority because she is the teacher."

In the first instance, because authority is earned, the teacher must consistently prove the characteristics that give her authority. These characteristics may vary across cultures, but in the black community they tend to cluster around several abilities. The authoritative teacher can control the class through exhibition of personal power; establishes meaningful interpersonal relationships that garner student respect; exhibits a strong belief that all students can learn; establishes a standard of achievement and "pushes" the students to achieve that standard; and holds the attention of the students by incorporating interactional features of black communicative style in his or her teaching.

By contrast, the teacher whose authority is vested in the role has many more options of behavior at her disposal. For instance, she does not need to express any sense of personal power because her authority does not come from anything she herself does or says. Hence, the power she actually holds may be veiled in such questions/commands as "Would you like to sit down now?" If the children in her class understand authority as she does, it is mutually agreed upon that they are to obey her no matter how indirect, soft-spoken, or unassuming she may be. Her indirectness and soft-spokenness may indeed be, as I suggested earlier, an attempt to reduce the implication of overt power in order to establish a more egalitarian and nonauthoritarian classroom atmosphere.

If the children operate under another notion of authority, however, then there is trouble. The black child may perceive the middle-class teacher as weak, ineffectual, and incapable of taking on the role of being the teacher; therefore, there is no need to follow her directives. In her dissertation, Michelle Foster quotes one young black man describing such a teacher:

> She is boring, boring. She could do something creative. Instead she just stands there. She can't control the class, doesn't know how to control the class. She asked me what she was doing wrong. I told her she just stands there like she's meditating. I told her she could be meditating for all I know. She says that we're supposed to know what to do. I told her I don't know nothin' unless she tells me. She just can't control the class. I hope we don't have her next semester.[10]

But of course the teacher may not view the problem as residing in herself but in the student, and the child may once again become the behavior-disordered black boy in special education.

What characteristics do black students attribute to the good teacher? Again, Foster's dissertation provides a quotation that supports my experience with black students. A young black man is discussing a former teacher with a group of friends:

> We had fun in her class, but she was mean. I can remember she used to say, "Tell me what's in the story, Wayne." She pushed, she used to get on me and push me to know. She made us learn. We had to get in the books. There was this tall guy and he tried to take her on, but she was in charge of that class and she didn't let anyone run her. I still have this book we used in her class. It has a bunch of stories in it. I just read one on Coca-Cola again the other day.[11]

To clarify, this student was *proud* of the teacher's "meanness," an attribute he seemed to describe as the ability to run the class and pushing and expecting students to learn. Now, does the liberal perspective of the negatively authoritarian black teacher really hold up? I suggest that although all "explicit" black teachers are not also good teachers, there are different attitudes in different cultural groups about which characteristics make for a good teacher. Thus, it is impossible to create a model for the good teacher without taking issues of culture and community context into account.

And now to the final comment I present for examination:

"Children have the right to their own language, their own culture. We must fight cultural hegemony and fight the system by insisting that children be allowed to express themselves in their own language style. It is not they, the children, who must change, but the schools. To push children to do anything else is repressive and reactionary."

A statement such as this originally inspired me to write the "Skills and Other Dilemmas" article. It was first written as a letter to a colleague in response to a situation that had developed in our department. I was teaching a senior-level teacher education course. Students were asked to prepare a written autobiographical document for the class that would also be shared with their placement school prior to their student teaching.

One student, a talented young Native American woman, submitted a paper in which the ideas were lost because of technical problems—from spelling to sentence structure to paragraph structure. Removing her name, I duplicated the paper for a discussion with some faculty members. I had hoped to initiate a discussion about what we could do to ensure that our students did not reach the senior level without getting assistance in technical writing skills when they needed them.

I was amazed at the response. Some faculty implied that the student should never have been allowed into the teacher education program. Others, some of the more progressive minded, suggested that I was attempting to function as gatekeeper by raising the issue, and had internalized repressive and disempowering forces of the power elite to suggest that something was wrong with a Native American student just because she had another style of writing. With few exceptions, I found myself alone in arguing against both camps.

No, this student should not have been denied entry to the program. To deny her entry under the notion of upholding standards is to blame the victim for the crime. We cannot justifiably enlist exclusionary standards when the reason this student lacked the skills demanded was poor teaching at best and institutionalized racism at worst.

However, to bring this student into the program and pass her through without attending to obvious deficits in the codes needed for her to function effectively as a teacher is equally criminal—for though we may assuage our own consciences for not participating in victim blaming, she will surely be accused and convicted as soon as she leaves the university. As Native Alaskans were quick to tell me, and as I understood through my own experience in the black community, not only would she not be hired as a teacher, but those who did not hire her would make the (false) assumption that the university was putting out only incompetent Natives and that they should stop looking seriously at any Native applicants. A white applicant who exhibits problems is an individual with problems. A person of color who exhibits problems immediately becomes a representative of her cultural group.

No, either stance is criminal. The answer is to *accept* students but also to take responsibility to *teach* them. I decided to talk to the student and found out she had recognized that she needed some assistance in the technical aspects of writing soon after she entered the university as a freshman. She had gone to various members of the education faculty and received the same two kinds of responses I met with four years later: faculty members told her either that she should not even attempt to be a teacher, or that it didn't matter and that she shouldn't worry about such trivial issues. In her desperation, she had found a helpful professor in the English Department, but he left the university when she was in her sophomore year.

We sat down together, worked out a plan for attending to specific areas of writing competence, and set up regular meetings. I stressed to her the need to use her own learning process as insight into how best to teach her future students those "skills" that her own schooling had failed to teach her. I gave her some explicit rules to follow in some areas; for others, we devised various kinds of journals that, along with readings about the structure of the language, allowed her to find her own insights into how the language worked. All that happened two years ago, and the young woman is now successfully teaching. What the experience led me to understand is that pretending that gatekeeping points don't exist is to ensure that many students will not pass through them.

Now you may have inferred that I believe that because there is a culture of power, everyone should learn the codes to participate in it, and that is how the world should be. Actually, nothing could be further from the truth. I believe in a diversity of style, and I believe the world will be diminished if cultural diversity is ever obliterated. Further, I believe strongly, as do my liberal colleagues, that each cultural group should have the right to maintain its own language style. When I speak, therefore, of the culture of power, I don't speak of how I wish things to be but of how they are.

I further believe that to act as if power does not exist is to ensure that the power status quo remains the same. To imply to children or adults (but of course the adults won't believe you anyway) that it doesn't matter how you talk or how you write is to ensure their ultimate failure. I prefer to be honest with my students. I tell them that their language and cultural style is unique and wonderful but that there is a political power game that is also being played, and if they want to be in on that game there are certain games that they too must play.

But don't think that I let the onus of change rest entirely with the students. I am also involved in political work both inside and outside of the educational system, and that political work demands that I place myself to influence as many gatekeeping points as possible. And it is there that I agitate for change, pushing gatekeepers to open their doors to a variety of styles and codes. What I'm saying, however, is that I do not believe that political change toward diversity can be effected from the bottom up, as do some of my colleagues. They seem to believe that if we accept and encourage diversity within classrooms of children, then diversity will automatically be accepted at gatekeeping points.

I believe that will never happen. What will happen is that the students who reach the gatekeeping points—like Amanda Branscombe's student who dropped out of high school because he failed his exit exam—will understand that they have been lied to and will react accordingly. No, I am certain that if we are truly to effect societal change, we cannot do so from the bottom up, but we must push and agitate from the top down. And in the meantime, we must take the responsibility to *teach,* to provide for students who do not already possess them, the additional codes of power.[12]

But I also do not believe that we should teach students to passively adopt an alternate code. They must be encouraged to understand the value of the code they already possess as well as to understand the power realities in this country. Otherwise they will be unable to work to change these realities. And how does one do that?

Martha Demientieff, a masterful Native Alaskan teacher of Athabaskan Indian students, tells me that her students, who live in a small, isolated, rural village of less than two hundred people, are not aware that there are different codes in English. She takes their writing and analyzes it to features of what has been referred to by Alaskan linguists as "Village English," and then covers half a bulletin board with words or phrases from the students' writing, which she labels "Our Heritage Language." On the other half of the bulletin board she puts the equivalent statement in "Standard English," which she labels "Formal English."

She and the students spend a long time on the "Heritage English" section, savoring the words, discussing the nuances. She tells the students, "That's the way we say things. Doesn't it feel good? Isn't it the absolute best way of getting that idea across?" Then she turns to the other side of the board. She tells the students that there are people, not like those in the village, who judge others by the way they talk or write.

> We listen to the way people talk, not to judge them, but to tell what part of the river they come from. These other people are not like that. They think everybody needs to talk like them. Unlike us, they have a hard time hearing what people say if they don't talk exactly like them. Their way of talking and writing is called "Formal English."
>
> We have to feel a little sorry for them because they have only one way to talk. We're going to learn two ways to say things. Isn't that better? One way will be our Heritage way. The other will be Formal English. Then, when we go to get jobs, we'll be able to talk like those people who only know and can only really listen to one way. Maybe after we get the jobs we can help them to learn how it feels to have another language, like ours, that feels so good. We'll talk like them when we have to, but we'll always know our way is best.

Martha then does all sorts of activities with the notions of Formal and Heritage or informal English. She tells the students,

> In the village, everyone speaks informally most of the time unless there's a potlatch or something. You don't think about it, you don't worry about following any rules—it's sort of like how you eat food at a picnic—nobody pays attention to whether you use your fingers or a fork, and it feels *so* good. Now, Formal English is more like a formal dinner. There are rules to follow about where the knife and fork belong, about where people sit, about how you eat. That can be really nice, too, because it's nice to dress up sometimes.

The students then prepare a formal dinner in the class, for which they dress up and set a big table with fancy tablecloths, china, silverware. They speak only Formal English at this meal. Then they prepare a picnic where only informal English is allowed.

She also contrasts the "wordy" academic way of saying things with the metaphoric style of Athabaskan. The students discuss how book language always uses more words, but in Heritage language, the shorter way of saying something is always better. Students then write papers in the academic way, discussing with Martha and with each other whether they believe they've said enough to sound like a book. Finally, students further reduce the message to a "saying" brief enough to go on the front of a T-shirt, and the sayings are put on little paper T-shirts that the students cut out and hang throughout the room. Sometimes the students reduce other authors' wordy texts to their essential meanings as well.

The following transcript provides another example. It is from a conversation between a black teacher and a Southern black high school student named Joey, who is a speaker of Black English. The teacher believes it very important to discuss openly and honestly the issues of language diversity and power. She has begun the discussion by giving the student a children's book written in Black English to read.

TEACHER: What do you think about that book?

JOEY: I think it's nice.

TEACHER: Why?

JOEY: I don't know. It just told about a black family, that's all.

TEACHER: Was it difficult to read?

JOEY: No.

TEACHER: Was the text different from what you have seen in other books?

JOEY: Yeah. The writing was.

TEACHER: How?

JOEY: It use more of a southern-like accent in this book.

TEACHER: Uhm-hmm. Do you think that's good or bad?

JOEY: Well, uh, I don't think it's good for people down this-a-way, cause that's the way they grow up talking anyway. They ought to get the right way to talk.

TEACHER: Oh. So you think it's wrong to talk like that?

JOEY: Well . . . {Laughs}

TEACHER: Hard question, huh?

JOEY: Uhm-hmm, that's a hard question. But I think they shouldn't make books like that.

TEACHER: Why?

JOEY: Because they are not using the right way to talk and in school they take off for that, and li'l chirren grow up talking like that and reading like that so they might think that's right, and all the time they getting bad grades in school, talking like that and writing like that.

TEACHER: Do you think they should be getting bad grades for talking like that?

JOEY: {Pauses, answers very slowly} No . . . no.

TEACHER: So you don't think that it matters whether you talk one way or another?

JOEY: No, not long as you understood.

TEACHER: Uhm-hmm. Well, that's a hard question for me to answer, too. It's, ah, that's a question that's come up in a lot of schools now as to whether they should correct children who speak the way we speak all the time. Cause when we're talking to each other we talk like that even though we might not talk like that when we get into other situations, and who's to say whether it's—

JOEY: {Interrupting} Right or wrong.

TEACHER: Yeah.

JOEY: Maybe they ought to come up with another kind of . . . maybe Black English or something. A course in Black English. Maybe Black folks would be good in that cause people talk, I mean black people talk like that, so . . . but I guess there's a right way and wrong way to talk, you know, not regarding what race. I don't know.

TEACHER: But who decided what's right or wrong?

JOEY: Well that's true . . . I guess white people did.

{Laughter. End of tape.}

Notice how throughout the conversation Joey's consciousness has been raised by thinking about codes of language. This teacher further advocates having students interview various personnel officers in actual workplaces about their attitudes toward divergent styles in oral and written language. Students begin to understand how arbitrary language standards are, but also how politically charged they are. They compare various pieces written in different styles, discuss the impact of different styles on the message by making translations and back translations across styles, and discuss the history, apparent purpose, and contextual appropriateness of each of the technical writing rules presented by their teacher. *And* they practice writing different forms to different audiences based on rules appropriate for each audience. Such a program not only "teaches" standard linguistic forms, but also explores aspects of power as exhibited through linguistic forms.

Tony Burgess, in a study of secondary writing in England by Britton, Burgess, Martin, McLeod, and Rosen, suggests that we should not teach "iron conventions . . . imposed without rationale or grounding in communicative intent," but "critical and ultimately cultural awareness."[13] Courtney Cazden calls for a two-pronged approach:

1. Continuous opportunities for writers to participate in some authentic bit of the unending conversation . . . thereby becoming part of a vital community of talkers and writers in a particular domain, and

2. Periodic, temporary focus on conventions of form, taught as cultural conventions expected in a particular community.[14]

Just so that there is no confusion about what Cazden means by a focus on conventions of form, or about what I mean by "skills," let me stress that neither of us is speaking of page after page of "skill sheets" creating compound words or identifying nouns and adverbs, but rather about helping students gain a useful knowledge of the conventions of print while engaging in real and useful communicative activities. Kay Rowe Grubis, a junior high school teacher in a multicultural school, makes lists of certain technical rules for her eighth graders' review and then gives them papers from a third grade to "correct." The students not only have to correct other students' work, but also tell them why they have changed or questioned aspects of the writing.

A village teacher, Howard Cloud, teaches his high school students the conventions of formal letter writing and the formulation of careful questions in the context of issues surrounding the amendment of the Alaska Land Claims Settlement Act. Native Alaskan leaders hold differing views on this issue, critical to the future of local sovereignty and land rights. The students compose letters to leaders who reside in different areas of the state seeking their perspectives, set up audioconference calls for interview/debate sessions, and, finally, develop a videotape to present the differing views.

To summarize, I suggest that students must be *taught* the codes needed to participate fully in the mainstream of American life, not by being forced to attend to hollow, inane, decontextualized subskills, but rather within the context of meaningful communicative endeavors; that they must be allowed the resource of the teacher's expert knowledge, while being helped to acknowledge their own "expertness" as well; and that even while students are assisted in learning the culture of power, they must also be helped to learn about the arbitrariness of those codes and about the power relationships they represent.

I am also suggesting that appropriate education for poor children and children of color can only be devised in consultation with adults who share their culture. Black parents, teachers of color, and members of poor communities must be allowed to participate fully in the discussion of what kind of instruction is in their children's best interest. Good liberal intentions are not enough. In an insightful 1975 study entitled "Racism without Racists: Institutional Racism in Urban Schools," Massey, Scott, and Dornbusch found that under the pressures of teaching, and with all intentions of "being nice," teachers had essentially stopped attempting to teach black children.[15] In their words: "We have shown that oppression can arise out of warmth, friendliness, and concern. Paternalism and a lack of challenging standards are creating a distorted system of evaluation in the schools." Educators must open themselves to, and allow themselves to be affected by, these alternative voices.

In conclusion, I am proposing a resolution for the skills/process debate. In short, the debate is fallacious; the dichotomy is false. The issue is really an illusion created initially not by teachers but by academics whose worldview demands the creation of categorical divisions—not for the purpose of better teaching, but for the goal of easier analysis. As I have been reminded by many teachers since the publication of my article, those who are most skillful at educating black and poor children do not allow themselves to be placed in "skills" or "process" boxes. They understand the need for both approaches, the need to help students establish their own voices, and to coach those voices to produce notes that will be heard clearly in the larger society.

The dilemma is not really in the debate over instructional methodology, but rather in communicating across cultures and in addressing the more fundamental issue of power, of whose voice gets to be heard in determining what is best for poor children and children of color. Will black teachers and parents continue to be silenced by the very forces that claim to "give voice" to our children? Such an outcome would be tragic, for both groups truly have something to say to one another. As a result of careful listening to alternative points of view, I have myself come to a viable synthesis of perspectives. But both sides do need to be able to listen, and I contend that it is those with the most power, those in the majority, who must take the greater responsibility for initiating the process.

To do so takes a very special kind of listening, listening that requires not only open eyes and ears, but open hearts and minds. We do not really see through our eyes or hear through our ears, but through our beliefs. To put our beliefs on hold is to cease to exist as ourselves for a moment—and that is not easy. It is painful as well, because it means turning yourself inside out, giving up your own sense of who you are, and being willing to see yourself in the unflattering light of another's angry gaze. It is not easy, but it is the only way to learn what it might feel like to be someone else and the only way to start the dialogue.

There are several guidelines. We must keep the perspective that people are experts on their own lives. There are certainly aspects of the outside world of which they may not be aware, but they can be the only authentic chroniclers of their own experience. We must not be too quick to deny their interpretations, or accuse them of "false consciousness." We must believe that people are rational beings, and therefore always act rationally. We may not understand their rationales, but that in no way militates against the existence of these rationales or reduces our responsibility to attempt to apprehend them. And finally, we must learn to be vulnerable enough to allow our world to turn upside down in order to allow the realities of others to edge themselves into our consciousness. In other words, we must become ethnographers in the true sense.

Teachers are in an ideal position to play this role, to attempt to get all of the issues on the table in order to initiate true dialogue. This can only be done, however, by seeking out those whose perspectives may differ most, by learning to give their words complete attention, by understanding one's own power, even if that power stems merely from being in the majority, by being unafraid to raise questions about discrimination and voicelessness with people of color, and to listen, no, to *hear* what they say. I suggest that the results of such interactions may be the most powerful and empowering coalescence yet seen in the educational realm—for *all* teachers and for *all* the students they teach.

NOTES

1. Such a discussion, limited as it is by space constraints, must treat the intersection of class and race somewhat simplistically. For the sake of clarity, however, let me define a few terms: "black" is used herein to refer to those who share some or all aspects of "core black culture" (see John Gwaltney, *Drylongso,* New York: The New Press, 1993), that is, the mainstream of black America—neither those who have entered the ranks of the bourgeoisie nor those who are participants in the disenfranchised underworld. "Middle-class" is used broadly to refer to the predominantly white American "mainstream." There are, of course, nonwhite people who also fit into this category; at issue is their cultural identification, not necessarily the color of their skin. (I must add that there are other nonwhite people, as well as poor white people, who have indicated to me that their perspectives are similar to those attributed herein to black people.)

2. *Multicultural Britain: "Crosstalk,"* National Centre of Industrial Language Training, Commission for Racial Equality, London, England, John Twitchin, producer.

3. See, for example, M. W. Apple, *Ideology and Curriculum* (Boston: Routledge and Kegan Paul, 1979).

4. See E. V. Siddle, "A Critical Assessment of the Natural Process Approach to Teaching Writing," unpublished qualifying paper, Harvard University, 1986.

5. See E. V. Siddle, "The Effect of Intervention Strategies on the Revisions Ninth Graders Make in a Narrative Essay," unpublished doctoral dissertation, Harvard University, 1988.

6. Shirley Brice Heath, *Ways with Words* (Cambridge, Eng.: Cambridge University Press, 1983), p. 280.

7. C. E. Snow, A. Arlman-Rup, Y. Hassing, J. Josbe, J. Joosten, and J. Vorster, "Mother's Speech in Three Social Classes," *Journal of Psycholinguistic Research* 5 (1976), pp. 1–20.

8. Heath, *Ways with Words,* p. 280.

9. I would like to thank Michelle Foster, who is presently planning a more in-depth treatment of the subject, for her astute clarification of the idea.

10. Michelle Foster, "'It's Cookin Now': An Ethnographic Study of the Teaching Style of a Successful Black Teacher in a White Community College," unpublished doctoral dissertation, Harvard University, 1987, pp. 67–68.

11. Ibid., p. 68.

12. B. Bernstein makes a similar point when he proposes that different educational frames cannot be successfully institutionalized in the lower levels of education until there are fundamental changes at the postsecondary levels (see "Class and Pedagogies: Visible and Invisible," in B. Bernstein, *Class, Codes, and Control,* vol. 3 [Boston: Routledge and Kegan Paul, 1975]).

13. J. Britton, T. Burgess, N. Martin, A. McLeod, and H. Rosen, *The Development of Writing Abilities* (London: Macmillan Education for the Schools Council, and Urbana, Ill.: National Council of Teachers of English, 1975/1977), p. 54.

14. Ibid., p. 20.

15. G. C. Massey, M. V. Scott, and S. M. Dornbusch, "Racism without Racists: Institutional Racism in Urban Schools," *The Black Scholar* 7.3 (1975), pp. 2–11.

16

REFINING THE CRAFT
OF TEACHING

Vito Perrone

THIS DISCUSSION IS INTENDED to describe activities that can enlarge your understandings of practice and through which you can gain fuller control of a more inspiring and generative language of teaching and learning. In this regard, it is more about becoming the "students of teaching" that the schools need.

In the early 1970s, more than a hundred North Dakota teachers and I, along with several other University of North Dakota faculty members, engaged ourselves in focused conversations around John Dewey's formulation of "becoming students of teaching." This work serves as a base for this chapter. Even though it is a twenty-year-old experience, it fits well many current interests. Among the products of this activity, which I will describe more fully later, were a *Teacher Interview* (Center for Teaching and Learning, 1972) and a *Staff Development Handbook* (Center for Teaching and Learning, 1979), which were used extensively in North Dakota and in many other parts of the United States. The interview and the handbook, while long out of print, still get enthusiastic responses from teachers, who see in them many renewing possibilities.

I can't describe easily the long days we talked together about what it meant to be a student of teaching. The summer seminars at the University of North Dakota, where we read a variety of philosophical essays and books, shared our various understandings with each other, and engaged in collective exercises oriented toward "staff development," were particularly intensive. The decision making around the handbook and the teacher discussion groups that formed and met regularly in many different communities around the state were particularly inspiring to me. A powerful community of teachers emerged, made up of individuals who came to understand well the critical nature of their work as they became increasingly more authoritative about their practice. The control they gained over their teaching craft was remarkable.

The friendships that developed among us in those years endure. One of the teachers in this group, a person with a good ear for children's language, called me recently because she knew I would want to hear some interesting conceptual language from children in her kindergarten class who were discussing the "growing of rocks." She was right: the dialogue she recounted was indeed delightful, particularly because it was so rich in detail. Many of the other teachers from those years also keep me up-to-date on their work, continuing, it is clear, to be careful observers of children who reflect deeply on their practice.

So much for background. Now I will move directly to some of the literature and ideas that provided a context for our work together.

Seymour Sarason, in his *Culture of the Schools and the Problem of Change* ([1973] 1982), a book I recommend, notes that teachers, after five years, "felt as competent as they ever were to feel and they verbalized no expectations that they would be teaching or thinking differently in the future . . . these teachers indicated that they rarely experienced any more a sense of personal and intellectual growth. The shape of the future was quite clear . . . a routine with which they were already quite familiar" (pp. 163–164). While most of us, I suspect, might acknowledge that such conclusions have some foundation, especially at a time when so much is being mandated from sources beyond individual schools, we need also to resist them. Most teachers I know desire much more from their professional lives and if provided reasonable opportunities and professional support would maintain their enthusiasm for teaching and continue to be productive learners.

Given the conditions that exist in many of our schools and the limited support teachers receive in many communities, it is actually surprising that so many *have* survived as learners, growing personally and professionally. But their continued growth and sense of optimism are more often a tribute to their individual initiative and perseverance than to any particular design of a school system, colleges and universities, or state educational agencies.

Some school administrators protest such a belief, suggesting that inservice education is an item of high priority in *their* districts. And colleges and universities, as well as state education agencies, may also feel that they have creative inservice programs for teachers. Good intentions abound, and often stimulating programs are presented. But even when well done, the capacity of most large-scale inservice education activities to cause teachers to alter in any significant manner the nature of their classroom practices or their knowledge of ways to extend children's learning or their own is relatively small.

Largely this is because most inservice activities are too general. They are typically organized externally by school administrators, colleges and universities, state education agencies, or districtwide teacher committees around learning activities *they* believe teachers (as a general population within a particular district or school) need. The needs are often determined by a desire to introduce, for example, a new curriculum or a new reading series. In some school districts, however, inservice activities are based on "needs assessment" data gathered from large numbers of teachers. My experience with this latter process is that the specific needs and interests provided by an *individual* teacher ("I would like assistance in getting my second-graders into writing") assume very broad, more general form when they are summarized at a central office ("Teachers say they want assistance in language arts"). The result is that *few* teachers receive in the resulting inservice workshops precisely what they identified as being important to them.

More positive inservice and staff development directions, organized and developed by teachers themselves, are possible and could bring about for many teachers renewed enthusiasm for learning and renewed confidence in their capacity to make educational decisions. Before suggesting some of these directions for stimulating teacher growth, at least two assumptions (drawn in part from Bussis, Chittenden, and Amarel, 1974) need to be established: first, that the quality of teachers' understandings influences to a large degree what teachers do in the classroom; second, that the best source for teachers to learn more about teaching and learning, growth and development of children, materials and methods, is through an examination of their own practice and their own classrooms.

Maxine Greene in *The Teacher as Stranger: Educational Philosophy for the Modern Age* (1973) provides a clear extension of those assumptions: "Teaching is purposeful action . . . [the teacher's] intentions will inevitably be affected by the assumptions he makes regarding human nature and human possibility. Many of these assumptions are hidden; most have never been activated. If he is to achieve clarity and full consciousness, the teacher must attempt to make such assumptions explicit; for only then can they be examined, analyzed and understood" (pp. 69–70).

I have come to understand, more now than ever before, that teachers have not had many opportunities, nor have they been encouraged, to systematically examine their purposes and practices. Such an understanding was affirmed in the early 1970s through the use of our *Teacher Interview,* a structured, open-ended protocol that provides a context for individual teachers to reflect on their intentions, use of materials, relationships with children, and organization of time and space, as well as perceptions of difficulties and successes. I have used the teacher interviews again in recent years, experiencing similar responses.

The interview was designed initially as a program evaluation instrument, but it rather quickly became a useful staff development tool. Teachers then as now have described the interview experience as one of their most intense and revealing inservice activities.

The interview (two to four hours long) causes teachers to consider, among other things, why they organize their classroom as they do, why they use specific materials as opposed to other materials, why they pursue particular goals and not other goals. It has stimulated many teachers to articulate educational directions they want to pursue and has encouraged them to organize the necessary resources to go forward. I have provided below a small sample of the questions and probes in the interview (see Exhibit 1). You will probably think of many others that can help you and colleagues get more deeply into the interior of your practices.

The interview activity tended to foster a variety of documentation practices. This was especially true in the early 1970s, when the project I am using as the base for this discussion had so much support built into it. Some teachers began to keep daily journals in which they noted particularly important occurrences, positive and negative responses of children, peer interaction, children's use of various materials, and questions asked by children. Others began to document specific aspects of their instructional programs—reading, writing, the creative arts.

The following account comes from one teacher's efforts to document aspects of his practice (Perrone, 1977b).

> I began by observing various activities in my classroom for short periods of time each day. I made anecdotal records of my observations in a notebook. The results were not astounding but the entries helped me to confirm many of the notions I had and also raised some questions.

Exhibit 1. Sample Teacher Interview Questions.

Question

Probes

1. Let's begin with a description of your classroom. As a stranger, what would I see if I walked into your room? How is the room arranged or organized?

   a. What would I see as I looked around the room at the walls?
   b. How is the furniture arranged?
   c. Where is your desk?
   d. What kinds of books, resource materials, construction materials are there?
   e. Where do they come from?
   f. How often are they used?

1a. Has the arrangement of the room or the kinds of materials present changed any over the course of the year? How has it changed?

   a. How did these changes come about?

2. We know that no two days are alike, but we'd like to get a general picture of what a typical teaching day (or class) is like. Would you describe for me how a day (or class) is organized?

   a. When would you usually do that?
   b. How long would that usually last?
   c. Are there specific times scheduled for particular activities? When?
   d. Why have you organized in that way? What other possibilities have you considered?

3. Let's change our focus now. Could you discuss the sorts of things that you want your students to learn? In other words, what areas of learning are most important to you as a teacher?

3a. Okay, you mentioned [*list the areas of importance mentioned*]. Now, let's talk about how you try to accomplish these in terms of specific activities, materials, questions. Let's start with [*select one of the areas mentioned*]. What sorts of things do your students do in _____? [*This can be followed by a second or third.*]

   a. How do these activities get started?
   b. How are the students organized during these activities? If I came in while that was going on what would I see? Would the students be working alone, in small groups, or all together as a class?
   c. How many would be involved in these activities?
   d. What would others be doing during that time?
   e. How often would these activities go on in the classroom, or how often has that happened?
   f. What would you be doing while these activities were going on?
   g. What materials or resources are used during these activities?

Exhibit 1. Sample Teacher Interview Questions (*continued*)

Question	Probes

Question / Probes

h. Where do these materials or resources come from?

i. How do you evaluate progress in these activities? What would cause you to say that the students have enlarged their understandings?

4. Do you find ways of integrating the learning activities in your classroom? (For example: reading activities with science, history with literature.)

    a. Can you describe the way that happens?

    b. How often does that happen?

    c. Does it occur in other areas as well?

4a. How has the integration of learning activities changed over the course of the year?

    a. Why has there been change?

    b. How do you feel about that?

9b. What roles do you feel competition and cooperation should play in the classroom?

    a. Do you find the words "competition" and "cooperation" useful in describing children's behavior and classroom interaction?

    b. Can you describe activities in your room which promote competition? Which promote cooperation?

    c. How do you feel about the role competition and cooperation play in your classroom?

14. Now, we'd like you to reflect upon opportunities you may have to talk about important aspects of your teaching experience with others. For example, with teachers in your building, with your principal, or others at conferences or meetings. [*Pause.*] Are there persons you try out your ideas on; ask for help; share both your doubts and failures as well as your aspirations and accomplishments as a teacher? Could you give some examples?

    a. How valuable are these opportunities to you?

    b. Do you wish there were more opportunities to talk with others about your teaching?

    c. How could this be made to happen more often?

    d. In general, do you feel that the kind of things you are trying to do in your classroom are understood and supported in your school?

We'd like to shift our focus now to think about the growth of individual children in your classroom. Could you select the tenth child in your class list. Think about that person for a moment. Now, could you tell me something about him or her?

Exhibit 1. Sample Teacher Interview Questions (*continued*)

22. How would you assess the quality of his or her learning?

22a. How would you characterize the quality of his or her thinking? (Examples?)

22b. What kinds of questions does he or she raise in the classroom? (Examples?)

22c. Does he or she select projects and activities that challenge him or her to think? (Examples?)

22d. What does he or she seem to value highly? What are his or her strongly held beliefs? Does he or she seem aware of those values, beliefs?

22e. How does he or she interact with others?

22f. How does he or she react to rules?

> After making many broad observations . . . I decided to investigate . . . math because that subject was least appealing to the children. I began observing and recording both my activities and the children's . . . my observations indicated an inconsistency between my philosophy and my practice. In spite of my strong belief that manipulative math experiences help children to understand math concepts, I was doing little in the way of teaching with these materials or encouraging their use in independent study. . . . [Some new directions were begun.] Since my first attempt as a teacher-researcher, I have continued to experiment with alternative manipulative experiences in math, using a variety of settings and levels. Through careful observation and recording, I have come to more specific conclusions about the purpose and use of manipulative experiences. Using the same process during the past five years I have become involved in research on lab approaches to social studies and science, vocabulary development, language experience, parent-child-teacher conferences, values clarification, multi-age grouping, parent meetings [p. 4].

The kinds of documentation activities implied in that account have assisted many teachers in their classroom-based reflections. And in many settings teachers pursuing such documentation activities began to come together to share their insights with each other, to discuss education as "students of teaching." This collective work was particularly constructive.

We began very early to use the "teacher as researcher" notion as a way to describe the documentation activities. It was a particularly useful way of giving credence to the ways teachers were beginning to examine their work. The conception of teacher research that is currently in vogue typically denotes a researcher-teacher collaboration. While acknowledging then that such a formulation could be constructive, we saw the teacher research directions within our project as a critical precursor to this recent method, helping teachers gain greater independence and more co-equal status with external researchers from the colleges and universities.

In regard to teacher research, Ann Cook and Herb Mack ask in *The Word and the Thing: Ways of Seeing the Teacher* (1974), "Are teachers becoming more self-reliant, able to determine not only what to do with children but why to do it? Are they able to evaluate the degree of their success in a particular subject or with a specific child?" (p. 7). Many of the teachers who participated in the teacher interview and subsequent documentation activities could certainly have answered yes to such a question. They traveled far toward becoming thoughtful, analytical, independent professionals relying on their own initiative and critical judgment.

Approximately thirty of the teachers who had been involved in the teacher interviews and the early documentation activities came together in the summer of 1974 to discuss their reflective efforts. They became the core group responsible for developing a *Staff Development Handbook*. The handbook was designed to assist other classroom teachers in organizing their *own* efforts to become students of teaching.

Their initial draft was subsequently reviewed by several hundred North Dakota teachers and, over a year's time, the handbook went through at least eight different revisions. The final product was, I believe, an exemplary sample of what teachers can do when provided an opportunity to act as professionals.

It is hardly possible here to share the handbook in its entirety; yet I believe that a sample of its contents might be useful. The basic organizational construct of the handbook reflected the growth of the teachers who worked on it; fittingly, they used components of growth as their framework. The components and some operational definitions are shown as Exhibit 2.

For each of these six components, a series of theoretical-philosophical statements and corresponding practical suggestions was developed. The intention of using both was to create a dialectical exchange. A small sample of the suggestions (without the philosophical statements) appears as Exhibit 3. They are taken from sections of the handbook related to awareness and reflection, opportunities for growth, and working plans.

These suggestions are by no means all-inclusive but they should provide a flavor of the handbook and its basic orientation. None of us who worked on it suggested that it should serve as *the* basis for a staff development effort for which individuals and groups of teachers might take

Exhibit 2. Components of Growth, Teacher Handbook.

Awareness/Reflection

Beginning to wonder, to question, to search, to step back and view ourselves as we actually are.

○ What are my strengths as a teacher?

○ What do I know about how children learn?

○ How do my beliefs and attitudes about teaching guide the decisions I make about my classroom practice?

Trust

Feeling safe enough to experiment, discuss, admit problems, fail, ask questions, seek help, maintain faith in ourselves and others. Trust develops in an atmosphere where you are known for what you are, understood for where you've been, accepted for whom you've become, and *still* are gently invited to grow.

○ Where can I find support as I reflect upon the uncertainties and questions I have about my teaching?

○ Are there others with whom I can share ideas, questions and concerns?

Opportunities for Growth

Being able to recognize the value of new experiences, to create opportunities for growth where they do not seem to exist.

○ Who are the people who can assist me to grow personally and professionally?

○ How can I arrange my day so that I will have time to seek out opportunities for growth?

Risk

Gambling that you'll be successful in an attempt to work with children in a different manner. It is taking a chance and leaving yourself open to failure.

○ How do I develop a sufficient level of confidence to take some risks?

○ Why is it so difficult to begin new patterns of doing things?

Working Plans

Implementing one's beliefs and intentions about teaching and learning; reflecting about the needs of individual children; organizing materials which support children's learning.

Exhibit 2. Components of Growth, Teacher Handbook (*continued*)

o How can I put into practice what I believe about children's learning?

o What kind of relationship do I want with children? How should I organize the classroom? How should time be organized? What kinds of materials should be available?

o How can I divide my really big ideas into parts that are small enough so that I dare to make a beginning? Whom can I talk with about my ideas?

Conflict

Experiencing personal uneasiness and anxiety when dealing with risk taking. Finding the internal and external resources and strength to resolve puzzling questions and apprehensions.

o How can I know that my teaching practice is really assisting children with their learning?

o How can I respond to the many questions and concerns of my colleagues as well as the parents of children with whom I work?

Exhibit 3. Sample Suggestions, Teacher Handbook.
Awareness and Reflection

Think about and write down five learning experiences of your own you can recall.

Why was it important?

In what setting did it occur?

Were others involved in the experience?

Was there anything special about what you learned?

Was there anything unique about you at that time?

Draw generalizations about the conditions under which you learn best.

Share your learnings with someone else.

Does this help you to look differently at the way children in your classroom learn?

Exhibit 3. Sample Suggestions, Teacher Handbook (*continued*)
Deliberately and systematically reflect on your classroom practice.

- Take 15 minutes at the close of your morning (or day) and write all the important things you can think of that happened in your classroom. Notice how much more observant you become after a week or two.

- Use the questions on the teacher interview to examine and clarify your classroom experiences.

  – Describe your classroom. How is it arranged and organized? Why do you have it this way?

  – In your classroom, how are children involved in making decisions about their learning?

  – In your classroom, what happens when a rule isn't followed?

- Observe some element of your classroom over a long period of time (peer interaction). Keep a log of your observations.

- Document carefully some aspect of your program; for example, reading or creative arts.

  – Write a statement of purposes.

  – Keep logs on daily activities.

  – Maintain samples of children's work.

Opportunities for Growth

Survey your real interests, the things you do outside of school. Take one of your personal interests into your classroom tomorrow.

Organize staff development and teacher growth groups in your school.

- A small group of teachers and principals get together and discuss particular children and their learning every Thursday afternoon.

Use the teacher interview as a tool for reflection and personal evaluation.

- Use questions from the interview with one other person.

- Use questions from the interview as a base for discussion.

Do action research and documentation in your classroom in order to clarify what you do in the classroom and explore its effects on children.

Exhibit 3. Sample Suggestions, Teacher Handbook (*continued*)

○ Take note of a specific part of your classroom experience over a period of time (or invite someone else to observe this element on a regular basis).

– A student who puzzles you.

– The way students spend their time, the choices they make, the effect or results of a particular teaching method, the kinds of questions students ask.

○ Collect data related to a concern you have.

Samples of a student's writing over a period of time.

Samples of children's artwork.

Videotape or tape record your class in action.

Working Plans

Use the community as a resource.

○ Invite local people to explain their work, the tools they use, how they spend their day, what sorts of things they do when they're not working.

○ Visit a variety of community resources.

○ Plan with a business for children to spend an extended time with them (maybe a week)—a sort of short-term apprentice program.

Plan and implement a different evaluation and reporting system.

○ Keep anecdotal records of children's classroom activities, behavior, interactions with other people.

○ Regularly collect samples of children's work.

○ Use narrative reporting and frequent formal and informal conferencing with parents and their children.

○ Hold as many parent conferences as possible in the classroom during the school day while the children are working.

○ Meet with parents and children in their homes.

responsibility. Growth, after all, is a highly personal process, which occurs as individuals find ways to reflect, as well as act, on their experiences. But the handbook does represent a starting point for growth; in addition, and this I believe is significant, it attempts to encourage teachers to rely more on their own personal resources and those of their colleagues.

You might want to work with some of the ideas. You might also share with colleagues what you learned. And over time you and your teaching colleagues might well become the thoughtful teachers you most wish to be. In the end, the schools will get better as teachers themselves become students of teaching, able to assume the principal responsibility for all aspects of teaching and learning.

BIBLIOGRAPHY

Bussis, A., Chittenden, E., and Amarel, M. "Reflection on Teaching." *City College Notes,* Spring 1974, 2–7.
Center for Teaching and Learning. *Teacher Interview.* Grand Forks, N. Dak.: Center for Teaching and Learning, 1972.
Center for Teaching and Learning. *Staff Development Handbook.* Grand Forks, N. Dak.: Center for Teaching and Learning, 1979.
Cook, A., and Mack, H. *The Word and the Thing: Ways of Seeing the Teacher.* Grand Forks: North Dakota Study Group on Evaluation, 1974.
Greene, M. *The Teacher as Stranger: Educational Philosophy for the Modern Age.* Belmont, Calif.: Wadsworth, 1973.
Perrone, V. "Documentation: A Source of Personal/Professional Learning and Staff Development." *Insights,* Apr. 1977b, pp. 1–15.
Sarason, S. B. *The Culture of the School and the Problem of Change.* Boston: Allyn & Bacon, 1982. (Originally published 1973.)

17

CALEXICO, CALIFORNIA

Mike Rose

I

I DROVE OUT OF LOS ANGELES on the 405, two hours or so, curving through San Diego, close to the Mexican border, heading east onto Highway 8, where the road narrowed from four lanes to two. I passed an abandoned government kiosk, various twists of scrap metal, and a thousand configurations of rock and brush, and began the slow descent onto the desert floor of the Imperial Valley. There were signs for—but no sight of—Lake Moreno, Kitchen Creek Road, the Tecate Divide, Manzanita, Jacumba, and Ocotillo. The sky was clear, deep blue, and the sun played off the rockface in the distance. I was the only car on the road. The air was warm and dry. In the distance: ROAD 98. The road that takes you along the border to Calexico.

Calexico is an American city that speaks two languages, a truly bicultural city. Border culture. Of the 21,000 residents, most are of Mexican ancestry, and the majority of Anglos speak so-so–to–fluent Spanish. This whole area of the Imperial Valley was converted from desert to arable land through water diverted from the Colorado River. The project began just after the turn of the century. Calexico was the surveying camp on the Mexican border—the name blends *Cali*fornia and *Mexico*—and in 1908 was incorporated as a city. A few of the early buildings still stand on First Street, just this side of Mexicali.[1]

Though many families in Calexico are poor—income is low and seasonal—and the school district is always scrambling for funds, the elementary schools exceeded the Imperial County average on recent statewide tests of language arts, mathematics, and science, and the high schools have the lowest dropout rate of any predominantly Latino school district in California. In fact, they are 9 percentage points below the statewide average for *all* schools. A significant number of graduates go on to two- and four-year colleges. One explanation has to do with the unanimity of goals between district administration and school board. Another with an effective bilingual education program. And a third has to do with the way teacher education develops out of respect for local history.[2]

The Imperial Valley Campus of San Diego State University took up one square block of land six short blocks from the Mexican border. It was located on the site of the old Calexico High School, which had been boarded up and broken into for a long time. The campus retained three original, though refurbished, buildings—archways, white stucco, tile roofs—and had built a few classrooms and brought in some portable structures for administration, student services, and faculty offices. There were plans in the works for a complete reconstruction, but for over twenty-five years this small satellite campus, with its patchwork of buildings and bungalows, has served as the only means for Valley residents to get a four-year degree. Walking down Seventh Street, you came upon it like a park or a historical preserve, nestled between houses and parked cars and an occasional delivery van. Maybe you'd hear the buzz of a lawn mower. Little more.

Students at the campus would usually begin their work at IVC, Imperial Valley College, a two-year school about twelve miles north of Calexico, right up Highway 111, and transfer over to complete degrees in humanities or social science. They majored in liberal studies or Latin-American studies, English or Spanish or criminal justice administration, psychology or history, to prepare themselves for careers in business or law enforcement or education. Many hoped to teach. They were a serious student body—numbering four to five hundred in any given year—and they came to school in order to lead a better life here in the Valley. Most worked, and night classes were popular. Hardly anyone hung out. So unless you walked across campus right at those times when classes were starting up or winding down—noon, say, or four or seven or ten—you might, in fact, think the place *was* a historical monument. There would be the shade and rustle of Mexican fan palms and date palms and eucalyptus, and you might stop to hear the birds chirping in the trees and cooing in the red tile. As you made your way toward the north side of the campus—it's a short walk—you'd begin to hear faint music from behind the closed doors of the service bungalows: the hectic advertisements of

Mexican *rocanrol* stations or trumpets and guitars or the lyrics of North American oldies—"Angel Baby" or "Blue Velvet." A little farther, over toward the plywood and corrugated metal, and you'd come upon the faculty offices, faded and baking in the sun. . . .

II

The streets in Calexico were calm and lightly traveled. At the end of the day, there was a predictable jam at Imperial, the main drag to the border, as Mexicali workers crossed back over *la linea*, the line. Birch Street, too, got a little hectic where it met State Highway 111. But otherwise traffic was blissfully light; you'd barely hear the honking of a horn. Every morning, though, Monday to Friday, there would suddenly develop this convergence of cars and trucks on usually quiet streets around the city, those where the district's elementary schools were located—like Encinas, running north and south, just a few blocks away from the college. It would be quick and fleeting, a vehicular whirl of wind: parents and aunts and older brothers dropping off the young ones, pulling in and out of white zones, double parking, stacking up, blinkers on. But no horns. They'd holler and wave to each other, neighbors and bloodlines, generation to generation.

Evangelina recommended I visit the school on Encinas, Dool Elementary—named after another of those early developers. "There's a teacher there you should see," she said. "Elena Castro. She has a good reputation in the district. She teaches bilingual third grade and has mentored a lot of our students. She's a pistol. You'll like her, I think. And, besides, Dool is right down the street." While in Calexico I stayed with an old college roommate, Matt Contreras, now a superior court judge. When I mentioned that I'd be visiting Dool, he laughed and told me a story. He had to transfer to Dool when he was entering the fourth grade, and he was worried. "You'll come in with me, right?" he nervously asked his father. His father mumbled something, apparently not taking this request seriously—after all, the young Matias was an assured and athletic kid. Why worry? "No, I mean it, Dad. You'll walk in there with me, OK?" It seems that Dool had a reputation as a tough school. It was on the wrong side of town. Matt laughed again. "*La Dool!*"

I called Elena Castro. Not long after, I watched the cars on Encinas cluster and pull away, kids running across the sidewalk with books and lunch pails. It was a small, clean school, white and industrial tan, green lawn, on the poor side, but kept up. I turned up the walkway hearing the unsteady bleat of a trombone from the cafeteria, and entered a stream of children coming in from the curb. Other groups gathered around the tree in front of the gate or just inside at the tables by the dissonant cafeteria, talking and bouncing and laughing. The main office was so full that the door was held half open by kids clumped against the jamb. Then came four or five rows of classrooms, some portable buildings—the library and the Writing Center, both the results of grants and donations—and the expanse of asphalt and grass that loudly signified the freedom of the playground. Kids were shooting baskets with a mix of awkwardness and grace, playing tether ball and foursquare and hopscotch, and running every which way on the broad stretch of lawn. Walking among them, ignored and intermittently jostled, I felt the unbridled joy of physical play. I thought about Matt and wanted, right then and there, to call him up and tell him about this. *La Dool.* I don't know how the school looked and felt then—especially to a fourth-grader—but it had the cast of decency to it now. Who knows? It was nice to believe that a school could take a turn for the better.

I found Elena out in the field, two or three kids around her. She handed me the key to her room and said they'd be in shortly. "Make yourself at home," she called after me; then the children pulled her back in. From our earlier conversation I knew that she structured her curriculum around general themes that the students themselves had a hand in selecting. The various subject areas—language arts and science, for example—were integrated and the students studied them in contexts that were interesting to them. The theme they were currently working on was sea life. Evangelina had alerted me that Elena's room itself would knock me out. "Stimulus-rich" was the term she used. I found Room 42 and opened the door. Evangelina was right: the place was vibrant. The walls, the blackboard, even the sliding doors on the cabinets were covered with charts and posters: "Ocean Wonders" and "Milagros del Mar." Blue, orange, and red fabrics formed a backdrop for the copious display of children's art and writing. Books were stacked and leaning everywhere; a sign with coral drawn around it said, "You don't have to read every day, just on the days you eat!" Across the ceiling, a clothesline was crisscrossed, and cut-and-pasted drawings of fish dangled— the Crayola butterfly fish, the newsprint manta ray—seeming to swim in the breeze that came in behind me. I thought of Ariel's song in *The Tempest.* This tan room had undergone a sea change. An ocean of color and language. Spanish and English. The shark, *el tiburon,* and *la anguila,* the eel, and the jellyfish, *el aguamar.* The bell rang and I took a few steps inside, into a surround of print and art-paper water.

The children filed in, hot and antsy from play, and headed for the long rectangular tables in the middle of the room on which their chairs were stacked. Clatter and clang and the chairs came down. The flush of the school yard was starting to fade, but not quite, and while the children reached for their books, there was a jibe in Spanish and a questionable tug and nudge. One boy wore a sweatshirt that said MOTOCROSS POWER; another boy had ATTACK FORCE on the heels of frayed sneakers. There were two Beverly Hills 90210 T-shirts, and a pullover from the Salt Lake City Zoo, and an old rugby shirt, and some simple checks and stripes. The boys wore jeans and cords, mostly, and the girls had on pastel jeans and stretch pants and cotton dresses. One girl's dress puffed out at the shoulders; another dress had three ribbons down the front, white against a background of pink and blue verbena.

Elena Castro moved to the front of the room and, while the children did some work at their tables, quickly took roll. Everyone was present. Then she tallied those who would be eating in the cafeteria and had the children stand for the Pledge of Allegiance. Mrs. Castro's voice was strong and precise—"and to the Republic for which it stands"—but tempered by a throaty quality, a lounge singer's rasp, consequential, melodious. These classroom preliminaries were handled with brisk efficiency. Then, in a softening of demeanor, Mrs. Castro said it was time for a story and reached for a chair close to the blackboard. The children got up from their tables and gathered around her. I grabbed a little chair from one of the tables and moved in closer to the half-circle of children. The book was about deep-sea divers. It looked as if it had some years on it. Elena began. She read in English, then translated into Spanish or asked a bilingual child to "explain to us what's happening here." During these moments, she would turn the book around to face the children, using the illustrations as guides to comprehension, tracing the tentacles on the octopus, *tentaculos del pulpo,* and the broad curving wing of the manta ray. She encouraged interaction through comments and questions—"Carlos, you're working on the manta ray, *verdad?*" or "Why is salt left when the water dries on the boat?"—and the students would respond, sometimes adding observations of their own. At one point, a bubbly girl named Irianna noted that the divers' suits are *soooo* old, Miss Castro, and later Andres, sharp-featured and handsome, observed, in Spanish, that a sinking ship looked like the *Titanic.* Elena acknowledged these and other comments, weaving them into the story when possible, sometimes laughing with the children—a low and easy *heh heh heh*—and continued, the children sitting rapt, legs crossed, elbows on knees, toying with their fingers or cradling their chins. One girl, Arely, reached up as Mrs. Castro read and traced with her finger the octopus on the cover, cocking her head and watching her teacher's eyes widen as the divers went down toward the ocean floor.

Mrs. Castro finished the book at nine o'clock straight-up, folded it in her lap, and called for the first rotation. The children uncrossed their legs and, in springing extensions and ungainly turns, stood up and headed for their stations. What happened from that point on was a study in the way an environment can be organized to foster learning. Though Mrs. Castro usually opened her class with some sort of group activity—a reading or a math lesson, perhaps a discussion of current events—a fair amount of the work the students did was accomplished individually or in small groups. There were eight stations. Starting at the door, and moving counter-clockwise, there was the Listening Station (two old-time tape recorders and ear sets on a small table by the door), the Publishing Center (a computer and printer with large, occasionally wobbly script, covers and plastic spines, and a binding machine), and the Writer's Table (actually four small tables pushed together to make one uneven square). Then came the front of the room and the blackboards. Next, the Reader's Corner (shelves crammed with books leaning every which way, a big rocker, a worn red Persian rug), a Math Station and a Research Station, where volumes from two different encyclopedias have been interleaved to create an almost complete set. Then the Teacher's Workshop, where Mrs. Castro did a good deal of her close work with the children. This placed you at the back wall, covered with information about fish, just behind the teacher's desk, which Elena used mostly for the stacking of papers. A red felt apple lay knocked over. "I ♥ my teacher" was printed across it; a green smiling worm curled out and up its side. A few more steps and you have returned to the door and the Art Station, where blue and orange and yellow watercolors had left little ribbons of stain on the tile.

To provide sequence and structure to their day, and to receive close instruction from Mrs. Castro, the students shifted, every half hour or so, from one major task—and one station—to another. They moved in groups or "rotations." Depending on the task, the groups might be composed only of English-speakers or of Spanish-speakers—for example, for writing instruction. Or they might be mixed, combined with fluently bilingual kids (Elena called them "brokers"), the children conversing back and forth, helping each other with a math lesson on sets and sorting. There was a good deal of fluidity here, though Elena, who was meticulous in her organization and record keeping, seemed to be on top of the activity. A visit to the classroom, then, might yield one group of children bent over stories in progress at the Writer's Table—with one of the students, brow furrowed, editing a story on the computer at the Publishing Station. A second group might be working on mathematics, one or two receiving audio-taped guidance at the Listening Station. A third group might be sitting around Mrs. Castro at the kidney-shaped Teacher's Workshop, doing research on the particular sea creatures that caught their fancy. Elena Castro controlled the clock and moved the children through the range of activities, but within these activities, children were free to follow their interests and take responsibility for completing their work in the way they thought best.

Before returning to Mrs. Castro, who was now setting her book back on its shelf, a word on how the curriculum was developed. Although the children helped determine the organizing themes, Elena gave them a sense of how this would work by beginning the year with a unit of her own choosing but of relevance to them, the Imperial Valley. (In a blue basket by the computer, I saw a stack of booklets the students had written collaboratively on the histories of the towns of their birth: Mexicali, Calexico, Brawley, Holtville, Heber.) After studying the Valley for a month, the students voted on the topics they'd want to study through the year. These topics became the conceptual skeleton of the curriculum. A list of them was taped to the door.

Themes We Will Study
Temas Que Estudiaremos

Earth

La Tierra

Sealife

Animales Marinos

Energy

Energia

Pollution

Contaminacion

Cultures

Culturas

And so on. As a particular month progressed, then, the books Elena Castro begged, borrowed from the library, salvaged, and bought from her own pocket would change somewhat, as would the charts and posters and plentiful work of the children that adorned the walls and hung in the air. There was much that was stable, of course—from the multiplication chart to the computer to that incomplete encyclopedia—but this was a classroom always in a state of orderly evolution, structured and unpredictable.

Mrs. Castro walked back to the corner by her desk, the Teacher's Workshop. She wore a black jacket, silver bracelets a bright blue dress, and heels. She was about five foot two, and moved quickly—though she could stop on a dime to listen to a child's question, seeming to block out everything else. Andres headed her off and asked if he could take the book about the divers home that night: "*Maestra, me puedo llevar el libra a la casa, por favor?*" Sure he could, she said, touching his shoulder, complimenting him for giving the English book a try. Then she settled in at her workshop to help the nine students gathering around her with their marine research.

The students had in front of them booklets Mrs. Castro made to guide their inquiry. Each booklet had four sections: What You Know, What Do You Want to Know?, Bibliography, and Research Notes. Across the top of each section swam a line of sketched fish, each about to gobble the other—a cartoon food chain. Mrs. Castro took a booklet, creased it open, and turned it toward the children, the top of the cover resting on her shoulder. She began slowly turning the pages, explaining the purpose of each section: How you listed all the things you already knew about your puffer fish or manta ray or great white shark. How, on page two, you listed all the things you want to know, what you're curious about, what puzzles you. ("For example, Alex, you wanted to know how the jellyfish eats. You'd put that question here.") Next came the Bibliography, and bubbly Irianna, who had just recently begun acquiring English, leaned across the table and said that was where you put the books you read. "Very good, *mija*," said Mrs. Castro—using the common term of endearment, "my daughter"—and Irianna smiled in a dimpled way that brought her chin to her chest. Then Elena Castro turned to the final section, Research Notes, and talked a little about how important research was in helping us to learn about the world. "I'm always looking things up—in my dictionary, in my encyclopedia, at the library. *Ay*, we learn a *lot* that way." She paused here and drew herself up in the chair for emphasis. "In fact, when you boys and girls do research, I learn so much." She looked at Irianna. "Yesterday, Irianna showed me something she found on the starfish. Do you want to read it to us, Irianna? It's so interesting!" And Irianna lit up, reached for her book, and read to the group about the eye at the end of each arm of the starfish.

When Irianna finished, Mrs. Castro reached to the center of the table, where she had piled two stacks of books on marine life. On mysteries of the sea, on dolphins and sharks and killer whales, the F volume of an old encyclopedia, a book on coral, and one on the octopus. Books and books, the dirt of innumerable fingers ground into the covers. Books she sorted out like a giant deck of cards. "Alex, here's something on the jellyfish . . . and, let's see, Irianna, look at this, another book on the starfish . . . and, hey, Arely, we're in luck, here's the W volume of the encyclopedia—see if your walrus is in it." As the kids flipped through the books, she showed them how to use a table of contents and an index—and some got this and some didn't yet—and then she gave what brief assistance she could when a book was beyond the third-grade reading level. The children started writing in their Research Notes.

Alex got up and came over to look at the charts on the cabinet doors behind Mrs. Castro's desk. I followed his gaze. On the door closest to me, closed at an angle, off its runners, layers of sea life descended from the barracuda to the mid-level octopus to the sea urchin and deep-sea angler. The door next to that displayed the "Whale Wall Chart" where the hundred-foot blue whale swam past the fifty-foot humpback whale, which curled toward the fifteen-foot narwhal. The blue whale "is believed to be the largest animal that ever lived." The humpback whale emits a low-pitched moaning "song" that can last up to thirty minutes. One of the teeth in the male narwhal develops into a long spiral tusk. On the next door, opened slightly, revealing bags of cookies, was a chart of "Ocean Wonders": the flying fish and the oarfish with its long dorsal fin and the weird luminescent snake dragonfish. And—the jellyfish! Bingo. Alex stopped and folded his booklet, trying to steady it on his forearm, writing irregularly, looking back and forth from chart to page.

Maria, tall for her age and pretty, untangled her feet from her chair and walked over to the Research Station. She sat down and looked up at the wall over the encyclopedias. There was a large hand-drawn sketch of fish anatomy, something I hadn't noticed yet—I'd be discovering new things each day I was here—and Maria settled her chin in her cupped palms and studied a bit longer: heart/*corazon*, aorta/*aorta*, gills/*agallas*, fins/*aleta*. I let myself drift, thinking how rich this was, half-listening to Elena and the students at the Teacher's Workshop. I thought about how radically this classroom clashed with so many of our stock representations of school: monochromatic, trivial, regimented, dull. To the side of the children at the Teacher's Workshop was a broad stretch of wall Mrs. Castro had covered with swirling blue-violet fabric. "Creatures of the Sea" was printed above it. Over the week it would become populated, like a slow-motion nature film, with drawings that had cartoon-like blurbs above them, first-person accounts of what it's like to be a squid or an electric eel or a puffer fish. A few were already done. Arely's skillfully rendered walrus said, through its big tusks and whiskers:

> I am a walrus. I live in the ocean and I eat fish. I am brown and I have big teeth called tusks. I like to be in the ocean and swim a lot. I also live on the land.

On a little table under the display sat a cluster of objects, material for postlunch show and tell: a stuffed, fuzzy dolphin with "Sea World" scripted on its belly, a few pieces of coral, and a construction of four frogs, about six inches high, playing guitars and trumpets—frog mariachis?—made entirely out of seashells. Fat seashell bodies, thin seashell lips, tiny spiral seashell horns. It's a lot of fun under the sea.

III

Just to the south of the San Diego State Campus is a little park called Rockwood Plaza. If you took a turn out of the snug metal doors of the Rodney Auditorium and cross Rockwood Plaza, you would be at the border in about five or ten minutes. Maybe a little longer in the dead heat of summer. Brief as it is, the walk would provide the beginnings of a sketch of Calexico's history.[3] Rodney Auditorium, built in 1927, was part of the city's first high school. Rockwood Plaza, like Rockwood Street, which you would soon cross, was named after Charles Robinson Rockwood, the chief engineer of the first project to irrigate the Valley. This area used to be the more prosperous part of the city: it held the old homes of middle-class Anglos and Mexican Americans. To the east—where Dool Elementary is now—there was poorer housing and the new arrivals from Mexico. To the west, across the Southern Pacific railroad tracks, there was once an agricultural shanty town called La Garra—a colloquialism meaning "the rag"—where Mexican immigrants settled in the early part of the century.

You could walk straight to the border along Heber—the town northwest of Calexico named after the early developer—or you could veer diagonally, crossing Heffernan (Dr. W. T. Heffernan was one of Rockwood's financiers) and pass by the Hotel De Anza, with its Spanish arches and mission-style cupola. Juan Bautista de Anza was the first Spaniard to cross the desert in search of a land route to the coast. (He would continue northward and found the city of San Francisco in 1776.) My friend Héctor Calderón, a native Calexican, now a professor at UCLA, has childhood memories of being dressed in buckskin and feathers and marching in the Calexico Desert Cavalcade, a pageant re-enacting De Anza's journey to bring, as the late 1930s' promotional literature put it, "God and civilization to the Southwest."[4] The Cocopah Indians, who, in fact, did not wear feathers or buckskin, but who, I assume, Héctor was dressed to represent, served as guides for De Anza and, over a hundred years later, worked on the Valley's irrigation project. During World War I they were declared aliens and exiled to Mexico. Few of them survived.

From the De Anza you would continue south through one more block of modest houses, quiet, sunny, and upon crossing Third Street, hit the energetic business district, which extended, in full commercial tilt, right up against the chain-link fence that marked this particular stretch of the two-thousand-mile border. These few blocks have been the site of Calexico's buying and selling for over sixty years. Walking along First Street, with its weathered shops and storefronts, you would slip in with shoppers from both sides of the border, moving among rows of boxes, jammed and folded, tilted full view toward the street, piled with boots and shoes and slippers, purses, thongs, socks, sandals, bundles of bright fabric, spools of ribbon, of thread, T-shirts with Bart Simpson, the UCLA logo, Michael Jordan, Madonna. "Cash and Carry." Soon, without any fanfare, you would come upon an opening in the fence and a simple concrete walkway. You could, if you wished, cross the line and shop in Mexicali. People have been going back and forth for a long time.

Most of the people I met in Calexico had relatives living in Mexicali, and Calexicans frequently crossed the border to visit them or to shop or dine or secure professional services. For many years, Mexicali's agricultural and industrial laborers have been traveling daily through Calexico, and you could see them cashing checks on First Street, dusty from a day's work in the fields. The arrival of foreign assembly plants, *maquiladoras,* in Mexicali has brought more women into the work force, and some of their meager but steady wages are spent in Calexico. In fact, Calexico's merchants are dependent on shoppers from Mexicali—Kress, Inc.'s most profitable store in the nation is on Second Street—and Calexico's economy wrenches with changes in the peso. "When Mexicali sneezes," a saying goes, "Calexico catches a cold.

Originally a labor camp, then a cow town, Calexico, by the late 1920s, had become an established border city with the extensive agricultural base those early developers had envisioned. It is not surprising, then, that the city's old local histories lavishly celebrate the "courage," "ingenuity," and "pioneering spirit" of Rockwood, Heber and the other engineers and businessmen who founded Calexico. They had, in fact, pulled off an extraordinary technical achievement: turning a desert into lush farmland. Like the writers of those histories, the entire leadership of Calexico was Anglo and would remain so well into the 1950s. Though there was a significant number, eventually a majority, of Mexican Americans in Calexico, the city fathers—and the historians—chose to enhance the city's history through a romanticized portrait of the Spanish past, rather than the Spanish-Indian, Mestizo past and present. Witness the Desert Cavalcade, the Hotel De Anza, and the architecture of the old buildings on the San Diego State campus. Mexican Americans had limited influence: the city council, the judiciary, the police force, the teachers were all White. Classes in the schools were, in effect, segregated, as they were throughout the Southwest, by race.

Change began in the mid to late 1950s. Both Héctor Calderón and Matt Contreras, the judge who acted as my guide through the Imperial Valley, recall the beginnings of Chicano political activity via activist groups that brought Mexican-American families together for a dance, a barbecue, and some grass-roots organizing. In addition, the Viva Kennedy campaign in 1960 mobilized the vote, and the farm workers' movement, which developed a major power base in the Valley, got poor people involved in the political process. Early affirmative action programs gave Mexican-American youth a greater sense of the possible and led to the recruitment of high school students into higher education and subsequent jobs in law enforcement, education, and business. Matt still remembers the strange pride he felt when, in the late 1950s, Rollie Carillo was appointed the first Mexican-American mayor of Calexico.

"Extra!" "Extra!" announced the newspaper banners pinned to the wall way up above the sink where Art Station paints ran pink and orange in the draining water. "Extra! Read All About It!" Tuesday through Friday, right after the Pledge of Allegiance, Elena Castro's students reported on current events in their neighborhood, in the city, county, or state, in the United States, or in the world. They followed a schedule posted on a free patch of wall over the Art Station, their names listed by day—Arely on Tuesday, Carlos on Thursday—monolingual and bilingual speakers mixed on any given day, holding the floor together.

This was one of the ways Elena connected her classroom to the flow of events in the community and beyond. During the week before their presentation, students would be on the lookout for news stories that interested them—from print media, TV or radio, or from the elaborate oral networks of friends and family. Then they would fill out sheets available in a large envelope pinned to that wall beneath the headlines, indicating the focus of the story—city, state, world—and its source: newspaper, radio, and so on. Then they answered journalism's central questions: who (*quien*), what (*que*), when (*cuando*), where (*donde*), why (*por qué*), how (*como*). Finally, they considered how the event affected their lives. When their day of the week arrived, each would read aloud their responses and answer questions posed by fellow students or by Mrs. Castro. There was a lot of interchange between Spanish and English, with Elena acting as facilitator. The schedule was posted on the wall, but by the time of my visit, the students pretty much knew who was up when, and they came forward in the morning to talk about the news, to field questions, to think on their feet about the world beyond themselves.

Sometimes the news was very local. Carlos reported on his aunt being mugged on the streets of Mexicali; Andres's grandmother visited from Heber, and his headline read: *La Visita de la Abuela de Heber*. Elena and the others would then listen to the "where," "why," and "how" of these events and proceed to ask their questions: "Is she OK, Carlos?" and "Why do you think such things happen?" and, for Andres, "*¿Que pasa en la casa cuando visita su abuela?*" or "What happens in your house when your grandmother visits?" City news came primarily from the region's newspapers: the *Calexico Chronicle*, the *Imperial Valley Press, La Vo de la Frontera*, and *El Mexicano*—the last two printed in Mexicali but sold as well in Calexico—or from the local radio stations, KQVO down Highway 111 or XEAO and XED, *La Grande*, across the border. Ricardo reported on the pesticides used in agriculture and the way they can hurt us; Arely told everyone about the fair that was then in progress; Maria said that the school board was trying to get more money so that there could be more aides in schools, and "that would be good for all of us."

State news and beyond tended to come from television: *President Clinton Visits Europe* or *People From Haiti Turned Back To Their Home*. Irianna told the class about AIDS: that people all over the world were dying every day, that it made her very sad because it was hard to find a medicine to cure them. Veronica reported on "the hole in the ozone layer": that it came from spray cans, that we can get skin cancer because of it, and that we can help by not using stuff that comes in spray cans. Jorge reported on smog in "*las grandes ciuadades como Los Angeles y Mexicali*," explaining that it comes from "*el humo del las fabricas y el humo de los automoviles*," and observed that it affects everyone, causing much illness, "*muchas enfermedades.*"

Elena would be sitting against the board, behind the presenter, leaning in occasionally to ask one of her bilingual "brokers" to rephrase and comment, or to add some information that would place a presentation in context, or she would pick up on a child's question or add one of her own. So, during the report on Haitian refugees, she pulled down the map and pointed out the island, then asked the students whether they thought the United States should turn the people away or let them in. (Let them in was the consensus.) During the discussion of the ozone layer, she asked the class to brainstorm on what they could do to curtail the use of aerosol cans. During the presentation about the school board, she explained what a school board was and how people got elected to it. Then she would slide down a little in her chair, feet together, hands folded, attentive as the next child came forward to engage the news.

Elena Castro moved with her family to Calexico in 1959, just as the power base in the city was beginning its slow shift toward the Mexican-American majority. She entered kindergarten in 1961, a monolingual speaker of Spanish, six or seven years before the advent of bilingual education in the Imperial Valley. (The first bilingual program in modern American public schools was launched in Dade County, Florida, in 1963. Lyndon Johnson signed the Bilingual Education Act in January 1968, and Calexico's first experimental programs were started up in late 1969.[5]) Elena struggled through kindergarten and first grade, not catching on, confused, reprimanded. "She's not trying," the first-grade teacher told her mother through an interpreter. "She doesn't know how to pay attention. She has no discipline." Elena remembers being made to stand outside the classroom; she remembers a particular look in the teacher's eyes. Once, she was trying to shape a plaster handprint, one of those curios kids make for Mother's Day or Christmas, and she was having a hard time of it. She didn't understand the instructions and moved her hand, blurring the mold. The teacher took the mold away and threw it in the trash can, fed up with her intransigence. By sheer luck, Elena's second-grade teacher was a Mexican-American woman, one of the few beginning to enter the teaching force, and though, at that time, the use of Spanish in the schools was forbidden, the woman encouraged Elena and explained lessons to her in her native tongue. Elena credits her with saving her academic life.

When Elena Castro talked about bilingual education, then, she spoke with an authority grounded in the beginnings of her own history in the classroom, a history that developed out of the multilayered history of the border town that became her home. These are histories of power and language, of emerging participation. Participation. One of the things you noticed, you *felt,* right away when you sat in Elena's classroom was the excitement of young minds working. Many of her students came from poor families; a fair number were the children of migrant workers and laborers—people who have very hard lives and little or no opportunity to learn English. In schools across the Southwest, such children often sat silent, uncomprehending, withdrawn—lost to the possibility of the classroom. Like Elena years before. But in Room 42 in Dool Elementary, Andres and Jorge and Irianna and the others were alive, caught up in the flow of words and images and numbers.

On an overhead projector, Elena was reviewing the telling of time. There was a clock on the transparency with no hands; she drew in one, then the other. "What time is it, class, *que hora es?*" The children responded quickly. She erased with a small cloth and drew in a new hour, then a new minute hand. A number of the students answered at once, "Ten-twelve." "Aw, Miss Castro," someone pleaded, "make 'em harder." "OK, OK." She laughed, and wrote 3:15 on the bottom of the transparency, asking Jorge to come forward to draw in the hands. "*Por favor, Jorge, dibuje quince despues de last tres.*" Jorge sprang to his feet, tripping a little on Carlos who was lodged in close. He took the grease pencil from Mrs. Castro and quickly executed the answer. Then came the hands waving for the next round. "Pick me!" "Oooooh, let me, Miss Castro!" "*Permite me, Maestra.*" The eager voices. The sharp eyes.

After a halting but auspicious start in the late 1960s and early-to-mid 1970s, bilingual education evolved both as a philosophy and a set of methods, always controversial, marked by both incompetence and dogged brilliance, conceptual confusion and real insight into the dynamics of culture and schooling—evolved through a combination of legal decision and legislation into a powerful pedagogy, only to be undermined during the Reagan presidency. Now, lobbying groups like English Only and U.S. English present the most organized opposition to bilingual education, arguing that it will contribute to ghettoization, divisiveness, or, in the worst-case scenario, a balkanized America. The charges stir deep fears in the United States, playing as they do to anti-immigrant and anti-Latino sentiments, but, in one way, they are curious, for there is a long, if neglected, history of bilingualism in our country.

Though English became the dominant language in the colonies, many languages were spoken—German, Dutch, French, Swedish, Polish, and various Indian languages among them—and it was common for pre-Revolutionary War colonials, from indentured servants to the elite, to be fluent in several tongues. It was common, too, for official documents to be published in more than one language. The Articles of Confederation, for example, were printed in German as well as English. By the late seventeenth century, German colonials had opened private schools in

Philadelphia in which their native language was the medium of instruction, and throughout the eighteenth century other linguistic minorities
developed such schools. With the emergence of comprehensive public education in the nineteenth century, groups with sufficient political clout lob-
bied for monolingual or bilingual instruction in their local schools, and
though such instruction was, at times, contested by other ethnic and religious groups (for example, the Irish versus the French in Massachusetts),
it was often granted, primarily to keep students in the newly developing
public school system. So, German-language instruction was conducted in
public schools in Cincinnati, Cleveland, Baltimore, Saint Louis, Chicago,
and San Francisco; French in Louisiana, three counties in Wisconsin, and
San Francisco; Spanish in New Mexico. To be sure, such instruction was
opposed before our time by policymakers wary of foreign influence, but
the most significant force threatening our nation's linguistic diversity was
a potent early twentieth-century nativism fueled by increasing Central and
Southern European immigration and, finally, the advent of World War I.
It was not until those 1960s' experiments in Dade County—urged by a
powerful Cuban-American constituency—that bilingual education re-
emerged in our country as an educational program of any consequence.

The primary concerns raised by U.S. English, English Only, and similar groups are that bilingual education retards the learning of English and
the entrance of non-English-speaking children into the social and institutional flow of American life and that it encourages linguistic and social
isolation and divisiveness. To be sure, there are bilingual programs that
are poorly conceived and poorly taught—though their limitation, ironically, tends to be their focus on rudimentary functional English in lieu of
educationally rich bilingual curricula. And a small number of Latino cultural nationalists in the past have tried to incorporate bilingual education
into a separatist political agenda. But when you sit in Elena Castro's classroom, it's hard to believe that what you're seeing will lead to exclusion
and separatism.

There were, of course, scuffles and cheap shots in Room 42, the nasty,
personal injuries children inflict on one another. But, overall, this was a
cohesive class. You saw children working together in groups, helping each
other, listening while the other spoke, and the one Anglo child was right in
the thick of it all. There did not seem to be a pronounced separation of children who could speak English and Spanish from those who were monolingual—though in Calexico itself there was some friction between established
Mexican-American families and poorer new arrivals. In Room 42 there was
much translating and other cross-linguistic exchange. The children's native
Spanish was appreciated and utilized, and the use of English encouraged

and guided. Both were used to communicate, solve problems, learn things, reflect on intellectual work, and make connections to the world outside. There was a belief here, as in other effective bilingual classrooms I've seen, in the power of participation, a belief that engagement in the classroom will lead to rich cognitive and linguistic development, extending outward to the world beyond. "Extra! Read All About It!" The children in Room 42 were becoming civic beings.

It occurred to me after a day or two in Calexico that the city could be imagined as an English Only nightmare. Walking down Heber or Rockwood or Heffernan, spending a few minutes outside Dool Elementary, or shopping on Second Street, you would be likely to hear Spanish more than English. Most of the signs in the business district were in Spanish and English, but sometimes just in Spanish. "*Ahorre comprando con nosotros,*" it said above the Pronto Market, located at Calle Primera y Heffernan. If you entered a ma-and-pa restaurant with a local, the owner might well greet you in Spanish. Your friend would probably order for you.

But when you went to pay your bill at that restaurant, you'd see eight-by-ten color photographs of John Kennedy and Ronald Reagan behind the cash register. Those parents chatting outside Dool Elementary were more than likely bilingual, choosing—as ethnic groups in America have always chosen—to speak their native tongue in informal or private situations. (In this regard, it's interesting to note that in 1911 a federal commission worried that the new immigrants—Italians and Central Europeans, characterized now as model assimilationists—were not learning English quickly enough.) And those parents who spoke only Spanish encouraged their children to learn English, for, as one mother struggled to explain to me, "it will help them get ahead." If you visited English composition courses at Imperial Valley College, or at the San Diego State campus, you would meet young people like Izela, who worked with children in a Mexicali school, or Claudina, who wanted to get a degree in business—both fluently bilingual, working hard after work to master the conventions of written English.

Though infused with Spanish language and Mexican culture, Calexico defied, in its complexity, the kinds of political and social generalizations that are made about such communities. Attitudes toward English ranged from intimidation and resentment to admiration and a desire for fluency. There was a strong Mexican work ethic fused with an American "can do" attitude. There was despair and weariness, alcohol and violence, and a fierce commitment to the possibility of a better life: "Take care of yourself and work hard," was one old man's philosophy. "I never could have owned a home like this in Mexico," said another. There was provincialism, yet there was respect for those who went away to acquire specialized knowledge and brought it back to the community. There were communitarian bonds and a deep commitment to family, yet a strong individualist ethic as well, a belief that, as one woman explained: "You have to show what you can do. You can't be one of so many. You have to stand out." There was talk of solidarity, of *la raza,* and there were class conflicts. There were a wide range of reactions to historical inequities and racism: from fury to denial, with many believing that they could effect change by entering professional and managerial and service ranks and doing things differently. (I heard this especially from people hoping to become teachers.) There was cynicism about politics and pride in citizenship—with many old timers having voted in every election. The power base had changed: all the above played itself out on a Mexican-American political landscape marked by infighting and compromise. The Spanish language was no longer denigrated; the Mestizo heritage honored. But you knew the moment you came back across the border from Mexicali that you were in a city in the United States. It was hard to explain why; something you felt, the movement of the people on the street, the look of things. "You know," one civic leader explained to me, "if you stood up in a council meeting and proposed that we become part of Mexicali, you'd get hooted out of the room."

Rafael Jacinto picked at the crease in his gray flannel slacks, worn, the crease ironed in—he picked as if to say "See what I mean?" He was leaning against a desk in the Music Room, where he and his wife had just completed another session of Evangelina Jones's course in the teaching of reading. Stacked on shelves behind him, warped and dusty, was a library of old record albums—Ralph Marterie, Blossom Dearie, Broadway hits, *Songs of Ireland*—left from another time in the Music Room at the San Diego State University Imperial Valley campus. He looked from his trousers up to me—*see what I mean?*—explaining how this decision to go back to school had limited the hours he can work, how he and his wife have to spend so many hours studying, so he wears these old pants, and this windbreaker, staying up late, tired, the crease carefully ironed in once the kids have gone to bed.

He was telling me the story of his decision. It was made in 1985. He was working in the fields, packing cauliflower. It was past midnight, and he was driving through the desert. Late, tired, those little hallucinatory wisps flitting in from the periphery of the beams of his headlights. "I started thinking about my life. What I had achieved so far. What I would probably achieve in the future. And just like that"—he snapped his fingers—"just like *that,* I knew I had to make a change." When he went home, he woke up his wife and told her what he wanted to do. He asked her to join him, and they began taking high school equivalency classes at the local adult school. They applied for citizenship and enrolled in ESL classes at Imperial Valley College. Five years later, with associate arts degrees in hand, they entered San Diego State. They have both passed the difficult English composition proficiency exam. Last semester, each got a 3.0. They want to become teachers.

Guadalupe Jacinto, who had been outside in the warm evening talking to Evangelina, walked in and took a seat beside Rafael. She was polite, engaging, full of thoughts that she expressed slowly, measuring her expression, conscious of her spoken English, but gaining fluency and fervor as she spoke. She was born in Mexicali, married Rafael at sixteen, had four children—one of whom Evangelina taught when she was still at the elementary school. "My father always wanted me to go to school," she explained, "but . . . " She shrugged and smiled. "She's very smart," Rafael said softly. "The English is very hard," she said, leaning forward, "but we work on it together. We study together." She looked simultaneously weary and poised, in the evening, a warm breeze, dark outside. They have about two more years to go for the bachelor's degree. Then certification. "It's like you're in a dream," she said. "I can't believe it sometimes." There was exhaustion in her voice—as though every word of English came with oppressive weight—but anticipation, too. To be a teacher. Pride and disbelief. "San Diego State University," Rafael said, pausing on each word, melodious, a Spanish lilt to his English.

IV

Elena Castro usually ate lunch in her classroom. Other teachers would drop by for a minute or two or for the duration of a quick meal. There were three regulars, the school's three first-year teachers. They were there most of the time. Carmen Santos was twenty-five and taught first grade. She had a serious, almost studious, demeanor that registered in her gaze and in the slight pursing of her lips. Thin, about five-two, full brown hair; one of her friends called her Carmencita. Veronica Zwart, whose mother was Mexican and father Dutch, taught third grade next door to Elena. She was thirty, five-seven or -eight, angular face, high cheekbones. Jessie Carillo, twenty-five, taught a combined fourth-fifth class in the very room where she was once a fifth-grade student. Jessie's eyes were round, big, and she had a quick smile. When she asked her students to write, she wrote along with them, raising her hand, as they did, when she wanted to read her paper.

The teachers sat at the Writer's Table, spreading sandwiches or burritos or microwaved leftovers out on paper towels grabbed from the sink by the Art Station. There were chips and colas and fruit juice from the cafeteria. Carrot sticks or a salad or soup for the dieters. Pencils. A stray crayon. Like Elena, the three new teachers were all born in the Valley, were all bilingual, and all graduated from the SDSU campus, where they either took courses from or were supervised by Evangelina Jones—Evangelina, who one late afternoon told me, "Your first real teaching job is crucial. It forms you. If you're lucky, you'll find a place that will nurture you and teach you things. It'll shape the kind of teacher you'll become."

On the days I was observing Elena's class, she would ask me to join her and the others for lunch. The group had a casual warmth to it, low-key and inviting. Sometimes they would talk about a shopping expedition to San Diego, two hours west, or exchange local gossip—stopping to explain to me the context of a story—or discuss a union issue, for Elena was Dool's representative. But they also talked a lot about teaching. They talked about particular students or lessons or about upcoming statewide tests and how to prepare for them. And they swapped materials: books, wall displays, the advertisements they found in their mailboxes. So in the easy flow of conversation a lot of advice drifted around the table. Although Elena was by far the most experienced teacher there, the mentor, it didn't show in her bearing. "She's willing to share everything," Jessie told me one day. "She's very knowledgeable, but, you know, she doesn't brainwash you. She definitely has her opinions; she'll say, 'This is what I think,' but then she asks *you* to talk." Isolated in their rooms, young teachers easily get overwhelmed by their notions of success and experiences of failure. Elena's table created a common space for them, familiar, set in shared history, alternately light and serious. And hopeful— I got the sense that competence was taken for granted here. "When I first started," Veronica explained, "I'd go home feeling hopeless. But, now, well, now I'm excited." If one of the young teachers came in defeated, the setback was assumed to be momentary, a problem to be solved. And sometimes a request for direct intervention arose from the problem, a request that seemed natural, part of the give-and-take. That's the way it was when Carmen asked Elena to visit her class and help her with Felipe.

Carmen had her first-graders around her at the front of the room, all singing along to a well-worn record by children's musicians Greg and Steve:

The world is a rainbow
With many kinds of people
And when we work together
It's such a sight to see.
The world is beautiful when
we live in har-mo-ny.[6]

As they sang, the children waved their hands back and forth in the air, sweeping the sky with the curve of the rainbow. Carmen swept the sky as well, rocking her head, a little grin on her face, into it, but with a hint of amusement. Her room was set up like Elena's with a range of work stations—*Estación de Escuchar,* the Listening Station, *Estación de Arte,* the Art Station, and so on—and the walls were filled with print, and overhead hung colorful samples of the children's work.

After the song and a quick stretch—"reach beyond the rainbow, higher, higher"—Carmen began the rotations. Small groups of students went to the *Estación de ABC* and the Listening Station. A larger group went to the Writer's Table where some would be setting down the words of their first stories while others would be dictating more elaborate stories to the aide Carmen had that morning: leaning over the table, stringing events together excitedly with "and . . . and . . . and then . . . " And still others would be joining Carmen at the Teacher's Workshop to continue to learn to read in Spanish. On a shelf behind Carmen sat a short stack of books: *Los Animales de Don Vincencio, Azulin Visita a Mexico,* and a book about a kite, *El Papalote.* Alongside them was a large book, bound in art paper, entitled *Mi Extraterrestre.* I quietly pulled it out. It was a collection of student drawings accompanied by Carmen's neat script; from what I could tell, students had to imagine what their own private extraterrestrial might be like. The creatures they conjured up had multiple legs and heads, long ears, fangs, huge purple hands, big red eyes—lots of them. In English and in Spanish the children described Ets that would knock things down and "spin around to get to the earth" and attend a birthday party and fly to the mall.

Right at the second rotation, Elena came in. The children knew her; she had visited before, so there was no uneasiness. She walked over to the table where students were writing in their journals—the idea here being that they would write, as best they could, about something that happened to them, and then the teacher or an aide would respond, thus demonstrating to the children that writing did things, was interactive. Elena worked with two or three children, then moved next to Felipe. Carmen drifted over.

"Felipe," Elena said, "can I write in the journal with you?"

"Yes."

"What would you like to write about?"

Silence.

"Did you go to the fair last weekend?"

A big "Yes."

"What did you see?"

And Felipe began to write—slowly, awkwardly—while Elena helped him along. "Saw. Sawww. What letter makes that *www* sound, *mijo?*"

Eventually Felipe wrote, "I went to the fair and saw a bull."

"Felipe, what else did you see?" Felipe fell silent again.

Elena took a different tack. "Felipe, did you eat anything at the fair?"

An enthusiastic "I ate corndogs!"

"*Ay!*" exclaimed Elena. "Write about that!"

And so it went. After Felipe produced another sentence or two, Elena said to him, "I'm going to respond to you now, OK?" Under Felipe's sentences she began to write—reading out loud what she was writing—"I went to the fair last year, but I'm not going this year." She paused and looked at him, all serious. "Do you know why, Felipe?"

"No, *Maestra.*"

Here she picked up the pen again, talking as she wrote, "Because I ate tooooo many corndogs!"

She laughed her throaty *heh-heh-heh* and turned back to Felipe, who was grinning in skeptical pleasure.

They finished up and, as the aide continued to work with the journals, Elena took Carmen out of earshot and said, "He just needs a little more. Three or four days of intensive work. Then leave him be. But, now, be persistent." Carmen listened, nodding. "Be persistent," she said under her breath and walked Elena to the door. Then she went back and sat with Felipe.

Eddie Hernandez taught kindergarten on the south end of Dool, a couple of hundred feet from Elena, Veronica, and the rest. He had been teaching for ten years; Elena Castro was his master teacher. Now he's known throughout the district and serves as a master teacher for others. Eddie was born in Calexico—one of a family of ten—went to Imperial Valley College, then to the San Diego State campus up the street. In fact, his kindergartners play on a grassy enclosure that was once the site of his grandmother's house; where there used to be a tool shed and a garden, there were now swings and a slide and a burro and parrot, both saddled, ready to ride, on iron poles rising out of the ground.

Evangelina had sent a lot of students to Eddie, and based on their reports and her own observation, she described him this way: "Eddie is the epitome of the master teacher. He shows trainees how to think about teaching. He expects a lot from his class, and at the end of every week he sits down with his student teacher and thinks out loud about how things went, or about new things that cropped up, or about what he had to modify to help So-and-so understand a concept. It's really something, you know, because Eddie looks so effortless, but really he's always thinking, and the new teacher gets to see how that works."

The philosophy guiding Eddie's classroom—and guiding the way Elena, Carmen, and the others ran their classes—was called "whole language." Proponents of whole language believe that teachers should create environments in which students are immersed in language and are given numerous opportunities to use it: talking, reading, writing, and taking chances with print, telling a story, responding to a reading, writing with and to others, compiling information on topics of personal interest. To be sure, work on discrete skills was done in the whole language classrooms at Dool—Eddie and Elena, for example, helped kids sound out words phonetically—but, as Elena explained, such work was done "in the service of something bigger," was done as children were trying to write stories or pursue the narrative line in a book. So a new teacher in Eddie's room would learn this philosophy and the range of approaches that came with it. A way to think about the teaching of language and a set of beliefs about what students can do under the right conditions.

One of the first things that struck visitors to Eddie's class was how sophisticated it seemed, how much academic work the kids were doing. There were ditties, of course, and snacks, and happy faces everywhere—and half the time the stars Eddie gave the kids ended up on forearms or foreheads, rather than on the fronts of shirts and blouses. But in addition to practicing the formation of letters, the children were trying to write stories; along with learning the ABC's, they were being guided through simple narratives and giving their opinions about them. Spanish and English was all around them—as in Elena's room—and they were expected to try to solve problems with words. Eddie had covered one section of his west wall with samples of print that the children would recognize from their home environment: there was a box of Lucky Charms and a label from Campbell's Sopa de Polla and a package of Blue Bonnet and other food and household products. So when, one morning, a little girl was writing a story and got stuck on the word *blue*, Eddie turned her around and asked her to find the word on the display. She did, and copied it down. "See?" he said to the intern who was there that day. "There's all kinds of ways they can learn to spell. The whole idea is to get them to think, to look around at the language that surrounds them and use it."

One day I asked Carmen, Jessie, and Veronica to speculate on the ideal training program for elementary school teachers. "They'd put you in the schools earlier—observing, tutoring, something to get you around kids sooner." "It would be more hands-on." "Reading books alone doesn't do it. Books can't tell you what to actually expect in the classroom." The training would involve a lot of role playing and simulation, for "it's important to go through what the kids go through." Who should conduct this training? "People who have been in the classroom, who have a lot of techniques." Evangelina Jones and Elena Castro were cited as exemplars, as was Eddie Hernandez and a woman named Jane Carpenter, a local teacher who had developed a training program in children's literature for the district. The topic of in-service workshops came up several times, and the young teachers made it clear that they were *not* talking about the typical one-day presentation, usually given by an outside consultant. What they had in mind was an ongoing series—like Carpenter's—where teachers could come, learn some things, try them, and come back, discuss the results, fine-tune, modify, or abandon what they tried, and learn more. This sort of training, said Carmen, Veronica, and Jessie, especially should be in place during a teacher's first few years in the classroom. "So what is it," I asked, "that makes people like Evangelina, Elena, and Eddie so good?" The answers: "They know so many things to do." "They make learning fun." "They have a great relationship with their kids." "They care."

Probably because of the demands of their immediate situation and the early phase of their own growth as teachers, Carmen, Veronica, and Jessie focused their discussion on practice. This made sense. No matter how well they might master a teacher-ed class, or how high they might score on a test, or how skillfully they could talk about teaching in the abstract, they still had to walk into a room full of children five days a week and *do* things, engage in an extraordinarily complex activity fraught with the uncertain and conditional. Developing effective ways to generate and guide discussion, provide feedback on reading and writing, put together a test, even take roll and collect homework—procedures and routines, big and small—these and a formidable number of other activities would determine their success or failure as classroom teachers. And central to that success, and to their sense of themselves as competent teachers and decent human beings, were the ways they could find to manage the classroom and to connect with the children in it. The social dimension of teaching.

How could they foster relationships with the children that were caring yet professional, that would enable them to manage the room and touch individual lives? No wonder they admired Elena's warmly attentive but efficient classroom style.

What was interesting to me, and it took a while to grasp it, was the degree to which these concerns about practice and relationships, while certainly emerging from immediate needs, were also reflecting deeply held values and beliefs about children and learning. At first, I wondered—because I didn't hear much specifically about it—I wondered about the importance for these young teachers of the conceptual or moral dimensions of teaching. Did they see themselves primarily as technicians, caring technicians, but technicians nonetheless? Or was there more? What I came to appreciate was that their concerns about practice were embedded in wide-ranging moral imperatives. Take, for example, the talk about "caring."

When Carmen and company praised Elena's "care," they were referring not only to their mentor's affection for kids—though that was part of it—but more so to Elena's absolute regard for children, her unfaltering belief in their potential. "Caring" had as much to do with faith and cognition as with feeling. All children, no matter what their background, had the capacity to learn. And this belief brought with it a responsibility: it was the teacher's intellectual challenge to come to understand what must be done to tap that potential. All this was so basic a tenet of these teachers' beliefs about their work that most of the time it went unsaid. It was simply acted upon. Thus the need for skill, techniques, smart practice. When Felipe wasn't writing, Carmen went to Elena for help in eliciting a story—for Felipe's capacity to produce written language was not in question.

Every time interns watched Elena teach, they saw these beliefs in action, in even the most commonplace encounters—for it's often in the asides, the offhand questions, the microlessons that a teacher's most basic attitudes toward students are revealed. Carlos had written a shaggy dog story. Elena was slowly scrolling up the computer screen, praising the story as she read. Once done, about to move onto the next child, she tapped a key, taking the story back to a line at the beginning in which Carlos described the dog as a "troublemaker." "You know, Carlos," she reflected, "I found myself wondering what Penny did that caused so much trouble?" "She tips over garbage cans," he said. "Good. Anything else?" Carlos giggled. "What?" she asked. "What is it?" "She makes messes!" Elena laughed. "Put that in, too, Carlos. That way your reader will *really* know what you mean by trouble." Another time, Elena was reading to the class in Spanish the story of a marvelous garden, and she came across a description of a beet that was six inches wide. She paused for a moment and reached across the desk for a ruler, handing it to Arely. "*Mija*, show us how big that beet was." Arely counted four, five, six on the ruler. "Whoa!" said Alex. "Big, huh?" And yet another time, Elena was working with a group of students on their marine research when Alex walked over from the Writer's Table to get her attention: he needed a definition of *admire*. She looked up, defined it, and, as he was walking away, called to him and asked if he admired the farmer in a story they had read that morning. He turned back and thought for a moment: "No." No he didn't, thereby applying the new definition to a familiar character. She was masterful at extending a child's knowledge at every turn of the classroom day.

This affirmation of potential was deeply egalitarian. It did not stratify children by some assessment of their readiness or ability or by judgments based on their background or record. It assumed ability and curiosity; learning, in this belief system, became an entitlement. In Elena's words, "You can't deny anybody the opportunity to learn. That's their right." Bilingual education gained special meaning in this context. There is a long history in California schools, and Southwestern schools in general, of Mexican culture, language, and intelligence being deprecated. (Mexican children, one representative educator wrote in 1920, "are primarily interested in action and emotion, but grow listless under purely mental effort."[7]) The profound limits on the quality of education that stemmed from such practice and perception made all the more understandable the commitment of these Calexico teachers to bilingual education. Bilingual education was not just a method; it was an affirmation of cultural and linguistic worth, an affirmation of the mind of a people. It fit into a broader faith that, as Evangelina said before her Teaching of Reading class one afternoon, "all children have minds and souls and have the ability to participate fully in the society, and education is a way to achieve that."

These egalitarian beliefs, from what I could tell, had multiple origins and played out in life and work in complicated ways.

There was a civic base to the teaching of Elena and her colleagues. They took seriously their nation's best promise, held to it against that same nation's abuses of equality. There were pictures of Washington and Lincoln in their classrooms, the flag, the Pledge of Allegiance—icons and credos placed against those forces which have created barriers to the growth of children like the ones in Calexico. Teaching was a means of effecting social change. "Any child can learn," said Carmen. "Any child. They have to be given a fair chance."

On a more personal level, each teacher spoke about a teacher of her own who validated her intellectual worth, who demonstrated to her the power of having someone believe in a student's ability. For Carmen, it was a Mrs. Self; for Jessie, a Mrs. Hems, someone "who gave me the incentive to try my best." Also of critical importance was that Elena, Carmen, and the others shared a history and a community. They knew the families of the kids they taught, knew the streets they lived on and the cultural pathways open or closed to them. This familiarity, of course, widened their sphere of influence—as Jessie said, it's easy to "see a kid on the street and tell him to come by"—but on a deeper level, where heart and instruction intersect, they identified with the children they taught. As Evangelina explained, "When you see that third-grader, you're seeing yourself. You think, 'If someone had done this for me when I was in third grade, how much better my education would have been.' " This was an identification that had significant pedagogical consequences.

Though the teachers certainly had strong community bonds—and in their professional lives they overcame the isolation of the classroom by working together and by involving themselves in unions and educational lobbies—though these bonds were strong, Carmen and the others defied easy ideological distinctions by also putting great weight on individual responsibility. They believed that if one was self-reliant and worked hard, one would succeed. "It's a big thing here to be a teacher," Evangelina explained, "and it's achievable." There seemed to be few illusions about the effects structured social inequalities could have on this success. "You have to work twice as hard," as Elena put it. Because of race and class, it would be a difficult life; all the more reason to develop a resilient inner core. Their family histories were histories of hard work, and they respected those histories, derived from them a personal mythology of strength and endurance. In turn, they have worked hard to enter a profession and develop a sense of institutional efficacy. They believed they could make a difference and pushed themselves to do so.

Given this blend of egalitarianism and individualism, it was no surprise that they had high expectations for their students. This was surely true for Elena. The majority of the children I saw in Room 42 had entered in September with the designation "low achiever" or, in some cases, "slow learner." Elena's response was to assume that they had developed some unproductive habits and were sabotaging their own intelligence. "The first two weeks, it was difficult," she explained one noontime when we were all sitting around the Writer's Table. "I'd put them here to write—and they'd fool around. It took them a while to figure it out, it took time, with me talking to them. 'This is *your* education,' I'd say. 'It's your responsibility. I'm here to support you, but you have to do the work.'" It was warm that day, Elena's sleeves rolled up, the paper fish hanging motionless. She spoke emphatically, with a nod or an exclamation or a quick laugh, her finger tapping the table, her hand slicing the air. "I had to keep some in at recess to finish the work. I had to talk to them. But then . . . look at them now. They're bright kids. They're not underachievers; they're not slow. They were just used to doing what they could get by with." Her room was constructed on work and opportunity. "You can't say 'I can't' in this classroom. You have to try." And that cut both ways.

If you believe so firmly in the potential of all your students, you have few ready explanations for their failure. The first line of scrutiny is oneself. "What you do is not necessarily good for everyone," Elena would say. "You have to try different things. You have to ask yourself, 'What can I change that will work for a child who's not learning?'" When a student was not doing well, Elena would assume she was failing and put herself through a rigorous self-assessment. "Why am I not teaching him," she would ask, her record book open, the child's work spread out in front of her.

Elena's sense of the role of the teacher fit with my own, but spending time with her helped me understand the tension inherent in such a position, the power and the limits of individual force of mind.

Roberto was a sweet, quiet boy who seemed to understand his classwork, would do it when Elena was assisting him, but would just not complete it on his own. "I don't know what to do to get him motivated," she said. "I tried structuring things more, and I tried letting him pursue whatever he wanted. He's a smart boy—I'm doing something wrong. What am I missing?" One day when Elena was sitting with Roberto, encouraging him to write a little more on a story, he suddenly started crying. His mother had left home, and he was sent to stay with his grandmother. He missed his mother terribly and was afraid that his grandmother, who was ailing, would die and leave him alone. How could he concentrate, Elena thought, when his very security was threatened? This was beyond anything she could influence. It was telling, though, that Elena didn't entirely let up. She told him he could talk to her anytime he felt sad, and that she would ease off a little—on him, I suspect, more than herself—but that "they both had a responsibility to teach and learn," and that the best thing he could do was to learn what he could so he would someday be able to take care of himself. "We both have to try," she said, holding him, wanting to make for him, as best she could, her classroom a place of love and learning. In Elena's mind, the consequences for Roberto's future of his not learning to read and write and compute were too great to ignore, even in sorrow.

Among the teachers I got to know in Calexico, the response to hardship was a firm resolve to try harder. On the day of my visit to Carmen's classroom, a San Diego newspaper ran a story on the social and economic problems plaguing the California Latino community and the impact those problems were having on education. She and I talked about the article. "You know, Carmen," I finally said, "some would say that teachers like you are battling insurmountable odds." "The problems *are* big ones," she answered, "and they make me very angry. But everybody's got a job to do. The problems are not going to stop me from teaching."

All this was what it meant to care.

V

I sat in the booth across from Emily Palacio in the large, bright coffee shop of Hollie's Fiesta Motel. There were a few businessmen around us— insurance agents, merchants—and some of the mechanics from the Pep Boys down the street. From our window we could see the traffic lining up on Imperial, eight blocks from the border, and it felt good to settle into the thick Naugahyde cushions in the quiet dining room. Emily was the director of Curriculum Development for the Calexico Unified School District, and she was going to take me to a meeting of the school board. We had some time to kill, dallying with Pepsis, and at one point I asked her to talk about the classrooms I had been visiting, to give me the perspective from the district office. "You have to understand," she said, "the number of things that had to be put in place so that those teachers you saw can flourish." Emily's posture and movement suggested an athletic deliberateness—the result, I would learn, of a back injury—but her strong, almost formal, bearing was counterpointed by a friendly directness.

"Bilingual education," she continued, "is a good example. When I first started teaching, in 1969, we still weren't allowed to use Spanish in the classroom. And, to be honest, when we got our first bilingual ed money, I wasn't sure it would work. There was resistance from some of the Mexican parents too—it's really important to them that their kids learn English—and, well, I was skeptical." She paused, twirling the wrapper from her straw around her fingers. "But then I started reading some research that impressed me, and I looked closely at our kids who were being taught to read in Spanish—and paradoxically they were learning English better than those we moved into English early. I knew then what we had to do." She smoothed out the wrapper and started over. "Nothing came easy. We convinced the parents to let us try things, but got a lot of resistance from some teachers who were monolingual and from some of the city leaders in Calexico. We had to work very hard. It was a struggle. But the leadership was changing here, and slowly, slowly things turned around."

As we continued to talk, me asking her about her own history as well as the more recent history of the district, I heard the same affirmations of potential I had heard from the teachers—"we just don't believe that our kids can't succeed"—spoken from the same kind of personal base. "My father stressed that his children would get an education so that we could help our people." And I heard, as well, a broad linguistic range put to the service of those beliefs. In our time in the restaurant, and during a subsequent visit to her office, I listened as Emily spoke both informal and highly educated Spanish and English, shifted into policy-speak on the phone to the state capital, and adopted the language of educational research—she had done graduate work at Claremont—when talking to a reporter. I would sit back, thinking about the ways in which that fluency affected the classrooms in which Elena, Carmen, Veronica, and the others did their work.

Emily was right: even the most individually brilliant teaching takes place in a historical and political context. There was so much that had to be achieved: the changes in Calexico's power base; the federal-level policy and legislation involving bilingual education, affirmative action, and increased support for education and the resulting availability of loans and scholarships for economically disadvantaged students; the movement of bilingual teachers, both Latino and Anglo, into the work force; new blood in administration; a decent working relationship between the school board and administration (this was recent—a not-so-old joke had it that in Calexico there were three superintendents, the one who just left, the one here now, and the one on the way); the documented successes the schools were having and the sense of pride and purpose this evidence gave to the community about its schools. Hard-won achievements that made further achievement possible.

Emily and I haggled a little over who would pay the bill. We split it, and headed for the offices of the Calexico Unified School District, down Highway 98 to Andrade Avenue on the outskirts of town. I followed Emily's car, the sun low in the sky. Driving through the city, away from the center of things, I thought more about what Emily said, about all the lines of history and power that intersect in one classroom—or circles, concentric circles moving inward from the activism of a previous era, the pain and optimism that made a good classroom possible. Emily's blinker came on, and I turned with a bounce onto Andrade. Palm trees. Open fields. The district office.

The meeting opened with a greeting by the two student representatives on the school board—Lorena and Lizette, both from Calexico High—and proceeded to presentations of awards for Student of the Month. The meeting was taking place right at the time of a regional science fair, so a display of some of the work of Calexico students came next. One young woman told us about studying the reproductive cycle of the whitefly, an insect that had devastated crops in the Valley. A young man explained a research project on the relation between hormone levels in cows and the production of milk. The members of the board sat back while the students spoke. Their posture seemed to say: This is our reason for being.

Then Roberto Morales, the board member with the longest tenure, thanked the students and turned the board toward its administrative agenda. After a number of items dealing with planning and budget came new business: the head of the Chamber of Commerce wanted to honor the schools by putting a photo of the district office on the cover of a promotional brochure. More business. Then another board member, Refugio Gonzales, the director of the University of California Agricultural Extension in the Valley, steered the meeting on a different course. The national meeting of the Mexican-American Legal Defense and Education Fund, MALDEF, was to take place soon, and he wondered whether someone from the board could present data on Calexico's success. "There is so much press about Hispanic failure, I'd like to let people know that there are programs in which Hispanic students are doing well."

On the side of the meeting room, along the west wall, were two architectural models of the schools the district was planning to build. One, a middle school, was going to be named in honor of Willie Moreno, one of the 1960s' activists who worked hard to get Mexican Americans elected to Calexico's school board and city council. I thought about his legacy—evident in this board room—and about the growing importance of the achievements of Calexico's students. The community was inspired by its students, and it was this feeling of hope that made possible effective school governance: the effect of hope on structure and function, the way it can open political space and foster common cause.

But as Willie Moreno certainly knew, the alliances and commitments necessary for progress are tenuous. Previous boards and administrations had been at each other's throats—superintendents kept coming and going—and though that relationship has, during the last few years, been amicable, there were some conflicts brewing between the teachers' union and the administration over benefits. The conflict was potentially volatile, because California was in the middle of a financial crisis, and school budgets were being cut. Could the differences be worked through? On another front, would the long-standing friction between older Calexicans and new arrivals from Mexico worsen and be reflected in school politics? Or would personal rivalries among the city's power brokers erupt into crippling disputes? For now, this was only worrisome speculation; there was broad-based support for the schools and for new ideas. Alex, Arely, Carlos, Irianna, and the others were having an influence on school governance beyond what they knew, and what happened in this room over the next span of years would, in turn, have a profound influence on them.

Down the hall after the board meeting into the superintendent's office. Roberto Moreno (no relation to Willie) spoke easily, steadily. A tall, muscular man, quietly enthusiastic, sweeping his hair away from his eyes. He was born and raised in Calexico and married his high school sweetheart, who was now a counselor at a neighboring high school. As a teacher or administrator, he had been in the district for more than twenty years, except for some time at Stanford to do graduate work. He still looked young.

"We're not in a position," he was saying, "we don't have the resources to invent—it takes a lot of money to develop curriculum from scratch . . . we just can't do that. But we're great at implementing the good things that we find. We might have to beg, borrow, or steal it, but we can apply a good idea. And the board is supportive of innovation and risk.

"We've got some great teachers," he continued, rocking back in an old swivel chair. "A few of them are brilliant. But more so, it's a bunch of ordinary people rising to the occasion, ordinary people doing outstanding work. Our goal is to create the conditions for that to happen." He brought the chair forward, his elbows resting on his knees. "They're always on the lookout, and so are we. Something good appears, and we ask, 'What's this program about? What are the underlying concepts? Can we make it work for us?' Then"—he laughed—"then we try to find the funds to do it."

I had met the person who scouts for those funds, Mary Camacho, director of State and Federal Projects. The district couldn't survive without such assistance, and Mary was compiling an impressive record of securing it from government agencies, industry, and private foundations. Originally a home economics teacher at the high school, she had become an assistant principal, then moved into the district office, where she learned about grantsmanship. "I was told to try things," she said. "A lot of us here are home-grown. We might go away to school, but some come back, and we develop here. I just learned from a lot of people who were generous with their time. This is the kind of place where, if you have an idea, you're encouraged to pursue it."

One of the ideas that had been stirring excitement in the district office originated several years ago with an enterprising middle school English teacher, Gretchen Laue. Gretchen wanted to turn the summer session at her school into a lab school, a place where teachers could learn new methods and students would benefit from an enriched language arts curriculum. She applied for and received a grant from the state, and the project proved a local success. This past year, Roberto suggested to Emily Palacio that they apply Gretchen's idea to summer school for all the district's elementary grades. Get them early. "Be inventive," Roberto told Emily, so Emily decided to reconceive summer school for elementary students in Calexico's public schools.

Summer school had typically been remedial in nature, instruction in basics for kids who weren't doing well or for the children of new arrivals from Mexicali. But Emily didn't want it to be remedial; she wanted it to be an academy, a lab school for teachers and a site of enrichment for students. And she wanted to affect a number of subjects: math, language arts, music, and art. School restructuring that was not merely organizational but involved a new way of thinking about what children could do.

She developed a plan. There would be four expert teachers hired as coaches for each of the subjects. They would conduct workshops for the teachers, visit their classes, do demonstration lessons with their students, and consult with them. According to one pattern, the coach would conduct a lesson before a teacher's class; the teacher would do a follow-up lesson and then a third related lesson, with the coach observing and providing feedback. The new approaches would become part of the teachers' repertoires and, Emily hoped, would be carried over into the regular academic year, thereby extending the benefits of the experiment. Eddie Hernandez was hired as the art coach, and Evangelina Bustamente Jones was brought in to supervise language arts. One of the teachers, it turned out, was Jessie Carillo.

The program took place in the summer after my visit, and Evangelina told me about it by phone.

The language arts curriculum emphasized poetry, revising and editing, and various methods of collaboration. There were thirty teachers involved and about 850 students. From what Evangelina could tell, it was a big success, and Emily, Mary, and Roberto were thinking about funding for next year. The children wrote poetry, letters, and stories in Spanish, English, or both, and composed responses to each other's work. At the end of the program, the students in each class selected the writing they liked best, and it was displayed as part of a celebration that extended across several schools. They were given forms on which they could respond to the work of other children that struck them. "Your writing made me feel _____" was one item on the form; "I'd like to know more about _____" was another. These forms were then returned to the original author.

Evangelina read to me some pieces she had copied down. There were metaphors by first-graders, written as they were encouraged to let their imaginations play over a bowl of popcorn: "Popcorn tastes like haunted candy" and "Popcorn looks like crumpled flowers." There were majestic descriptions of fireworks—Fourth of July fare—produced by fifth-graders: "Under attack, neon fireballs turn with rays curving around them" and "Different colors of fluorescent confetti fall to the ground." And there was this reflection written by a third-grader as she listened to a recording of flute music:

> I was in the ocean and there were lots of leaves and trees.
> I was on a rock on the water. I was singing and touching
> the water by myself and I felt like the world barely started.

NOTES

1. On the history of Calexico and the Imperial Valley: Tracey Henderson, *Imperial Valley* (San Diego: Neyenesch Printers, 1968); Otis B. Tout, *The First Thirty Years: Being an Account of the Principal Events in the History of Imperial Valley Southern California, U.S.A.* (San Diego: Arts and Crafts Press, 1931; reprinted, Imperial County Historical Society, 1990).

2. School statistics: Emily Palacio, personal communication, August 1994; Ernesto Portillo, Jr., "In Calexico Schools, a Major Turnaround" *San Diego Union Tribune,* Aug. 9, 1992, pp. B1, B2.

3. "A sketch of Calexico's history": see note #1. Also see Albert Camarillo, *Chicanos in California: A History of Mexican Americans in California* (San Francisco: Boyd and Fraser Publishing, 1984).

4. "God and civilization": quoted in Héctor Calderón, "Reinventing the Border," in Barbara Roche Rico and Sandra Mano, *American Mosaic: Multicultural Readings in Context* (Boston: Houghton Mifflin, 1991, pp. 554–562).

5. On bilingual education: Kenji Hakuta, *Mirror of Language: The Debate on Bilingualism* (New York: Basic Books, 1986); François Grosjean, *Life with Two Languages: An Introduction to Bilingualism* (Cambridge: Harvard University Press, 1982); Heinz Kloss, *The American Bilingual Tradition* (Rowley, MA: Newbury House, 1977); James Crawford, *Bilingual Education: History, Politics, Theory, and Practice* (Trenton, NJ: Crane, 1989); Harvey A. Daniels, ed., *Not only English: Affirming America's Multilingual Heritage* (Urbana, IL: NCTE, 1990); Ira Katznelson and Margaret Weir, *Schooling for All: Class, Race, and the Decline of the Democratic Ideal* (New York: Basic Books, 1985).

6. "The World Is a Rainbow": Little House Music (ASCAP), 1978. Young-heart Music Education Service, Los Angeles. Written by Greg Scelsa.

7. "primarily interested in action": quoted in Charles Wollenberg, *All Deliberate Speed: Segregation and Exclusion in California Schools, 1855–1975*, p. 113.

18

THE PEDAGOGY OF POVERTY
VERSUS GOOD TEACHING

Martin Haberman

WHY IS A "MINOR" ISSUE like improving the quality of urban teaching generally overlooked by the popular reform and restructuring strategies? There are several possibilities. First, we assume that we know what teaching is, that others know what it is, that we are discussing the same "thing" when we use the word, and that we would all know good teaching if we saw it. Second, we believe that, since most teachers cannot be changed anyway, there must be other, more potent, teacher-proof strategies for change. Third, why bother with teaching if research shows that achievement test scores of poor and minority youngsters are affected primarily by their socioeconomic class; affected somewhat by Head Start, school integration, and having a "strong" principal; and affected almost not at all by the quality of their teachers?

The Pedagogy of Poverty

An observer of urban classrooms can find examples of almost every form of pedagogy: direct instruction, cooperative learning, peer tutoring, individualized instruction, computer-assisted learning, behavior modification, the use of student contracts, media-assisted instruction, scientific inquiry, lecture/discussion, tutoring by specialists or volunteers, and even the use of problem-solving units common in progressive education. In spite of this broad range of options, however, there is a typical form of teaching that has become accepted as basic. Indeed, this basic urban style, which encompasses a body of specific teacher acts, seems to have grown stronger each year since I first noted it in 1958. A teacher in an urban school of the 1990s who did *not* engage in these basic acts as the primary means of instruction would be regarded as deviant. In most urban schools, not performing these acts for most of each day would be considered prima facie evidence of not teaching.

The teaching acts that constitute the core functions of urban teaching are:

o giving information
o asking questions
o giving directions
o making assignments
o monitoring seatwork
o reviewing assignments
o giving tests
o reviewing tests
o assigning homework
o reviewing homework
o settling disputes
o punishing noncompliance
o marking papers
o giving grades

This basic menu of urban teacher functions characterizes all levels and subjects. A primary teacher might "give information" by reading a story to children, while a high school teacher might read to the class from a biology text. (Interestingly, both offer similar reasons: "The students can't read for themselves," and "They enjoy being read to.") Taken separately, there may be nothing wrong with these activities. There are occasions when any one of the 14 acts might have a beneficial effect. Taken together and performed to the systematic exclusion of other acts, they have become the pedagogical coin of the realm in urban schools. They constitute the pedagogy of poverty—not merely what teachers do and what youngsters expect but, for different reasons, what parents, the community, and the general public assume teaching to be.

Ancillary to this system is a set of out-of-class teacher acts that include keeping records, conducting parent conferences, attending staff meetings, and carrying out assorted school duties. While these out-of-class functions are not directly instructional, they are performed in ways that support the pedagogy of poverty. Since this analysis deals with the direct interactions characteristic of urban teachers and their students, I will limit myself to a brief comment about how each of these out-of-class functions is typically conceptualized and performed in urban settings.

- ○ *Record-keeping* is the systematic maintenance of a paper trail to protect the school against any future legal action by its clients. Special classes, referrals, test scores, disciplinary actions, and analyses by specialists must be carefully recorded. This slant is the reason that teachers are commonly prejudiced rather than informed by reading student records; yet the system regards their upkeep as vital. (In teacher preparation, neophytes are actually taught that student records will reveal such valuable information as students' interests!)

- ○ *Parent conferences* give parents who are perceived as poorly educated or otherwise inadequate a chance to have things explained to them.

- ○ *Staff meetings* give administrators opportunities to explain things to teachers.

- ○ *Assorted school duties* are essentially police or monitoring activities that would be better performed by hired guards.

The pedagogy of poverty appeals to several constituencies:

1. It appeals to those who themselves did not do well in schools. People who have been brutalized are usually not rich sources of compassion. And those who have failed or done poorly in school do not typically take personal responsibility for that failure. They generally find it easier to believe that they would have succeeded if only somebody had *forced* them to learn.

2. It appeals to those who rely on common sense rather than on thoughtful analysis. It is easy to criticize humane and developmental teaching aimed at educating a free people as mere "permissiveness," and it is well known that "permissiveness" is the root cause of our nation's educational problems.

3. It appeals to those who fear minorities and the poor. Bigots typically become obsessed with the need for control.

4. It appeals to those who have low expectations for minorities and the poor. People with limited vision frequently see value in limited and limiting forms of pedagogy. They believe that at-risk students are served best by a directive, controlling pedagogy.

5. It appeals to those who do not know the full range of pedagogical options available. This group includes most school administrators, most business and political reformers, and many teachers.

There are essentially four syllogisms that undergird the pedagogy of poverty. Their "logic" runs something like this.

1. Teaching is what teachers do. Learning is what students do. There-fore, students and teachers are engaged in different activities.

2. Teachers are in charge and responsible. Students are those who still need to develop appropriate behavior. Therefore, when students fol-low teachers' directions, appropriate behavior is being taught and learned.

3. Students represent a wide range of individual differences. Many stu-dents have handicapping conditions and lead debilitating home lives. Therefore, ranking of some sort is inevitable; some students will end up at the bottom of the class while others will finish at the top.

4. Basic skills are a prerequisite for learning and living. Students are not necessarily interested in basic skills. Therefore, directive peda-gogy must be used to ensure that youngsters are compelled to learn their basic skills.

Reform and the Pedagogy of Poverty

Unfortunately, the pedagogy of poverty does not work. Youngsters achieve neither minimum levels of life skills nor what they are capable of learning. The classroom atmosphere created by constant teacher direction and student compliance seethes with passive resentment that sometimes bubbles up into overt resistance. Teachers burn out because of the emo-tional and physical energy that they must expend to maintain their author-ity every hour of every day. The pedagogy of poverty requires that teachers who begin their careers intending to be helpers, models, guides, stimulators, and caring sources of encouragement transform themselves into directive authoritarians in order to function in urban schools. But people who choose to become teachers do not do so because at some point they decided, "I want to be able to tell people what to do all day and then make them do it!" This gap between expectations and reality means that there is a pervasive, fundamental, irreconcilable difference between the motivation of those who select themselves to become teach-ers and the demands of urban teaching.

For the reformers who seek higher scores on achievement tests, the pedagogy of poverty is a source of continual frustration. The clear-cut need to "make" students learn is so obviously vital to the common good and to the students themselves that surely (it is believed) there must be a way to force students to work hard enough to vindicate the methodology. Simply stated, we act as if it is not the pedagogy that must be fitted to the students but the students who must accept an untouchable method.

In reality, the pedagogy of poverty is not a professional methodology at all. It is not supported by research, by theory, or by the best practice of superior urban teachers. It is actually certain ritualistic acts that, much like the ceremonies performed by religious functionaries, have come to be conducted for their intrinsic value rather than to foster learning.

There are those who contend that the pedagogy of poverty would work if only the youngsters accepted it and worked at it. "Ay, there's the rub!" Students in urban schools overwhelmingly *do* accept the pedagogy of poverty, and they *do* work at it! Indeed, any teacher who believes that he or she can take on an urban teaching assignment and ignore the pedagogy of poverty will be quickly crushed by the students themselves. Examples abound of inexperienced teachers who seek to involve students in genuine learning activities and are met with apathy or bedlam, while older hands who announce, "Take out your dictionaries and start to copy the words that begin with *h*," are rewarded with compliance or silence.

Reformers of urban schools are now raising their expectations beyond an emphasis on basic skills to the teaching of critical thinking, problem solving, and even creativity. But if the pedagogy of poverty will not force the learning of low-level skills, how can it be used to compel genuine thinking? Heretofore, reformers have promulgated change strategies that deal with the level of funding, the role of the principal, parent involvement, decentralization, site-based management, choice, and other organizational and policy reforms. At some point, they must reconsider the issue of pedagogy. If the actual mode of instruction expected by school administrators and teachers and demanded by students and their parents continues to be the present one, then reform will continue to deal with all but the central issue: How and what are students taught?

The pedagogy of poverty is sufficiently powerful to undermine the implementation of any reform effort because it determines the way pupils spend their time, the nature of the behaviors they practice, and the bases of their self-concepts as learners. Essentially, it is a pedagogy in which learners can "succeed" without becoming either involved or thoughtful.

The Nature of Urban Children and Youth

When he accepted the 1990 New York City Teacher of the Year Award, John Taylor Gatto stated that no school reform will work that does not provide children time to grow up or that simply forces them to deal with abstractions. Without blaming the victims, he described his students as lacking curiosity (having "evanescent attention"), being indifferent to the adult world, and having a poor sense of the future. He further characterized them as ahistorical, cruel and lacking in compassion, uneasy with intimacy and candor, materialistic, dependent, and passive—although they frequently mask the last two traits with a surface bravado.

Anyone who would propose specific forms of teaching as alternatives to the pedagogy of poverty must recognize that Gatto's description of his students is only the starting point. These are the attributes that have been enhanced and elicited by an authoritarian pedagogy and do not represent students' true or ultimate natures. Young people can become more and different, but they must be taught how. This means to me that two conditions must pertain before there can be a serious alternative to the pedagogy of poverty: the whole school faculty and school community—not the individual teacher—must be the unit of change; and there must be patience and persistence of application, since students can be expected to resist changes to a system they can predict and know how to control. Having learned to navigate in urban schools based on the pedagogy of poverty, students will not readily abandon all their know-how to take on willy-nilly some new and uncertain system that they may not be able to control.

For any analysis of pedagogical reform to have meaning in urban schools, it is necessary to understand something of the dynamics of the teacher/student interactions in those schools. The authoritarian and directive nature of the pedagogy of poverty is somewhat deceptive about who is really in charge. Teachers seem to be in charge, in that they direct students to work on particular tasks, allot time, dispense materials, and choose the means of evaluation to be used. It is assumed by many that having control over such factors makes teachers "decision makers" who somehow shape the behavior of their students.

But below this facade of control is another, more powerful level on which students actually control, manage, and shape the behavior of their teachers. Students reward teachers by complying. They punish by resisting. In this way students mislead teachers into believing that some things "work" while other things do not. By this dynamic, urban children and youth effectively negate the values promoted in their teachers' teacher education and undermine the nonauthoritarian predispositions that led their teachers to enter the field. And yet, most teachers are not particularly sensitive to being manipulated by students. They believe they are in control and are responding to "student needs," when, in fact, they are more like hostages responding to students' overt or tacit threats of noncompliance and, ultimately, disruption.

It cannot be emphasized enough that, in the real world, urban teachers are never defined as incompetent because their "deprived," "disadvantaged," "abused," "low-income" students are not learning. Instead, urban teachers are castigated because they cannot elicit compliance. Once schools made teacher competence synonymous with student control, it was inevitable that students would sense who was really in charge.

The students' stake in maintaining the pedagogy of poverty is of the strongest possible kind: it absolves them of responsibility for learning and puts the burden on the teachers, who must be accountable for *making* them learn. In their own unknowing but crafty way, students do not want to trade a system in which they can make their teachers ineffective for one in which they would themselves become accountable and responsible for what they learn. It would be risky for students to swap a "try and make me" system for one that says, "Let's see how well and how much you really can do."

Recognizing the formidable difficulty of institutionalizing other forms of pedagogy, it is still worthwhile to define and describe such alternative forms. The few urban schools that serve as models of student learning have teachers who maintain control by establishing trust and involving their students in meaningful activities rather than by imposing some neat system of classroom discipline. For genuinely effective urban teachers, discipline and control are primarily a *consequence* of their teaching and not a *prerequisite* condition of learning. Control, internal or imposed, is a continuous fact of life in urban classrooms—but, for these teachers, it is completely interrelated with the learning activity at hand.

Good Teaching

Is it possible to describe a teaching approach that can serve as an alternative to the pedagogy of poverty? I believe that there is a core of teacher acts that defines the pedagogy one finds in urban schools that have been recognized as exemplary. Unlike the directive teacher acts that constitute the pedagogy of poverty, however, these tend to be indirect activities that frequently involve the creation of a learning environment. These teaching behaviors tend to be evident more in what the students are doing than in the observable actions of the teacher. Indeed, teachers may appear to be doing little and at times may, to the unsophisticated visitor, seem to be merely observers. Good teaching transcends the particular grade or subject and even the need for lessons with specific purposes.[1]

Whenever students are involved with issues they regard as vital concerns, good teaching is going on. In effective schools, the endless "problems"—the censoring of a school newspaper, an issue of school safety, a racial flare-up, the dress code—are opportunities for important learning. In good schools, problems are not viewed as occasions to impose more rules and tighter management from above. Far from being viewed as obstacles to the "normal" school routine, difficult events and issues are transformed into the very stuff of the curriculum. Schooling is living, not preparation for living. And living is a constant messing with problems that seem to resist solution.

Whenever students are involved with explanations of human differences, good teaching is going on. As students proceed through school, they should be developing ever greater understanding of human differences. Why are there rich people and poor people, abled and disabled, urban and rural, multilingual and monolingual, highly educated and poorly educated? Differences in race, culture, religion, ethnicity, and gender are issues that children and youths reconsider constantly in an effort to make sense of the world, its relationships, and their place in it. This is not "social studies." All aspects of the curriculum should deepen students' basic understandings of these persistent facts of life.

Whenever students are being helped to see major concepts, big ideas, and general principles and are not merely engaged in the pursuit of isolated facts, good teaching is going on. At all levels and in all subjects, key concepts can be made meaningful and relevant. Students cannot be successful graduates without having at some point been exposed to the various forms of knowledge. Historians deal with the nature of sources; artists, with texture, color, and design. A fundamental goal of education is to instill in students the ability to use various and competing ways of understanding the universe. Knowing how to spell is not enough.

Whenever students are involved in planning what they will be doing, it is likely that good teaching is going on. This planning involves real choices and not such simple preferences as what crayon to use or the order in which a set of topics will be discussed. Students may be asked to select a topic for study, to decide what resources they will need, or to plan how they will present their findings to others. People learn to make informed choices by actually making informed choices. Following directions—even perfectly—does not prepare people to make choices and to deal with the consequences of those choices.

Whenever students are involved with applying ideals such as fairness, equity, or justice to their world, it is likely that good teaching is going on. Students of any age can, at some level, try to apply great ideals to their everyday lives. The environment, war, human relationships, and health care are merely a few examples of issues that students can be thinking about. Determining what should be done about particular matters and defending their ideas publicly gives students experience in developing principles to live by. Character is built by students who have had practice at comparing ideals with reality in their own lives and in the lives of those around them.

Whenever students are actively involved, it is likely that good teaching is going on. Doing an experiment is infinitely better than watching one or reading about one. Participating as a reporter, a role player, or an actor can be educational. Constructing things can be a vital activity. We need graduates who have learned to take action in their own behalf and in behalf of others.

Whenever students are directly involved in a real-life experience, it is likely that good teaching is going on. Field trips, interactions with resource people, and work and life experiences are all potentially vital material for analysis. Firsthand experience is potentially more educational than vicarious activity, *provided* it is combined with reflection.

Whenever students are actively involved in heterogeneous groups, it is likely that good teaching is going on. Students benefit from exposure to cultural as well as intellectual heterogeneity, and they learn from one another. Divergent questioning strategies, multiple assignments in the same class, activities that allow for alternative responses and solutions all contribute to learning. Grouping in schools is frequently based on artificial criteria that are not used in life. Grouping can either limit or enhance students' self-concept and self-esteem and thus has a powerful effect on future learning.

Whenever students are asked to think about an idea in a way that questions common sense or a widely accepted assumption, that relates new ideas to ones learned previously, or that applies an idea to the problems of living, then there is a chance that good teaching is going on. Students are taught to compare, analyze, synthesize, evaluate, generalize, and specify in the process of developing thinking skills. The effort to educate thoughtful people should be guided by school activities that involve thought. The acquisition of information—even of skills—without the ability to think is an insufficient foundation for later life.

Whenever students are involved in redoing, polishing, or perfecting their work, it is likely that good teaching is going on. It is in the act of review, particularly review of one's own work, that important learning occurs. This technique may involve an art project or a science experiment as well as a piece of writing. The successful completion of anything worthwhile rarely occurs in a single trial. Students can learn that doing things over is not punishment but an opportunity to excel.

Whenever teachers involve students with the technology of information access, good teaching is going on. Teachers, texts, and libraries as they now exist will not be sufficient in the future. Computer literacy—beyond word processing—is a vital need. As James Mecklenburger points out, "Electronic learning must play a more important part in the mix, even at the expense of customary practices. Today, students and educators alike can create, receive, collect, and share data, text, images, and sounds on myriad topics in ways more stimulating, richer, and more timely than ever before."[2]

Whenever students are involved in reflecting on their own lives and how they have come to believe and feel as they do, good teaching is going on. Autobiography can be the basis of an exceedingly powerful pedagogy—one that is largely discarded after early childhood education. When critics dismiss my characterization of the pedagogy of poverty as an exaggeration, I am reminded of an immense sign hanging in an urban high school that has devoted itself totally to raising test scores: "We dispense knowledge. Bring your own container." This approach is the opposite of good teaching, which is the process of building environments, providing experiences, and then eliciting responses that can be reflected on. Autobiographical activities are readily extended into studies of family, neighborhood, and community. What could be more fundamental to subsequent learning than self-definition? Urban schools, in the way they narrowly structure the role of the teacher and restrict the content to be taught, too frequently repudiate the students and their home lives. The vision of good teaching as a process of "drawing out" rather than "stuffing in" is supported by diverse philosophies, including, most recently, feminist theories of the teaching/learning process.[3]

The Rewards of Not Changing

Taken individually, any of these indicators of good teaching is not a sufficient basis for proposing reform. We all know teachers who have done some of these things—as well as other, better things—for years. Taken together and practiced schoolwide and persistently, however, these suggestions can begin to create an alternative to the pedagogy of poverty.

Unfortunately, we must recognize that it may no longer be possible to give up the present authoritarianism. The incentives for the various constituencies involved may well have conditioned them to derive strong benefits from the pedagogy of poverty and to see only unknown risk in the options.

In the present system, teachers are accountable only for engaging in the limited set of behaviors commonly regarded as acts of teaching in urban schools—that is, the pedagogy of poverty. Students can be held accountable only for complying with precisely what they have specifically and carefully been directed to do. Administrators can be held accountable only for maintaining safe buildings; parents, only for knowing where their children are. Each constituency defines its own responsibilities as narrowly as possible to guarantee itself "success" and leave to others the broad and difficult responsibility for integrating students' total educations.

Who is responsible for seeing that students derive meaning and apply what they have learned from this fragmented, highly specialized, overly directive schooling? It is not an accident that the present system encourages each constituency to blame another for the system's failure. My argument here is that reforms will "take" only if they are supported by a system of pedagogy that has never been tried in any widespread, systematic, long-term way. What prevents its implementation is the resistance of the constituencies involved—constituencies that have a stake in maintaining their present roles, since they are, in effect, unaccountable for educating skilled, thoughtful citizens.

Continuing to define nonthinking, underdeveloped, unemployable youngsters as "adults" or "citizens" simply because they are high school graduates or passers of the General Education Development (GED) examination is irresponsible. Education will be seriously reformed only after we move it from a matter of "importance" to a matter of "life and death," both for society and for the individuals themselves. Graduates who lack basic skills may be unemployable and represent a personal and societal tragedy. However, graduates who possess basic skills but are partially informed, unable to think, and incapable of making moral choices are downright dangerous. Before we can *make* workers, we must first *make* people. But people are not *made*—they are conserved and grown.

NOTES

1. James D. Raths, "Teaching Without Specific Objectives," *Educational Leadership*, April 1971, pp. 714–20.

2. James A. Mecklenburger, "Educational Technology Is Not Enough," *Phi Delta Kappan*, October 1990, p. 108.

3. Madeleine Grumet, *Women and Teaching* (Amherst: University of Massachusetts Press, 1988), p. 99.

19

THE IMMENSITY
OF CHILDREN'S LEARNING

Frank Smith

DO YOU KNOW THE NUMBER of words children have learned by the time they get to school at the age of five or six? If all parents and teachers were familiar with this figure they might have some understanding of how much learning children are capable of accomplishing without formal instruction, tests, and all of the other rigmarole that goes along with our educational systems. The answer is that by the age of six children have a vocabulary of about 10,000 words.

They don't all know the same 10,000 words, of course. They know 10,000 words that their friends know. They don't know all the words their teachers know—but they probably know some words their teachers don't know. Since birth, children have been learning new words at the rate of 2,000 per year, without conspicuous effort or organized instruction—and without any forgetting. Psychologist George Miller calculated that infants are learning (and remembering) one new word for every hour they are awake. (If that is true, the children he studied couldn't have been sleeping very much.[1]

Why are most teachers unaware of all this inconspicuous learning, given that one of their primary concerns should be how much their students know? Part of the answer is that education professors—the teachers of teachers—usually focus on what they think teachers and students *can't do*. They emphasize the central role they believe must be played by outside experts (including themselves, of course).

Words Aren't Everything

I'm going to say a great deal about words, because that is one of the most conspicuous parts of anyone's language. It's not difficult to notice the relative richness or poverty of someone's vocabulary, and it is not much more difficult to estimate the size of it, though that is rarely done.

I shall also make some reference to grammar because that is another conspicuous aspect of language by which children, and adults as well, are frequently judged and compared.

But I don't want to suggest that language consists of just vocabulary and grammar, or even that they constitute the largest and most important part of our language learning. There is much about spoken language that is rarely talked about, such as phrasing, intonation, taking turns in conversation, and just how loud and long it is appropriate to say something, for the simple reason that it is *too complicated* to talk about. We don't know enough about these aspects of language to try to teach them so we tend to ignore them or to dismiss them as insignificant. The situation is the same in writing, where we concentrate on matters such as spelling and punctuation because they are conspicuous, but we give up on such vital but complicated matters as paragraphing, style, and the appropriate way in which to write different kinds of text for different audiences and different purposes, which all writers need to know about.

But the fact that there is much we aren't explicitly taught doesn't mean that we haven't been learning. We learn without knowing that we are learning. We learn without knowing *what* we are learning. In fact, there are many things we know that we don't know we have learned, though they dominate much of our behavior and our interactions with other people.

Take for example the matter of eye contact—how long you can look into someone's eyes and hold their gaze. This is an important issue for personal relationships. Two people gazing into each other's eyes are demonstrating intimacy. One person doing this while the other looks elsewhere is demonstrating authority. One person avoiding another's gaze is demonstrating embarrassment or wariness, if not shiftiness. The rules are incredibly precise—a couple of milliseconds makes a difference. But they are also incredibly complex—it makes a difference what you are talking about, with whom you are talking, and the circumstances in which you are talking.

The precise durations also differ from culture to culture—what is a respectful gaze in some societies is an insolent stare in another. The rules are not inherited, they are conventions that must be learned. Eye contact is so significant that babies are reluctant to give it before they learn how it is done in the community in which they find themselves. Try to look into a baby's eyes the first time you meet, and the baby will immediately look away. You will be allowed to hold a hand before you are permitted to hold a gaze.

There are other rules too—conventional rules about how close you may stand to another person, and how, where, and when you may touch them, all depending once again on the relationship between the participants, the business they are conducting, and where they are conducting it. And once again, the rules vary from culture to culture (as we often discover to our embarrassment). They must all be learned.

But whoever tried to teach us any of these things? How could they teach us, if we asked them to? How could we set about deliberately learning them for ourselves? This is all learning without awareness, without effort, without guidance or direction. Learning without knowing that we are learning, what we are learning, or what we have learned. It is learning from the classic point of view.[2]

Joining the Spoken Language Club

Children are effortlessly and inconspicuously learning an average of 20 words a day even before they begin school. So effortlessly and inconspicuously, in fact, that for a long time it was assumed that infants weren't learning anything or not learning very much, and anything they might be learning was probably wrong. The view fitted with a general picture of infants being ignorant and helpless, dependent on systematic instruction and formal education.

When it was realized that children were learning a great deal about language in the first years of their lives, another explanation was invented to take credit away from them. The argument was developed—and it is still prominent today—that little actual learning is involved in early language development because language is part of everyone's biological inheritance. It's in our genes. Some experts even assert that we are all born with a universal "language acquisition device" in our brains, from which the power to produce and understand speech unfolds practically fully formed.

This is nonsense. The language we speak is not a gift; we have to learn it, every bit. It has nothing to do with our ancestry. We may have Chinese forebears back to the year dot, but if we grow up in an English-speaking community we will learn English, and we will have as much difficulty as anyone else in learning Chinese later in our lives. Grow up in a Chinese-speaking environment and we will learn Chinese; Lithuanian and we will learn Lithuanian. More than 10,000 different languages are still in use throughout the world, and any child who is born anywhere in the world (with the rare and obvious exceptions of traumatized infants who can't learn any language at all) can learn any one of those 10,000 languages.

In fact, infants don't merely learn *language*. People don't speak languages, they speak dialects. I don't know how many hundreds of thousands of dialects there are in the world, but every child who is born is capable of learning a number of them—the dialects of the communities into which the child is born.

How do infants do it? The learning is, I think, rarely deliberately accomplished; it is not particularly desired. It is a byproduct, a consequence of something else far more important—the establishment of an identity. Infants are not born knowing the person they are, no matter how unique they might seem to us. Their identity is something to be learned, and they learn it from their observation of the people around them, the company they keep, in the clubs they join, from the people they take for granted they are like. And in the process of learning who they are, they learn about language and about many other things as well.

It begins at birth. Relatives and friends surround the baby and say in effect, "Welcome, stranger. You're one of us." And the baby looks up and responds, "Hi, folks. I must be just like you." That is all it takes—one single, mutual, unqualified act of affiliation and the baby is a fully-fledged member of a spoken language club, eligible to receive all the benefits.

The Benefits of Clubs

I employ the metaphor of a "spoken language club" to characterize the language community in which babies find themselves because the community offers babies exactly the kind of exclusive benefits or advantages that usually become available only through joining a club.

The first advantage of joining any club is that you find out what the club activities are. Before you join, what goes on in the club is a mystery, about which you can be ignorant if not misinformed. I am a member of a sailing club. Before I joined I assumed that the primary activity of the club was sailing. It wasn't until I was a member that I discovered that the closest some club members came to water was when they added a little to their whisky. Other members had a range of interests, from fiercely competitive racing to relaxed collaborative cruising. You don't need to be a particular kind of sailor to join a sailing club, you just have to identify with the other members. "You're one of us." "I'm just like you."

Language serves a number of purposes, none of which is self-evident. To say that the function of language is to communicate is a vast understatement—language can be used to create, conceal, narrate, or fabricate; to define and express oneself; and perhaps primarily, to establish relationships. And none of this is understood by infants before they join a language club; they aren't born with such knowledge and expectations. When infants join a spoken language club, established members reveal to them all the ways in which language is used, all of the things that it can do.

The second advantage of any club is that once you are a member and discover what activities are available to you, more experienced members help you to do those things that interest you. They don't *teach* you; they *help* you. There is no coercion, nor are there great expectations. No one cares how good you are (unless you choose to join a competitive team); you are simply accepted for who you are—a member of the club—and are helped to do what you are interested in doing. You gain security and confidence.

How Other Members Help

I'll be quite specific about the advantages of joining a spoken language club. No one forces you to talk in a particular way, nor are you evaluated on how well you are doing whatever you do. You are a member of the club. Instead, other members of the club

1. help you to say what you are trying to say,
2. help you to understand what you are trying to understand.

The helping to understand is the most important part. Children don't learn to talk by practicing talking—they hear other people talking and learn to talk like them. The learning is vicarious (this is *classic* learning). They don't have to do anything themselves. Other people talk—and the child begins talking like them.

Children don't often make mistakes as they learn to talk. From time to time they will invent a word, if they don't happen to know a convenient word that they want to use, and when they do invent, adults tend to think it is cute and tell one another about it. But most of the time children are learning silently and without error because the people around them are doing the talking and making the learning possible. The learning is so facile that most of the time we are not aware of it—until the child unexpectedly says something fluently outrageous and we ask ourselves, "Where on earth did she learn to say that?" We know immediately where she learned to say it, and we decide to start having our more intimate conversations in another room.

The basic requirement for effortless and essentially error-free learning from what others do is *understanding* what they are doing. To learn to say "Look at the big dog" or "Pass the ketchup, please" it's necessary to understand what other people are talking about when they say these things. And typically, this is what grownups (and older children) do when they talk in the presence of children. They spend a great deal of time giving *commentaries* on what they are doing and on the state of the world around them.

If there is anything innate about infant language learning, it is the compulsion that adults have to talk to babies before the babies can understand them. But if adults did not do this—if they waited for children's comprehension before they conversed with them—children would never learn to talk.

Introduced to a baby, most grownups immediately start a conversation: "So how are we today? Isn't that a great hat you're wearing? Look at the big dog over there." Grownups give commentaries: "Here's your juice. Let's change those wet socks. Isn't that the neighbor's cat coming down the driveway?"

At the same time, adults rush to help babies say whatever they think the baby is trying to say. An infant says, "Waw, waw, waw" and a grownup says, "Oh, you mean 'Please may I have a cookie.' "

The need of adults to engage in conversation with infants in no position to talk back to them seems so compelling that they will often borrow other people's babies to talk to, if they have none of their own. Or they'll talk to puppies and kittens.

Much of what is said around a child in the first few years of a child's life is self-explanatory. When an adult says to a child, "Here's your apple juice," it is usually obvious to the child what the adult is talking about— the adult is offering some juice. And when one adult says to another, "Here's your coffee," or, "I'll switch on the TV," it is again usually apparent what the adults are talking about.

It doesn't matter if the child misunderstands and makes a mistake of interpretation. No one knows that the child is learning in any case, and subsequent experience quickly puts the child right. And if the child has no idea about what is being said, so there is no possibility of learning, the child will quickly lose interest and turn attention elsewhere. The right to ignore anything that doesn't make sense is a crucial element of any child's learning—and the first right children are likely to lose when they get to the controlled learning environment of school.[3]

Learning Who We Are

Vocabulary isn't all that children learn without anyone knowing about it, and without practice. They learn how to put words together into powerful statements, assertions, and demands, which they express with authority and assurance. They don't put words together randomly, unless totally confused. All children talk systematically; they use grammar.

Children may not use the grammar their parents or teachers use, but their parents and teachers probably don't use the grammar *they* think they use. And no one speaks the grammar that is formally taught in schools. That is a grammar for autopsies, for the dissection of dead language on mortuary slabs of paper.

The grammar—or rather grammars—that all people learn to speak are dynamic grammars that enable us to produce and understand the language that expresses the identity and concerns of communities of people. The grammar and vocabulary that we learn is our cohesion with the communities with whom we identify. It is the reflection of who we are.

Most children, initially at least, learn to talk like their parents, with the same characteristic nuances, emphases, and intonation patterns. But very soon all children, in addition to (or instead of) speaking like their families, begin speaking like the people who will exert a far more powerful influence on their view of themselves and the world. They start talking like their friends.

Children start talking like the people with whom they most profoundly want to identify. They do so with exquisite precision. They do not learn to talk roughly like their friends or approximately like their friends. They learn to talk *exactly* like them, as if they were cloned. We may characterize the way they talk as bizarre or uneducated or even ignorant, but they do not make mistakes. This is very precise learning—and again it is accomplished without ostensible practice or conscious intention.

None of this is a behavioristic stimulus-response theory, incidentally. I am not saying that children learn to talk like the people they hear talking most. When they get to school children hear their teachers talking 90 percent of the time, with the other 10 percent divided up among the students. But children do not end up talking like their teachers—unless they would like to become teachers themselves.

Children learn many other things from their friends. They learn appropriate ways to walk, dress, and ornament themselves. They learn what to laugh at and what to take seriously. They learn values and aspirations, and what in general they might expect from life and from the world. All of this learning they do effortlessly, too—and it becomes the solid core of who they are. It is their identity—and the basis of all their confidence in facing the world.

Parents will know how difficult it is to get six-year-olds to wear T-shirts different from the shirts their friends wear or to do their hair differently. Do you think they have been studying and practicing fashion? They learn from the company they keep.

Learning Who We Are Not

The continual learning we do so effortlessly and inconspicuously is not always good for us. We can learn things that impair us—and we remember these things for the rest of our lives, too.

We can't pick and choose what we learn (though we can, to a point, be selective about the company we keep; we can choose what we hope to learn). The company we keep influences us whether we want it to or not. When people welcome us into their club or community we readily identify with them. But when people say, "You're not welcome in our club," or "You don't fit in around here," we learn that we don't belong, this is not the kind of person we are nor the kind of person we want to be.

We build our identity from the clubs we are excluded from as well as from those we join. We learn who we are as much from the people we don't want to be like as from those we do. And as we decide who we are, so we start to act those roles out.

Whether it is ultimately to our advantage or not, we become who we are from the company we keep and from the company we shun, or which shuns us.

Language gets so much attention because it is a primary way by which we establish our own identity and also the primary way by which we identify and categorize other people. It is perceived to be the core of everyone's identity. That is why one of the most offensive and destructive things that anyone can do is to try to change the way another person talks. Try to strip away people's language, and you attack the very core of their identity. Your intentions may be the best but they are mistaken and misguided. It is possible to learn more than one language—more than one dialect and particular way of viewing the world. We all do these things routinely in every club we join. But we don't do so by giving up all our emblems of affiliation in the other clubs to which we belong, certainly not in those that define most clearly who we are.

The way to change the way people talk is to make it possible for them to join new and (for them) desirable clubs, not to renounce the old and trusted ones.[4]

Learning Continues in School

Children's language expansion continues effortlessly and inconspicuously after they begin school. One third-grade teacher who had heard reports of early vocabulary development wondered how many words her students would learn during the school year they were with her.

She began by estimating the size of their vocabulary (not a difficult thing to do). She didn't wait around for her children to get a year older. She went to an adjacent classroom where there were fourth-grade students and estimated the size of *their* vocabulary. She then subtracted the third-grade average from the fourth-grade average and concluded, "This is approximately the number of words my students will be learning during the year they are with me."

She then divided that total by 365 (because it wasn't a leap year) and said, "This, roughly, is the number of words each of my students will be learning every day during the coming year." And the result—many people including myself have checked the teacher's arithmetic—was 27. On the average, her students would be learning *27 words a day.*

At this point you might want to question the teacher's reasoning. She divided by 365—including Saturdays, Sundays, and school holidays in her total. And she made no allowance for forgetting, counting only the words children were learning *and remembering.* Twenty seven words a day. If a child stayed in bed one day, she would have to learn 54 words the next, just to keep up.[5]

I make a point of reporting this research to teachers whenever I can, and I frequently receive vehement objection. A teacher will declare, "That must be wrong. It takes me an hour to teach 10 words on a word list, and I'm lucky if the little devils remember 5 words the next day and 2 at the end of the week. So how could children be learning 27 words a day, with no forgetting?"

And I say, "I suppose it's when they're not working on the word list."

The teacher is contrasting the consequences of the official theory that learning requires work and organization with learning as a member of the club, which is so unobtrusive that we require "research" to demonstrate that it is taking place. And even then some people will doubt it.

One group of researchers who were inclined to doubt all of these findings worked at the Center for the Study of Reading at the University of Illinois, a federally funded institution that might be said to have been dedicated to the proposition that children won't learn anything that isn't presented to them in a highly structured manner, diligently worked on, and constantly monitored.

These researchers expertly replicated and recalculated many of the studies of young children's informal vocabulary development, and to their credit they reported that they could not invalidate the general findings. They then did what might be considered a diabolical thing. They tested the vocabulary learning of high school students. Everyone knows that adolescents have other things on their minds in place of learning. Surely *they* can't still be expanding their vocabularies at such an incredible rate?[6]

Again to their credit, the researchers reported that teenagers still learn new words at an average rate of 3,400 words per year. You'd think they would run out of words. The average learning rate of all the thousands of students tested was still nearly 10 words per day, every day of the year.

Of course, 3,400 was an average. Some at the lower end of the range were learning "only" 1,500 words a year. If I'd told you at the beginning that high school students were capable of learning 1,500 new words a year, with no forgetting, you might have been incredulous and have wondered how anyone could learn that much. But these were the students at the *lower* end of the range. The ones at the other extreme were learning up to 8,500 new words a year, or well over 20 words per day. In fact, there is no indication that vocabulary learning ever stops, provided we can keep encountering new words in a comprehensible context.

Confronted by such a range, the researchers naturally wondered what made the difference. Why do some students learn "as few" as 1,500 new words a year while others learn up to 8,500? They rounded up the usual suspects—ethnic origin, socioeconomic status, parents' education, parents' occupation, family income, size of family, position in birth order—but none of these accounted for the difference. But they did find what seemed to be making the difference, possibly much to the surprise of some people but not to many others. What made the difference was *reading*, keeping the company of books.

The researchers published this as a great discovery. People who read a lot are likely to learn a large number of words. The researchers didn't find that you need a large vocabulary in order to read, or someone to teach you vocabulary while you read—all you need to become a reader is interesting materials that make sense to you. But if you read, your vocabulary will grow. The fact that you don't understand a few words doesn't matter; this is the time when you learn new words.

The researchers published other remarkable findings concerning what people learn while they read. They discovered that people who read a lot are likely to be good readers. Once again, they didn't find that you need to be a good reader in order to read a lot, but if you read a lot your readily ability increases. They discovered that people who read a lot also understand better what they read, tend to be better writers and spellers, and tend to have better academic skills. They didn't say this, but my conclusion is that if only we could encourage students to read more, it would take care of many of their problems in school.

The Advantages of Reading

One might object that evidence that people learn so much while they are unobtrusively reading disproves the classic view that you learn from the company you keep. Where is the company if you sit alone wrapped up in a book?

But reading is not a solitary activity. Readers are never alone. Readers can join the company of the characters they read about—that is the reason we read stories of people with whom we can identify or of situations in which we would like to be. When we read, we can join any club in the world—a powerful advantage of reading.[7]

When we read we can also join the company of authors. We can share ideas and experiences with them, often in considerably more comfort and security than the authors were in when they had their ideas and experiences or wrote their books. We can also employ authors as guides to help us to learn new words, to sharpen our skills of reading and writing, and to augment our abilities in the expression of ideas, in argument, and in thinking creatively.

Reading and writing are universally claimed to be useful if not essential parts of being a good citizen and a competent and desirable worker—sometimes exaggeratedly so in my opinion. The prime value of reading and writing is the *experience* they provide through which we may constantly and unobtrusively learn.

This inevitable learning when we are in the company of printed materials is unwittingly acknowledged every time there is a call for a book to be banned from a library shelf or for a particular point of view not to be published in a newspaper or magazine. Everyone recognizes that print is potent—it's part of the classic view of learning.

NOTES

1. See Miller's (1977) aptly titled *Spontaneous Apprentices: Children and Language* for more on children's language learning and the problems of studying it. Carey (1978) estimates that six-year-olds have mastered an average of 14,000 words "without much help from teachers." She documents the general process of learning. Children first hypothesize the probable meaning of a new word, then they gradually refine their knowledge and use in from 4 to 10 further encounters with the word in context. Rice (1990) reports that five-year-olds picked up the meaning of five test words such as *artisan, gramophone, makeshift, malicious, nurturant* and *viola,* each of which appeared seven times in a single 12-minute viewing of a television cartoon. Three-year-olds picked up an average of 1.5 words.

   The subtlety of children's word learning is discussed in Linda Smith (1995). She instances a two-year-old who is told a certain object is a tractor and is immediately able to recognize and name other tractors. How does the child know the word applies to the object and not to its color, size, noise, movement, big wheels, or anything else (an old philosophical conundrum)? The answer is that there is a bias in learning, a focusing of attention that puts constraints on hypotheses that the learner might make, ruling out many logical alternatives. Children know what word meanings are possible, not because they were born with the knowledge but because they have learned that names for common objects usually refer to objects of similar shape rather than to those of a similar size. This bias can sometimes be seen in "overgeneralizations," when a child calls all four-legged animals cats, for example. A large number of studies summarized by Bates, Bretherton, and Snyder (1988) demonstrate that children don't all learn language in a similar manner. The differences lie not in the rates at which children learn nor in dependence on comprehension but in the particular circumstances in which they find themselves. The learning is adaptive, interactive, continuous, constructive—and self-organized. It is not inborn nor is it a result of maturation. Infants are not "prewired" to learn to talk. Yet by the age of two, they have learned what they should attend to in language. In other words, they have learned *how* to learn language. Many observations of the complexity and subtlety of the ways in which individual children learn are contained in Bloom (1991). After a comprehensive introduction summarizing children's language learning between the ages of two and three, there are detailed and technical reports of many studies, showing, for example, how children focus first on nouns (naming) to get an initial mastery of language, then they focus on verbs in order to construct a grammar.

2. Edward Hall's classics *The Silent Language* (1959) and *The Hidden Dimension* (1966) explore the subtlety and pervasiveness of nonverbal signs and other conventions in cultural and personal development. Elsewhere, Hall (1986) discusses the role of education in the formation of ethnic identity, addressing himself particularly to Indian cultures in the United States. He concludes from his worldwide experience that the human species is a learning organism, and that it is patently untrue that children need motivating in order to learn. They love to learn, he says, though they may not always love school (p. 159). Hall's observations are in a book devoted to global perspectives on learning and development (Thomas and Ploman, 1986).

3. Krashen (1985, 1991, 1993) has published extensively to promote the argument that learning results from "comprehensible input" in first and other languages, spoken and written. Smith (1975) argues that comprehension and learning are inseparable.

4. The relationship of members of a linguistic minority to a dominant culture is always complex and problematic, fraught with emotion and preconceptions. Membership of some "clubs" or social groups can breed intolerance and paranoia. For a general review of these problems, focusing on Australia but examining situations involving language rights in the United States, bilingualism in Canada, and "semilingual" immigrant children in Sweden, see Kalantzis, Cope, and Slade (1989). They comment that while "there are no primordial cultural differences and no cultural gaps which ultimately and irretrievably thwart communication" (p. 17), there are worldwide problems of cultural and linguistic diversity in education and assessment as well as in society in general. Plurality is not always a diversity of equals, and difference often disempowers. The world doesn't need homogeneity, and would lose a great deal if differences among cultures and people were obliterated, but great pressure toward standardization is exerted through politics, advertising, and of course education. Another powerful collection of articles about linguistic interaction and conflict is provided by Wolfson and Manes (1985). Many specific situations in different parts of the world are examined, with examples of "linguistic genocide" where entire languages—and sometimes the people who speak them—may be wiped out.

Learning, whether viewed from the classical or the official point of view, is never neutral. We learn more than we expect to learn, and more than we know we learn, from every language interaction in which we are involved, from private conversations and public dialogues (or monologues) to reading various kinds of texts and engagement with different types of media. A specialized discipline called *discourse analysis* investigates what is going on in every kind of event involving language. Complex analyses probe beneath structure and content to the multilayered "textures" of social and cultural factors behind every language interaction, ranging from reader or listener expectations and interpretations to the assumptions and often hidden agendas of speakers, writers, and publishers. Many technical volumes and articles have been published on discourse analysis since the 1980s.

The relation between language and power is a particular focus of *critical discourse analysis*, which looks for ideological contexts surrounding all speech, reading, and writing activities. The critical view deplores many aspects of language study—as it would doubtless criticize the present book—for lack of an explicit social theory. The view asserts that there is nothing about language that is timeless or "pure." There is always an agenda. Critical discourse analysis demands from authors and researchers a "grounded" perspective with "closeness" to the reality of individual people's lives (something which in general I leave readers to do). Critical discourse analysis of children's language learning would look at imbalances in the power relations of children and teachers (as members of different clubs) and at the general dynamics of the situation and institution they are in. In a reading situation, for example, they would carefully dissect the text that is involved—interpreting its place in a general social and cultural situation. The approach has deep roots in the pioneering literacy and theoretical work of Brazilian educator Paulo Freire, who asserted that in learning to read children also learn to read the world. Until exiled from his own country by a military coup in 1964, Freire taught literacy by engaging his adult peasant students in the social and political problems of their own communities. His most influential books are *Pedagogy of the Oppressed* (1972) and *Education for Critical Consciousness* (1982).

Bloome and Talwalkar (1997) provide a helpful review article of a number of critical discourse analysis studies. They contrast "school-centered" views of literacy, which focus on its contribution to a student's progress in school and assumed "success" outside, with "community" views concerned more with tensions raised by the pursuit of success, not only in school but also in home and community. They consider problems of minority group members acquiring values and attitudes of a dominant culture and of the maintenance of language and culture of the learner's home and historical community in the face of school socializing pressures. Bloome, Puro, and Theodorou (1989) investigate classrooms to reveal how students "learn to be a student" and "learn to do school." See also Willinsky (1984) on the politics of standard English in the classroom and Willinsky (1990) on the politics of teaching literacy. Other relevant volumes with self-explanatory titles are Fairclough's (1989) *Language and Power,* and Lakoff's (1990) *Talking Power: The Politics of Language in Our Lives.*

5. The original 27-words-a-day study was done in Los Angeles by a teacher named Mary Smith (no relation) and was published in 1941 (M. Smith, 1941).

6. Nagy and Herman (1987) reviewed and validated earlier results as part of their own extensive research program, and they calculated that vocabularies of third-grade students ranged from 4,000 to 24,000 words, with a median annual growth rate of 3,500 words. In further studies, Nagy, Herman, and Anderson (1985) and Herman, Anderson, Pearson, and Nagy (1987) estimated that fifth-grade students are likely to encounter more than 1 million words a year, between 15,000 and 50,000 of which would be unknown. A "typical middle-grade" student would learn between 1,500 and 8,250 of these unknown words a year, an average of 4,875, regardless of whether direct instruction in vocabulary was provided by a teacher. White, Graves, and Slater (1990) reported that fourth-grade students who spoke "standard English" at a suburban school had an average annual increase of vocabulary of 5,200 words and knew an average of 16,000 out of 19,050 words on which they were tested. For "economically disadvantaged" students at an inner city school the average annual increase was 3,300 words, while similarly categorized students at a Hawaiian school, speaking mainly a Hawaiian Creole, achieved 3,500 words a year. Differences in all these rates were attributed to the general spoken and written language experience of the students, not to instruction, and were mainly related to infrequent words.

   Estimating vocabulary size is not time consuming. Start with the biggest dictionary you can find for the language in which you are interested. You will only look at 100 words, whatever the size of dictionary. Note the total number of pages in the dictionary, divide that number by 100, disregard any remainder, and look at the first word on every page that is a multiple of the result, up to 100 times the result. If there are 730 pages in the dictionary, for example, 730 divided by 100 is 7 plus a bit left over, so you look at the first word on page 7, the first word on page 14, the first word on page 21, and so on, until you reach page 700. When you have done, you will have examined 100 words spread throughout the dictionary. Don't test yourself on exact definitions, merely ask whether the word is familiar to you. Count or tally the result. Then ascertain or estimate the number of words in the dictionary. Since you sampled 100 words, you can say the number of words that were familiar to you is the percentage of words you know in the dictionary. (Now you know why you should use the biggest dictionary you can lay hands on; 68 percent of 100,000 words is better than 95 percent of 3,000.) Warning: Don't use this technique to compare yourself with anyone else, or to compare one child with another. Different people may use different criteria for saying that a word is familiar. But you can use the technique for comparing your own vocabulary before and after studying a foreign language for six months, or for comparing a group of fourth graders with an otherwise similar group of fifth graders, thereby estimating the number of words on average they must be learning in a year.

7. In an article subtitled "On Greek Gods, Cartoon Heroes, and the Social Lives of Children," Dyson (1996) shows how children develop their beliefs about the world and their identities from stories—and from such media symbols as superheroes. Adults, she notes, are often childlike in looking for "good guys" and "bad guys" in real-life situations.

REFERENCES

Bates, Elizabeth, Inge Bretherton, and Lynn Snyder. (1988). *From First Words to Grammar.* Cambridge, UK: Cambridge University Press.

Bloom, Lois. (1991). *Language Development from Two to Three.* Cambridge, UK: Cambridge University Press.

Bloome, David, Pamela Puro, and Erine Theodorou. (1989). Procedural Display and Classroom Lessons. *Curriculum Inquiry, 19,* 3, 265–291.

Bloome, David, and Susan Talwalkar. (1997). Book Reviews: Critical Discourse Analysis and the Study of Reading and Writing. *Reading Research Quarterly, 32,* 1, 104–112.

Carey, Susan. (1978). The Child as Word Learner. In Morris Halle, J. Breslin, and George A. Miller (Eds.), *Linguistic Theory and Psychological Reality.* Cambridge, MA: MIT Press.

Dyson, Anne Haas. (1996). Cultural Constellations and Childhood Identities: On Greek Gods, Cartoon Heroes, and the Social Lives of Children. *Harvard Educational Review, 66,* 4, 471–495.

Fairclough, Norman. (1989). *Language and Power.* London: Longman.

Freire, Paulo. (1972). *Pedagogy of the Oppressed.* New York: Herder and Herder.

Freire, Paulo. (1982). *Education for Critical Consciousness.* New York: Continuum.

Hall, Edward T. (1959). *The Silent Language.* New York: Doubleday.

Hall, Edward T. (1966). *The Hidden Dimension.* New York: Doubleday.

Hall, Edward T. (1986). Unstated Features of the Cultural Context of Learning. In Alan Thomas and Edward W. Ploman (Eds.), *Learning and Development: A Global Perspective*. Toronto, ON: Ontario Institute for Studies in Education.

Herman, Patricia A., Richard C. Anderson, P. David Pearson, and William E. Nagy. (1987). Incidental Acquisition of Word Meaning from Expositions with Varied Text Features. *Reading Research Quarterly, 22*, 3, 263–284.

Kalantzis, Mary, Bill Cope, and Diana Slade. (1989). *Minority Languages and Dominant Culture: Issues of Education, Assessment and Social Equity*. London: Falmer.

Krashen, Stephen D. (1985). *The Input Hypothesis: Issues and Implications*. New York: Longman.

Krashen, Stephen D. (1991). *Fundamentals of Language Education*. Torrance, CA: Laredo.

Krashen, Stephen D. (1993). *The Power of Reading: Insights from the Research*. Englewood, CO: Libraries Unlimited.

Lakoff, Robin. (1990). *Talking Power: The Politics of Language in Our Lives*. New York: Basic Books.

Miller, George A. (1977). *Spontaneous Apprentices: Children and Language*. New York: Seabury.

Nagy, William E., Patricia A. Herman, and Richard C. Anderson. (1985). Learning Words from Context. *Reading Research Quarterly, 20*, 2, 233–253.

Rice, Mabel L. (1990). Preschoolers' QUIL: Quick Incidental Learning of Words. In Gina Conti-Ramsden and Catherine E. Snow (Eds.), *Children's Language* (Volume 7). Hillsdale, NJ: Erlbaum.

Smith, Frank. (1975). *Comprehension and Learning*. New York: Holt, Rinehart and Winston.

Smith, Linda. (1995). Self-Organizing Processes in Learning to Learn Words: Development Is Not Induction. In Charles A. Nelson (Ed.), *Basic and Applied Perspectives on Learning, Cognition, and Development*. Mahwah, NJ: Erlbaum.

Smith, Mary K. (1941). Measurement of the Size of General English Vocabulary through the Elementary Grades and High School. *Genetic Psychology Monographs, 24*, 311–345.

Thomas, Alan, and Edward W. Ploman (Eds.). (1986). *Learning and Development: A Global Perspective*. Toronto, ON: Ontario Institute for Studies in Education.

White, Thomas G., Michael F. Graves, and Wayne H. Slater. (1990). Growth of Reading Vocabulary in Diverse Elementary Schools: Decoding and Word Meaning. *Journal of Educational Psychology, 82,* 2, 281–290.

Willinsky, John. (1984). *The Well-Tempered Tongue: The Politics of Standard English in the Classroom.* New York: Lang.

Willinsky, John. (1990). *The New Literacy: Redefining Reading and Writing in the Schools.* London: Routledge.

Wolfson, Nessa, and Joan Manes (Eds.). (1985). *Language of Inequality.* Berlin: Mouton.

CREDITS